Big Data's Big Potential in Developing Economies

Impact on Agriculture, Health and Environmental Security

FSC
www.fsc.org
MIX
Paper from
responsible sources
FSC® C013604

Big Data's Big Potential in Developing Economies

Impact on Agriculture, Health and Environmental Security

Nir Kshetri

The University of North Carolina at Greensboro, Greensboro, USA

CABI

CABI is a trading name of CAB International

CABI
Nosworthy Way
Wallingford
Oxfordshire OX10 8DE
UK

Tel: +44 (0)1491 832111
Fax: +44 (0)1491 833508
E-mail: info@cabi.org
Website: www.cabi.org

CABI
745 Atlantic Avenue
8th Floor
Boston, MA 02111
USA

T: +1 617 682 9015
E-mail: cabi-nao@cabi.org

A catalogue record for this book is available from the British Library, London, UK.

Library of Congress Cataloging-in-Publication Data

Names: Kshetri, Nir, author.
Title: Big data's big potential in developing economies : impact on agriculture, health and environmental security / Nir Kshetri.
Description: Boston, MA : CABI, [2016] | Includes bibliographical references and index.
Identifiers: LCCN 2016022766| ISBN 9781780648682 (hbk : alk. paper) | ISBN 9781780648705 (epub)
Subjects: LCSH: Big data--Developing countries. | Agriculture and state--Developing countries. | Medical policy--Developing countries. | Environmental policy--Developing countries.
Classification: LCC QA76.9.B45 K74 2016 | DDC 005.7094--dc23 LC record available at https://lccn.loc.gov/2016022766

ISBN-13: 978 1 78064 868 2

Commissioning editor: David Hemming
Editorial assistant: Emma McCann
Production editor: Tim Kapp

Typeset by AMA DataSet Ltd, Preston, UK.
Printed and bound in the UK by CPI Group (UK) Ltd, Croydon, CR0 4YY

Contents

Abbreviations

ACSS	Agricultural Census Sample Survey
AFBF	American Farm Bureau Federation
AfSIS	Africa Soil Information Service
AI	Artificial Intelligence
AKOL	Agricultural Knowledge On-Line
API	Application Program Interface
AWS	Amazon Web Services
BD	Big Data
BDSC	Big Data, Small Credit
BCDI	Booz & Company's Digitization Index
BI	Business Intelligence
BJP	Bharatiya Janata Party
CAGR	Compound Annual Growth Rate
CCAFS	Climate Change, Agriculture and Food Security
CDR	Call Data Record
CGAP	Consultative Group to Assist the Poor
CGIAR	Consultative Group on International Agricultural Research
CHAS	Clinical and Health Records Analytics and Sharing
CIAT	Centro Internacional de Agricultura Tropical
CKW	Community Knowledge Worker
CSP	Cloud Service Provider
DAWCO	Da Nang Water Company
EC2	Elastic Compute Cloud
EHR	Electronic Health Records
EIA	Environmental Investigation Agency
EMR	Electronic Medical Records
ERP	Enterprise Resource Planning
EU	European Union
EWEC	Every Woman Every Child

FAO	Food and Agriculture Organization
FDA	Food and Drug Administration
FIRM	Financial Identity Risk Management
FLAR	Fondo Latinoamericano para Arroz de Riego
FTA	Free Trade Agreement
GAP	Good Agricultural Practices
GCC	Gulf Cooperation Council
GCI	Global Cloud Index
GCM	Global Circulation Models
GDELT	Global Data on Events, Location and Tone
GFED	Global Fire Emissions Database
GFW	Global Forest Watch
GISC	Grower Information Services Cooperative
GMO	Genetically Modified Organisms
GNI	Gross National Income
GPS	Global Positioning System
HIS	Hospital Information Systems
IaaS	Infrastructure as a Service
ICD	Implantable cardioverter defibrillator
ICF	Intelligent Community Forum
ICT	Information and Communications Technology
IGF	Internet Governance Forum
IoT	Internet of Things
IP	Intellectual Property
IPZ	Intensive Protection Zone
IT	Information Technology
ITU	International Telecommunication Union
JIC	Joint Innovation Center
LDCs	Least Developed Countries
LST	Land Surface Temperature
MADIS	Mosquito Abatement Decision Information System
MADR	Ministry of Agriculture and Rural Development
MAS	Marker Assisted Selection
MDGs	Millennium Development Goals
MEA	Middle East and Africa
MFI	Microfinance Institution
MODIS	Moderate Resolution Imaging Spectroradiometer
MPA	Mobile Product Authentication
MSK	Memorial Sloan Kettering
NACAL	National Census of Agriculture and Livestock
NASSCOM	National Association of Software and Services Companies
NCCN	National Comprehensive Cancer Network
NECTA	National Examination Council of Tanzania
NGO	Non-Government Organization
NMA	National Meteorology Agency
NTAE	Non-Traditional Agricultural Exports
ODP	Open Data Portal

ODPS	Open Data Processing Service
PaaS	Platform as a Service
PII	Personally Identifiable Information
PPP	Public–Private Partnership
RAPID	Real-Time Antipoaching Intelligence Device
RFID	Radio-Frequency Identification
RHIN	Regional Healthcare Information Networks
SaaS	Software as a Service
SKA	Square Kilometre Array
SME	Small to Medium Enterprises
SSA	Sub-Saharan Africa
TNC	Transnational Corporation
UAV	Unmanned Aerial Device
UIDAI	Unique Identification Authority
UN	United Nations
UNESCO	United Nations Educational, Scientific and Cultural Organization
UNICEF	United Nations Children's Emergency Fund
UNOCHA	United Nations Office for the Coordination of Humanitarian Affairs
URSB	Uganda Registration Services Bureau
USSD	Unstructured Supplementary Service Data
VOIP	Voice Over Internet Protocol
VRS	Vital Records System
WEMS	Wireless energy management systems
WHO	World Health Organization
WRI	World Resources Institute

About the author

Nir Kshetri is a professor at the Bryan School of Business and Economics, The University of North Carolina-Greensboro, and a research fellow at the Research Institute for Economics & Business Administration – Kobe University, Japan. He is the author of five books and about 100 journal articles. His 2014 book, *Global Entrepreneurship: Environment and Strategy*, was selected as an Outstanding Academic Title by *Choice* magazine. Nir participated as lead discussant at the Peer Review meeting of the UNCTAD's *Information Economy Report 2013* and *Information Economy Report 2015*. Nir has taught classes or presented research papers in about 50 countries. He has been interviewed by and/or quoted in over 60 TV channels, magazines and newspapers.

Preface and Acknowledgements

While a lot of hype has surrounded the recent explosion of Big Data (BD), there clearly are some signs of BD-led economic and social transformation in developing countries. Early evidence has shown the huge potential benefits that can be realized by implementing BD in diverse fields that are critical to the future of these countries. Yet despite the huge potential benefits of data-driven decision making in the key areas of economic development such as agriculture, health and the environment, very little is known about how BD is being, can be and should be used in these activities.

A relatively low level of utilization of advanced technologies is one of the most important issues in the present discussion of BD in these countries. Unsurprisingly, in many areas where BD is deployed, the applications are in their infancy. Developing economies are thus far from achieving the full transformative potential of BD. An effective deployment and utilization of BD will require a greater understanding of the mechanisms involved and relationship of such mechanisms with various characteristics of BD.

It is thus important for researchers, practitioners and policy makers to have a deeper understanding of social, political and economic contexts that facilitate and inhibit BD's diffusion and effective utilization in vital sectors such as agriculture, health care and environmental protection. An understanding of the nature of various available data sources would also help utilize the best combination of data and information in a situation faced by a decision maker.

In light of the above observations, this book's goal is modest and is aimed at identifying and understanding the key factors and mechanisms involved in the diffusion and utilization of BD in key policy areas such as agriculture, health care and the environment in developing countries. These issues obviously are important to the livelihood of rural people. The book gives special consideration to the roles of BD in increasing access to credit and market for the rural population in the developing world. It also delves into the issues of privacy and data security. In order to achieve these goals, we present a review of academic literature, policy documents from government organizations and international agencies, and reports from industries and popular media on the trends in BD utilization as well as the worthwhileness, usefulness and relevance of this new technology.

Regarding the ideas, concepts and content presented in this book, I am grateful to several people for comments, suggestions, support and encouragement. I would like to express deep appreciation to David Hemming, Commissioning Editor, International Development, CABI Publishing, who inspired me to undertake this project. He shepherded the project with the greatest of care and professionalism through its various phases. I would like to thank Emma McCann, Editorial Assistant at CABI, for providing assistance with this project. Thanks are also due to anonymous CABI reviewers for their useful comments and excellent suggestions.

A special mention should be made of my graduate assistant, Bhuvaneswari (Bhuvna) Paladugu, at the University of North Carolina at Greensboro. Bhuvna did a very good job in the compilation of the bibliography.

My previous work as a consultant and trainer with the Food and Agriculture Organization (FAO), the German Technical Cooperation Agency, Gesellschaft für Technische Zusammenarbeit (GTZ) and Agricultural Development Bank of Nepal helped me to develop first-hand understanding of the diverse challenges faced by developing world-based smallholder farmers. I wish to express my sincere thanks to the farmers in Nepal, and employees of the Agricultural Development Bank of Nepal who shared their experiences, insights, perspectives and wisdom with me.

My family has been my source of strength and inspiration. My wife Maya deserves special thanks and credit. Without her love, encouragement, sacrifice, understanding and support, this book would not have been possible. Finally, I would like to dedicate this book in memory of my mother, Manamaya.

1 Big Data in Developing Countries: Current Status, Opportunities and Challenges

Abstract

This chapter reviews the current state, potential and applications of big data (BD) in developing countries. Definitions and explanations of key terms used in the book are provided. This chapter also looks at characteristics of BD. Key areas of BD deployment in developing countries are described. This chapter also focuses on the relationship between BD, mobility, the Internet of Things and cloud computing in the context of developing countries. Some major determinants of the development of the BD industry and market are considered. Various forces to overcome the adverse economic, political and cultural circumstances are explored. It also evaluates the intricate relationship between agriculture, health and the environment. Finally, this chapter argues that BD offers no panacea or magic pill for all the ills.

1.1 Introduction

Big Data (hereinafter: BD) is emerging as a means for governments, international development agencies, non-government organizations (NGOs) and the private sector to improve economic, health, social and environmental conditions in developing economies. Consequently, the BD application areas in developing economies are also numerous and growing steadily. A large and growing number of firms, both local and foreign, are offering diverse BD solutions in these economies.

A key benefit of BD is that large and sometimes unrelated sources of data can help discover relationships that were previously undetected. To take an example, researchers from Sweden's Karolinska Institute analysed data related to people's movement patterns before and after the January 2010 earthquake in Haiti, which killed more than 200,000 people. The data were obtained from Digicel, Haiti's largest mobile carrier. The data consisted of the call data records (CDRs) of 2 million phones from 42 days before to 158 days after the earthquake. Note that CDRs provide information about the number of users in a phone tower's coverage and origin–destination matrices representing phone users that move between two towers' coverage areas (Weslowski *et al.*, 2013).

The analysis of CDRs indicated that 630,000 people who were in Port-au-Prince on the day of the earthquake, 12 January 2010, had left the city within 3 weeks. A comparison of the movement patterns before and after the earthquake indicated that individuals who fled the city went to the same places where they had been on Christmas and/or New Year's Day. The researchers at the Karolinska Institute also demonstrated the capability to analyse data on a near real-time basis. For instance, within 12 hours of receiving the data, the researchers were able to tell the number of people that had fled an area that was affected by a cholera outbreak. They were also able to figure out where people went (Talbot, 2013).

Another retrospective analysis of the 2010 cholera outbreak in Haiti showed that mining data from Twitter and online news reports could have given the country's health officials an accurate indication of the spread of the disease with a lead time of 2 weeks (Chunara *et al.*, 2012). To take another example, a study of Serbian farmers by the Israeli company Agricultural Knowledge On-Line (AKOL) indicated a connection between drinking coffee and farm productivity. Farmers who did not drink coffee in the morning were less productive than those who did (Shamah, 2015).

In the past, decision makers needed to depend on data scientists, computer engineers and mathematicians to make sense of data (Fengler and Kharas, 2015). This is not the case anymore thanks to shared infrastructure such as cloud computing and the rapid diffusion of mobile phones. New programs and analytical solutions have put BD at the fingertips of any consumer with a smartphone. Another favourable trend is that personal computing devices such as smartphones are becoming cheaper. For instance, in 2014, a phone with GPS (global positioning system), Wi-Fi and a camera could be bought for US$30 (Caulderwood, 2014). Due to these recent developments, BD is becoming increasingly personal.

Perhaps the greatest advantage offered by BD in the context of development is that it helps us gain a better understanding of the extent and nature of poverty and devise appropriate policy measures. For instance, mobile data can make it possible to better understand the dynamics of slum residents. The CDR and other information can provide insights into the slum population, which would help forecast the needs for toilets, clean drinking water and other infrastructural facilities (bigdata-startups.com, 2013). To take an example, in Nairobi, Kenya, geocoded mobile phone transaction data are used by the Engineering Social Systems project to model the growth of slums, which could help the government to optimize resource allocation for infrastructural development and other resources (Bays, 2014). Alternative data collection and analysis techniques such as surveys have a very low degree of usefulness for such purposes, as they may take months and even years to get results and are often out of date.

An encouraging trend is that the tools and expertise that are employed to make decisions and take actions related to behavioural advertising based on consumers' real-time profiling are being used in addressing developmental problems. For instance, data generated by social media such as Twitter are being analysed in order to detect early signs that can lead to a spike in the price of staple foods, increase in unemployment, and outbreak of diseases such as malaria. Robert Kirkpatrick of the UN Global Pulse team referred to such signs as 'digital smoke signals of distress' and noted that they can be detected months before official statistics (Lohr, 2013). The importance of this technique is even more pronounced if we consider the fact that there are no reliable statistics in many developing countries.

BD deployment in the developing world is currently in the infant stage of development. According to International Data Corporation's Middle East Chief Information Officer Survey, in 2014 only 3% of the respondent organizations in the Gulf Cooperation Council countries had implemented BD (oilandgasbigdata.com, 2015). In some developing countries, the complete absence of a digital footprint renders BD irrelevant to a large proportion of the population. For instance, according to the International Telecommunications Union (ITU), as of 2014 Eritrea had a mobile phone penetration rate of 6.4% and an Internet penetration rate of 0.99% (see Chapter 2).

BD projects undertaken in the developing world vary widely in terms of the project's capital- and resource-intensiveness, sophistication, complexity, performance and impact. In order to illustrate this point, we make a brief comparison of BD deployments by China's Alibaba and a Kenyan-based mobile payment solution and service provider, MobiPay's cloud-mobile platform Agrilife. In the context of this book it is worth noting that the financial affiliate of Alibaba Group's MYbank, which is an Internet-only bank, aspires to provide credits to farmers to buy agricultural machines and tools.

It is fair to say that of the firms based in the developing world, Alibaba's BD tools are among the most advanced and sophisticated. In July 2014, Alibaba launched the Open Data Processing Service (ODPS), which allows users to remotely tap into Alibaba servers equipped with algorithms. According to Alibaba, the system had the capability to process 100 million high-definition movies' worth of data in 6 hours (Li, 2014). The program uses more than 100 computing models to process over 80 billion data entries every day. Alibaba mainly utilizes its huge online ecosystem that, as of early 2015, consisted of over 300 million registered users and 37 million small businesses on Alibaba Group marketplaces including Taobao and Tmall.com (alibabagroup.com, 2015).

Kenya's Agrilife, which connects farmers with value-chain partners such as dairy processors (who purchase milk), credit appraisers and local input/agrodealers, is technically less sophisticated than Alibaba's ODPS. Agrilife also helps farmers to assess market opportunities and get the information required to grow, manage and market their produce. A farmer can make credit requests via a mobile phone. The credit appraiser uses a range of data about the farmer, produce and status of farms to assess the creditworthiness. The input provider then makes a decision on credit. The platform facilitated credit lines to about 120,000 small farmers by 2013. As of 2014, Agrilife served farmers in Kenya, Uganda and Zimbabwe (fin4ag.org, 2014).

BD offerings of Alibaba and Agrilife exhibit different levels of resource intensiveness. Compared to Alibaba's ODPS, the Agrilife platform is simpler and cheaper. For instance, data volumes handled by Agrilife are not as big as those that Alibaba handles. Actions are taken on a near real-time basis rather than in a real-time manner. As of 2015, Alibaba had a market value of about US$233 billion, which made it the world's third-largest public Internet company, only behind Apple and Google (Schwarzmann, 2015). In 2014, Alibaba Group's online payment service, Alipay, handled payments worth US$800 billion (Kim, 2014). However, most organizations based in the developing world, such as MobiPay, tend to have limited access to the resources needed to set up BD-related businesses.

1.2 Definitions and Explanations of Key Terms

In this section, we clarify some of the key terms and concepts used in the book.

1.2.1 Algorithm

An algorithm is a procedure or formula for solving a problem. Algorithms are even more important than data as they convert data into actions and outcomes that can improve the effectiveness and efficiency of development efforts and improve the overall quality of lives of those living in the developing world.

1.2.2 Big Data

In order to define BD for the purpose of this book, we start with the technology research company Gartner's definition of BD, which is 'high-volume, high-velocity and high-variety information assets that demand cost-effective, innovative forms of information processing for enhanced insight and decision making' (gartner.com, 2013). With regard to volume, Boyd and Crawford (2012, p. 663) note that big data is a 'poor term' and argue that BD 'is less about data that is big than it is about a capacity to search, aggregate, and cross-reference large data sets'. In this book's context, we define BD as datasets that can provide insights into human well-being, which satisfy at least one of the following characteristics compared to datasets that have been traditionally used in developmental issues: (i) are of higher volume; (ii) are of wider variety; or (iii) enable us to make decisions and act faster. In this way, the term BD is used in the broadest possible sense in order to be inclusive and uncover any possible use of data and information to improve the welfare and livelihood of people living in the developing world.

1.2.3 Business model

A business model is a description of a company's intention to create and capture value by linking new technological environments to business strategies (Hawkins, 2003).

1.2.4 Cloud computing

Cloud computing involves hosting applications on servers and delivering software and services via the Internet. In the cloud computing model, companies can access computing power and resources on the cloud and pay for services based on their usage. The cloud industry is defined as the set of sellers/providers of cloud-related products and services. Cloud providers or vendors, which are suppliers of cloud services, deliver value to users through various offerings such as Software as a Service (SaaS), Platform as a Service (PaaS) and Infrastructure as a Service (IaaS). SaaS is a software distribution model, in which applications are hosted by a vendor and made available to customers over a network. It is considered to be the most mature type of cloud computing. In PaaS, applications are developed and executed through platforms provided by cloud vendors. This model allows quick and cost-effective development and deployment of applications. Some well-known PaaS vendors include Google (Google App Engine), Salesforce.com (Force.com) and Microsoft (Windows Azure platform). Some facilities provided under the PaaS model include database management, security, workflow management and application serving. In IaaS, computing power and storage space are offered on demand. IaaS can provide server, operating system, disk storage and database infrastructure, among other things. Amazon.com is the biggest IaaS provider. Its Elastic Compute Cloud (EC2) allows subscribers to run cloud application programs. IBM, VMware and HP also offer IaaS.

1.2.5 Developing economies

By developing economies, we mean low-, lower middle- and upper middle-income countries in the World Bank categorization (The World Bank Group, 2014). For the 2016 fiscal year, economies with a gross national income (GNI) per capita of US$1045 or less in 2014 based on the so-called Atlas method were categorized as low-income economies. Some examples include Eritrea and Haiti.

Lower middle-income economies are those with a GNI per capita of more than US$1045 but less than or equal to US$4125. Some examples of economies in this category are Kenya and Vietnam. Upper middle-income economies have a GNI per capita of more than US$4125 but less than US$12,736 (worldbank.org, 2016). Some examples in this category are China and Colombia.

1.2.6 Drip irrigation

Drip irrigation, which is also referred to as micro-irrigation or trickle irrigation, is a watering system that involves a network of pipes, tubing valves and emitters to deliver water directly to the soil at a gradual rate. Sensors track moisture in and around the root zone of each tree and water is delivered to the base. Water is thus used more efficiently. When a zone is saturated, the water supply is cut off.

1.2.7 Environmental monitoring

Environmental monitoring is defined as 'measurements of physical, chemical, and/or biological variables, designed to answer questions about environmental change' (Lovett *et al.*, 2007).

1.2.8 Institutionalization

Institutionalization is defined as the process by which a practice acquires legitimacy and achieves a taken for-granted status (Kshetri, 2009). This book uses the term in the context of BD utilization, data privacy and cybersecurity.

1.2.9 Least developed countries (LDCs)

The UN has recognized LDCs as a category of states, which are 'highly disadvantaged in their development process'. Compared to other countries, LDCs face a higher risk of deeper poverty and remaining in a state of underdevelopment. As of 2015, there were 48 LDCs with a combined population of around 880 million (unctad.org, 2016).

1.2.10 The Internet of Things

The Internet of Things (IoT) is the network of physical objects or 'things' (e.g. machines, devices and appliances, animals or people) embedded with electronics, software and sensors, which are provided with unique identifiers and possess the ability to transfer data across the Web with minimal human interventions.

According to Gartner, there are three components of an IoT service: the edge, the platform and the user. The edge is the location where data originates or is aggregated. Data may also be reduced to the essential or minimal parts. In some cases, the data may be analysed. The data then go to the platform, which is typically in the cloud. Analytics are often performed in the cloud using algorithms. Real-time data streaming decides if some actions need to be taken right away or if the data needs to be stored for future use. The user engages in a business action.

There are three possible ways in which data that have been analysed can move from the IoT platform to a user: (i) the user deploys an application program interface (API) to call or query the data, which specifies how software components of the user and platform should interact; (ii) if the IoT finds a predetermined set of events, it can announce or signal to the business user; (iii) it is possible to combine (i) and (ii) (Laskowski, 2016).

1.2.11 Machine-to-machine connections

Machine-to-machine (M2M) connections can be considered to be a subset of the IoT, which use wireless networks to connect devices to each other and with the Internet. The IoT can be viewed as an evolution of M2M, which requires the coordination of multiple vendors' machines, devices and appliances connected to the Internet through multiple networks (GSM Association, 2014).

1.2.12 Precision agriculture

Precision agriculture involves collecting real-time data on a number of relevant indicators such as weather, quality of soil and air, crop maturity, and costs and availability of equipment and labour using predictive analytics to make better decisions (IBM, 2015). This approach is different from traditional agricultural practices, in which various tasks (e.g. planting, harvesting) are performed based on a predetermined schedule.

1.2.13 Radio-frequency identification

Radio-frequency identification (RFID) uses electromagnetic fields in order to automatically identify and track tags that are attached to objects. A RFID tag stores unique numerical identification code, which can be scanned from a distance.

1.2.14 Sensor

A sensor is any device that responds to some type of stimulus input from the physical environment by emitting a signal. Some examples of inputs include location, atmospheric pressure, altitude, velocity, light, heat, temperature, pressure, illumination, motion, moisture, power, humidity, blood sugar, air quality, soil moisture, vehicular movement and other environmental phenomena. To act as a sensor, a device does not need to be a computer in the sense that most people understand it. However, the device may contain some or all elements of a computer (e.g. processor, memory, storage, inputs and outputs, software). The devices can communicate with the Internet directly or with other Internet-connected devices (McLellan, 2013). Any object such as a cow, a refrigerator, a car, a tree, a container, an air-conditioning unit, a patient's body, a lamppost or an elephant can be made a node in the IoT by attaching a sensor.

A key point from our perspective is that not long ago sensors' uses were mainly limited to large industrial systems such as electric utilities, power plants and jet engines. Nowadays, however, sensors are becoming smaller, more efficient and more cost-effective and thus increasingly pervasive. New and better algorithms are being developed to leverage low-cost sensors for developmental activities. The global availability of reliable wireless communication systems is another trend that has contributed to the rapid diffusion of the IoT in the developing world.

1.3 Characteristics of Big Data

The massive amounts of data generated by social media, mobile phones and other digital communication tools, which are being increasingly used in developing countries, are a true form of BD. While such data have not been traditionally used in developmental issues, they are likely to be useful indicators of human well-being and are thus relevant BD sources for development (UN Global Pulse, 2012).

It is first important to explain what BD is and how one can say that a dataset used for a specific, development-related purpose is BD. As noted earlier, Gartner has defined BD in terms of three Vs: volume, velocity and variety. The software company, SAS, has added two additional dimensions: variability and complexity (sas.com, 2013). The following discussion will examine how the various characteristics or dimensions of BD identified by Gartner and SAS are relevant in the context of agriculture, health care and the environment (Table 1.1).

1.3.1 Volume

There has been a colossal increase in the digitization rate of developing countries. Of particular importance to the present discussion is the rapid diffusion of mobile phones, which are probably the most important source of data in the context of development. One estimate suggested that the mobile data traffic generated by subscribers in emerging markets grew by over 100% in 2013 (cisco.com, 2014). According to the GSM Association, 79% of the world's total inhabited areas had mobile network coverage in 2012, which will increase to 85% in 2017 (GSM Association, 2012).

People with high disposable income in developing economies tend to spend a significant portion on topping up their mobile airtime credit. The monthly airtime expenses can provide background information on household income. This information provides guidance on how to best target appropriate services through advertising. It can be done anonymously. Monitoring airtime expenses for trends and sudden changes provides a measure of the early impact of an economic crisis and the impact of programmes designed to improve livelihoods (UN Global Pulse, 2013b).

Mobile phone-related data often provide high-quality, valuable information because a mobile phone is often the only interactive technology for most low-income individuals in developing countries. Moreover, it is easy to link mobile-generated data to individuals, which can help understand their needs and behaviours (WEF, 2012). The frequency with which calls are made and received with contacts outside of one's immediate community provides an in-depth understanding of the socioeconomic class (UN Global Pulse, 2013a).

Table 1.1. Relevance of big data dimensions in agriculture, health care and the environment.

Characteristic	Explanation	Some examples in the context of agriculture, health care and the environment
Volume	Huge amount of data created from a wide range of sources, such as transactions, unstructured streaming from text, images, audio, voice, VoIP, videos, TV and other media, sensor, historical weather data, satellite imagery and machine-to-machine data	Rapid diffusion of mobile phones, social media and other technologies has led to the creation of a huge amount of data
Velocity (fast data)	Some data are time sensitive and need to be collected, stored, processed, analysed and acted on quickly. In some cases, speed is more important than volume	Most decisions are based on data that are near real time
Variety	Data come in multiple formats such as structured, numeric data in traditional database and unstructured text documents; email, video, audio, financial transactions	Structured and unstructured data are being used in a number of developmental projects (e.g. Malaria Surveillance & Mapping project in Botswana and Water Watchers in South Africa)
Variability	Data flows can vary greatly with periodic peaks and troughs. These are related to social media trends, daily, seasonal and event-triggered peak data loads and other factors	Variation of data flow is related to certain developmental indicators (e.g. the correlation of the volume of tweets about staple foods and increase in the cost)
Complexity	Data come from multiple sources that require linking, matching, cleansing and transforming across systems	By matching and linking data from diverse sources such as CDRs, open portals, social media, government, NGOs and corporations (e.g. prediction of food shortages by combining data related to drought, weather conditions, migration patterns, market prices of staples, seasonal variation in prices and past productions), key insights can be gained regarding issues related to agriculture, health and environmental security

CDR, call detail record; NGO, non-governmental organization; TV, television; VoIP, Voice Over Internet Protocol.

Probably the most useful category of data is the CDR, which is automatically generated by mobile network operators for all mobile transactions. Each record contains attributes of the transaction, such as the start time and duration of a call. In addition, the operator records the mobile phone towers with which the phones of the caller and recipient are connected. This information makes it possible to use CDRs to know the location of both parties (UN Global Pulse, 2013a). CDRs have a number of potential uses. The information about mobile phone towers provides insight into the community's movement patterns, such as how people move from home, work, school, markets or clinics. More importantly, such information provides a basis for assessing the potential spread of a disease into the area and the movements of a disaster-affected population (UN Global Pulse, 2013b). This information provides key insights for relief efforts.

Mobile phones are the cornerstone of a large number of BD projects in developing countries. Mobile phone transactions, have been recognized as a major source of data for developmental issues. For instance, the characteristics of data related to microfinance transactions, such as the number and characteristics of clients, loan amounts and types, and default rate, arguably fall between traditional development data and BD (UN Global Pulse, 2012). With a more widespread use of mobile and online platforms for microloan transactions, a large amount of microfinance data can be digitized and analysed in real time.

Activity data generated by social media also constitute a major data source for developmental issues. For instance, most of Facebook's growth in recent years is coming from emerging markets. Among the ten countries with the most Facebook users in 2012, six were emerging markets. Five of them (India, Brazil, Indonesia, Turkey and the Philippines) accounted for 217 million Facebook users in 2012 (Mims, 2012). This growth can be partly attributed to initiatives such as Facebook Zero. Thanks to Facebook's collaboration with mobile operators from a number of emerging economies, users can access 0.facebook.com (Facebook Zero) completely free. Facebook Zero contains the key features of Facebook. The majority of users in developing countries use mobile devices to access Facebook. Most of these phones are feature phones that operate on a pay-as-you-go basis, rather than smartphones with app capabilities. Every phone app, which runs on around 3000 feature phone models worldwide, has made it possible for these users to access Facebook. As of July 2013, over 100 million people used this app. Some telecom carriers in countries such as India, the Philippines and Indonesia offer free or discounted data for Facebook Zero users (Byford, 2013).

1.3.2 Velocity

The idea here is that most of the data loses value if it is not quickly analysed. Velocity is considered as a 'competitive differentiator' for businesses using BD (Laney, 2001, p. 2). In this book's context, BD provides the possibility for real-time feedback, which can lead to important developmental outcomes. For instance, by monitoring a population in real time, it is possible to understand the areas where developmental policies and programmes are failing and to make required adjustments (Letouzé, 2012). A number of initiatives that have been launched to promote a BD ecosystem have focused on the velocity of data. In sub-Saharan African economies, the use of farm credits is reported to decline due to poor access to financial services, high borrowing costs and high risks associated with such credits (Oluoch-Kosura, 2010). The creation of high-velocity data has helped address some of these problems. For instance, as of September 2013, the information created by Agrilife, a cloud-mobile platform in Kenya that provides financial institutions and suppliers 'near real-time information' on farmers' ability to pay for services (capacity.org, 2013), facilitated over US$2 million in revolving credit lines to about 120,000 small farmers in Kenya and Uganda (G-Analytix, 2013).

As another example, the World Bank's 'Listening to LAC' (L2L) initiative in Latin America deployed mobile technologies to conduct real-time self-administered surveys. The surveys collect life-events data on a near real-time basis and generate panel data. The data are expected to inform policy makers on current indicators and help them to respond more quickly and effectively to key trends. The data collection instrument is also expected to help policy makers assess the impact of their programmes in real time and observe coping mechanisms in situations such as migration, school attendance, employment patterns and nutrition (The World Bank, 2010).

It is especially important to explain the benefits of BD in the context of the lack of availability of data on key developmental indicators. Most traditional development data come from surveys (e.g. household, labour market, living standard) and official statistics. In addition to high costs, the key problems of survey data include a relatively long time to collect and analyse the data. Developing nations often need to wait a decade or more to adjust the gross domestic product or estimate poverty indicators (Fengler, 2013). In this regard, more frequently collected and better organized data can be used to help assess the social and economic conditions faster.

1.3.3 Variety

It is important to first define structured and unstructured data. Structured data can be organized in an assigned format that can be used by a database management system such as Oracle and Microsoft SQL. Some examples include histories of mobile payment transactions and the date of a Twitter account creation. Such data can be arranged in a list, compared with other data, used to generate new data and retrieved for decision making. Unstructured data, on the other hand, is unformatted and lacks a predefined standard structure (e.g. cannot be organized in terms of rows and columns). Some examples include email messages, social media posts, pictures and videos. One estimate suggested that 80% of medical and clinical information about patients is in an unstructured form such as written physician notes, consultant notes, radiology notes, pathology results and discharge notes from a hospital.

It is also worth noting that some sources involving interactions between people and machines, such as web applications or social networks, may provide multi-structured data. For instance, web log data include unstructured data such as text and visual images as well as structured data such as transactional information (Arthur, 2013).

Structured and unstructured data are being increasingly combined in developmental projects. For instance, the Malaria Surveillance & Mapping project in Botswana was a pilot programme launched in 2011, which aims to move away from paper reports towards mobile clouds. Health-care workers are equipped with mobile phones to gather and upload malaria-related data to the cloud. The data can also be tagged with structured data such as GPS coordinates and unstructured data such as pictures, videos and audio. If there are signals of an outbreak of malaria, Ministry of Health officials and other health workers in the area receive a real-time notification via text message (mhealthinfo.org, 2011).

Another example that involves the utilization of structured and unstructured data is 'Water Watchers', an android app and portal developed in May 2013 by IBM and South Africa's City of Tshwane to report water-related issues. One estimate suggested that 60% of water worldwide is lost due to leaky pipes (Carew, 2013). The app's users take a picture that shows a water-related problem and answer three questions about the problem. These data are then uploaded in real time to a cloud server. The information generated can be expected to identify a water-leak 'hot spot' map (Carew, 2013). BD may hold great promise for finding appropriate steps to prevent or minimize this wastage.

1.3.4 Variability

The approaches in BD assume that correlations can be considered as pragmatic indications of relationships among variables (Mayer-Schönberger and Cukier, 2013). In this regard, one technique that has been of great interest in developing countries is anomaly (or outlier) detection based on the variability over time in the amount of data flow related to a given developmental indicator. Note that anomaly detection involves identifying items or events that fail to conform to an expected pattern. The idea here is that items or events that exhibit an anomalous behaviour (e.g. an unusually high rate flow of data of certain categories) may be associated with some kind of problem. To take an example, the data formats used in Twitter's API are such that they provide the dynamic anomaly detection features. The idea here is that the key metadata used in segmenting Twitter data such as hashtags (#) and replies (@) are user generated and thus are logical targets to follow in order to understand problems and crises that users face. In sum, observing patterns of anomalies inside the data flowing from the Twitter API, one can detect signals of a crisis (Madsen, 2013).

One example to illustrate this point comes from a research project undertaken by the UN Global Pulse, which indicated that analysis of Twitter data can provide information on an increase in food prices. An analysis of a data set containing thousands of tweets from Indonesia discussing the price of rice indicated that the volume of tweets about staple foods had a positive correlation with an increase in the cost (UN Global Pulse, 2013a).

1.3.5 Complexity

It would be helpful to first note that the really big difference between variety and complexity concerns multiple data types (variety) versus multiple sources of data (complexity). Matching and linking data from multiple sources such as CDRs, open portals, social media, government sources, NGOs and corporations can provide a whole picture of the economic and social conditions of the rural population and thus provide valuable and relevant new insights (bigdata-startups.com, 2013). To take an example, a study indicated that BD can be employed to predict food shortages by combining variables from a number of sources such as drought, weather conditions, migration patterns, market prices of staples, seasonal variation in prices, and past productions (hsph.harvard.edu, 2014). As another example, time-series analyses of CDRs can be combined with random surveys to provide better insights about the dynamics of rural economies and help devise appropriate government responses (bigdata-startups.com, 2013).

To take another example, remote sensing, which involves acquiring information about the Earth using remote instruments, such as satellites, is highly useful for disaster management. Satellites provide accurate, frequent and almost instantaneous data and cover large areas of the Earth (Lewis, 2009). For disaster mitigation and relief, images used in mapping, which often come from satellites, can be combined with information from drones to develop a better response.

1.4 Key Areas of Big Data Deployment in Developing Countries

While the focus of this book is on the agricultural, environmental and health-care sectors in developing countries, a number of other industries also provide interesting examples of BD development in these countries. BD deployment can be seen on CEO-agenda issues of the developing world's leading organizations across all major industries and sectors.

1.4.1 E-commerce

China's Alibaba has attracted vendors to its e-commerce websites Taobao Marketplace and Tmall.com by promoting BD- and cloud-based advertising and other services, which provide deep insights into shoppers' preferences (Lorenzetti, 2014). As of early 2015, Taobao had over 500 million registered accounts and over 7 million merchants, which sold 4800 items per minute. Tmall.com, which was launched by Taobao for international and Chinese brands to reach Chinese consumers, has also been highly successful. According to iResearch, Tmall was China's largest business-to-consumer retail platform in September 2013 in terms of the value of goods transacted. By 2014, Tmall captured over 50% of the Chinese market (Lorenzetti, 2014).

Another Chinese Internet service portal, Tencent, uses social data to identify the trendsetters among groups of friends. This information is used to target those people (xinhuanet.com, 2015). In 2015, Tencent also launched a third-party data management platform that gives advertisers open access to Tencent data. The data included the activities of 800 million QQ monthly active users and 500 million WeChat users (Loras, 2015).

1.4.2 Oil and gas

In September 2015, China's Huawei launched a new Joint Innovation Center (JIC) in Dhahran, Saudi Arabia, together with Saudi Aramco and King Fahad University of Petroleum and Minerals. The focus of the JIC will be on digital and intelligent oil fields, digital pipelines, intelligent refineries, high-performance computing, BD, mobility, safety and security, cloud computing and energy management (tradearabia.com, 2015). Some key areas for application include increasing production rates, reducing non-productive time, predicting the failure of equipment, decision support for project planning and trading, de-risking petroleum exploration and production (dealing with the uncertainty of outcome associated with knowing whether an area contains reserves of petroleum that are commercially recoverable), regulatory compliance and early event detection (environmentalleader.com, 2015). Unlike information-based industries, the approach to BD needs to be more targeted and tailored for the oil and gas industry.

1.4.3 Banking, finance and insurance

The banking, finance and insurance sector has been experiencing a high growth of BD deployment. For instance, in Brazil the demand for analytical solutions in banks, financial services and telecommunications companies is expected to grow more rapidly than in any other sectors (Couto, 2015). To take an example, Banco do Brasil has hired data scientists and created algorithms in order to better understand customer behaviour and predict their needs (Ozores, 2014).

The South African insurance firm Santam uses predictive analytics to process claims and spot frauds. It allowed the company to deal with legitimate claims within an hour, which was 70 times faster than it could before without using predictive analytics. It also reduced the frequency with which Santam's claims adjusters visited clients for low-risk claims. The company claimed that it saved US$2.4 million in the first 4 months after launching the programme (eu-africa-cc.org, 2014).

Another South African health insurance firm, Discovery, uses BD to interpret complex health-related data to predict its clients' problems. The operation sharpened Discovery's fraud-detection tools. Analysing data from pharmacies and health providers, it can spot potential 'phantom' drug prescriptions (eu-africa-cc.org, 2014).

1.4.4 Improving disaster mitigation and preparedness

During the period 1970 to 2008, developing countries accounted for over 95% all deaths caused by natural disasters (IPCC, 2015). Factors such as high-population densities, poor infrastructure, unstable landforms and exposure to severe weather events make these countries vulnerable to natural disaster and a high number of deaths (Lewis, 2009). BD can improve disaster mitigation and preparedness. For instance, when the Typhoon Bopha hit the Philippines in 2012, within 24 hours the Digital Humanitarian Network categorized 20,000 social media messages and created a map of the storm's impact, which was arguably the first official UN crisis map that was entirely based on data from social media (Meier, 2012). The map reportedly helped several UN agencies and the government of the Philippines in their relief efforts. To take another example, following the April 2015 Nepal earthquake, relief workers used data from drones and crowdsourced maps offered by volunteer groups to get emergency supplies to the affected survivors (Wang *et al.*, 2015). A non-profit organization, Code for Nepal, regularly updated an interactive map that showed the effects of the earthquake. The map used district-level data, which showed death counts, number of injuries and houses damaged, in order to help relief workers and the government agencies allocate resources (Kumar, 2015).

BD may provide additional details that help address key developmental issues, challenges and questions. For instance, it is possible to generate detailed poverty maps that can visually identify poor areas with greater accuracy. Accurate poverty maps can act as essential planning tools, which can enable the government, civil society and developmental agencies to identify poor areas and take appropriate actions (worldbank.org, 2015a). Current poverty maps are mostly based on household surveys. CDRs provide additional information about the communication and mobility patterns of people, which can be used to create more detailed poverty maps with a finer spatial resolution. Compared to household surveys, BD provides a more efficient way to construct such maps, which can facilitate improved diagnosis of poverty and help public policy planners to make appropriate interventions (Pokhriyal *et al.*, 2015).

1.4.5 Enhancing transparency and reducing corruption

The above discussion indicates the potential socioeconomic impacts of BD in a number of domains and sectors. The BD-led promotion of transparency and accountability can be included among the major impacts. Note that transparency involves making information about an entity's operations, structures and other attributes available to the public (Heald, 2006). Transparency has gained wide support among state decision-making bodies, international organizations and private companies (Finel and Lord, 1999).

In China, thanks to various private data sources, investors and the public have better means to rate the leadership's performance. Chinese citizens have a tendency to distrust information provided by the government. The market of privately produced data, such as the unofficial monthly purchasing-manager index produced by the Chinese financial media group Caixin, is increasing. The real estate company Soufun has built a private real estate price index, which is used to compare with official measures (Balding, 2015).

BD is evolving as an important tool for promoting transparency and reducing corruption in developing economies. In the village of Bagega in Nigeria, for instance, at least 460 children died due to lead poisoning associated with gold mining activity and nearly 2000 more became sick in 2010 (Mark, 2014). Two years following the tragedy, the area was not cleaned and the survivors had not received life-saving treatments. The local non-profit organization Follow the Money launched a social media campaign that featured government data on the disaster. The campaign gave an indication as to where the money should have gone. There was wide media coverage globally on the issue, and in January 2013 the government was forced to release US$5.3 million to alleviate the crisis (Firth, 2013).

In the context of this book, another intriguing area in which BD is likely to have a positive impact in promoting transparency and accountability is via fighting cruelty to animals. Discoveries and advancements in medications, steroids, hormones, pesticides, antibiotics, central air-conditioning systems, automatic feeders and other breakthroughs have delivered superior performance and unprecedented efficiency with which meat, eggs, fish and dairy products can be produced. For instance, chickens and pigs are being crammed into and raised in tiny coops and pens. Thanks to the scientific community's growing knowledge, animals' lives are being manipulated in such a way that they can efficiently serve the needs of humans. In this way, science has played a devastating and dismal role in this tragedy (Harari, 2015).

BD science can fight back. BD helps track agents who commit acts of cruelty against animals in a more systematic way and in a timely manner, which would help consumers and other groups pursue and impose economic and other sanctions to achieve the desired results. In summary, just like a diamond is the only material hard enough to cut another diamond effectively, BD science can be an effective tool to fight against science-driven cruelty to animals.

Greater transparency and accountability would help farmers to expand their markets. Access to precision data helps them export products to the European Union and other economies. There are differing standards regarding the amount of pesticides used on crops and the kind of feed/fertilizer given to animals/plants. There are also concerns about the use of child or slave labour to pick crops or produce milk or eggs (Shamah, 2015). Regulators, customers and other stakeholders are also interested in knowing how cows are milked or hens in the egg-laying stage are warehoused. For instance, animal activists have been pressuring poultry farming companies to stop the practice of warehousing egg-laying hens inside tiny wire cages.

In the Chinese securities market's electronic trading system, over 200 million investors generate more than 60,000 orders per minute. China Securities and Regulatory Commission and stock exchanges perform semantic analysis to detect more than 100 million social media data daily (SSE, 2013; SZSE, 2013). In December 2013, they detected 'rat trading' in Shanghai through an online monitoring system. ('Rat trading' refers to fund managers buying shares via their personal trading accounts ahead of large purchases of the same shares by their fund companies. Using this method, they can illegally profit from a rise in share price.) Some brokers study the relationship between Internet information, social media (e.g. Weibo) activity and stock market performance to identify stock market trends through public opinion analysis (Li *et al.*, 2014).

Data activism through BD is likely to make the government less corrupt, more efficient and less repressive, as well as more responsive to the needs of the people. A notable example is the Black Monday Movement in Uganda that was launched by a civilian organization in 2012. The organization publicized stories of corruption and the availability of money accessible to provide constituent services. The activists used Facebook and other social platforms in order to create awareness and engage in debates and criticism of negative social phenomena and political and corporate interest groups (Dutton, 2011).

1.5 The Relationship between Big Data, Mobility, the Internet of Things and Cloud Computing in the Context of Developing Countries

The growth of the BD industry and market in developing countries is associated with and facilitated by the diffusion of complementary technologies such as cloud computing, mobility and low-cost sensors. BD is thus intimately linked to these technologies. The combination of these technologies is likely to produce the greatest impact in the developing world (Khumalo, 2011).

The most notable trend is the sharp decline in the costs of sensors and other associated technologies. During the past decade or so, the cost of some types of sensors reportedly declined by a factor of 100 (Lesser, 2015). Some technologies associated with the IoT such as RFID tags cost just a few cents (McLellan, 2013). The favourable economics of cheap sensors are realized as a result of global availability of reliable wireless communication, better algorithms, cloud computing and BD. The use of tags on merchandise in stores is increasing due to the decline in the cost of readers and an expectation that most smartphones in the future will have built-in RFID readers (Swedberg, 2015).

In particular, BD and cloud computing play complementary roles. Each drives and feeds off advancement of the other. BD requires new processing and volume requirements, which translates into the need for additional infrastructure. The cloud makes it easier to scale up for processing power and storage (itnewsafrica.com, 2013).

1.6 Determinants of the Development of the Big Data Industry and Market

It is important to discuss the changing nature of the international digital divide. Hilbert (2014) identifies three complementary stages associated with the digital divide: (i) access to a technology; (ii) its effective usage; and (iii) social integration and impact of the technology. The fact that over 91.8% of the population in developing economies owned a mobile phone in 2015 means that the access-related digital divide has significantly narrowed down. However, the last two stages are characterized by a deep gap between industrialized and developing countries. Equality in access is thus necessary but not a sufficient condition to lead to a digital equality.

A related point is that the nature of the current digital divide is associated with and facilitated by the pattern of BD diffusion and its effective use. Hilbert

(2014) notes that the current inequality of technological capacity represents a more mature and also more persistent stage of the digital divide.

In order to better understand the above observations, it is important to note that the diffusion pattern of an innovation such as BD is a function of the environment and characteristics of the innovation (Rogers, 1995; O'Neil *et al.*, 1998). Regarding the environment, information infrastructure arguably has social, political and economic dimensions (Bowker, 1996). This means that different social, political and economic situations may give rise to significantly different rates of diffusion of BD in industrialized and developing countries. Such differences can explain the enormous gap between the developing and developed worlds in the utilization of BD.

1.6.1 Social and political dimensions

Factors such as the availability of skills and capabilities, social and cultural attitudes towards a technology, the institutional environment, and social reorganization are tightly linked to the ability to use the technology effectively and appropriately (DiMaggio *et al.*, 2004; Buente and Robbin, 2008; Robinson, 2009). The availability of skills and social support have also been recognized as key dimensions of the digital divide. Prior researchers have especially emphasized the role of 'Internet competence', which is related to the know-how, technical skills and capacity to exploit the Internet's potential by strategically responding to challenges and opportunities (DiMaggio and Hargittai, 2001).

Equality in usage does not necessarily translate to social equality. Some groups in a society are in a position to benefit more from information communication technologies (ICTs) than others. This implies the possibility of dominance by some social groups and may therefore lead to 'an increasing social divide' (Hilbert, 2014). For instance, one commentator noted that about 90% of the discussion at the 2013 Internet Governance Forum (IGF) referred to BD as a surveillance tool. At the same time, the debate focusing on developing countries treated BD as a means to 'observe' people to fight poverty. The argument provided by IGF participants was that data can help provide access to clean drinking water, health care and other necessities (Taylor, 2013).

Regarding political factors, governments in some developing countries have been active in promoting the use of BD and creating a favourable environment. For instance, in 2014 the Chinese People's Political Consultative Conference, the political advisory legislative body, organized a consultation forum in Beijing in order to gather ideas regarding the use of BD to improve governance capability (Cheng, 2014). In September 2015, Chengdu announced a plan to establish a local government agency that will be in charge of data held by the local authorities. Guangzhou and Shenyang announced the establishment of similar agencies in May and June of 2015. The establishment of the agency is expected to accelerate the local government's plan to open up its databases, which will create potential business for service providers of data analytics (wantchinatimes.com, 2015b). In September 2015, China launched its first BD zone in Guizhou. The Guizhou BD zone is expected to serve as a testbed for sharing, using, and engaging in innovation and security related to BD. Guizhou is also expected to build a cloud-based BD platform, known as Guizhou on the Cloud, which allows data from the provincial government to be shared and exchanged. By the end of 2016, the BD platform is expected to integrate data from city- and county-level governmental departments (telecomasia.net, 2015).

Chinese BD firms benefit from the government's favourable policy. The central government has decided to establish a unified platform for governmental data (BD platform) by 2018. The tech parks or zones in first-, second- and third-tier cities have also come up with policies to support the BD industry (wantchinatimes.com, 2015a).

1.6.2 Economic dimension

The developmental pattern of an industry is tightly linked to the forward linkages (demand), backward linkages (supply) and horizontal or inter-sectoral linkages (Markusen and Venables, 1999). This means that BD industries and markets are embedded in the broader economy and thus their development should not be viewed as a self-contained phenomenon with self-contained solutions.

Consumers in developing countries lack money to engage in activities that generate data. Organizations are not in a position to afford data. The limited access to BD has created new forms of digital divides (Boyd and Crawford, 2012).

Organizations in a country with a low degree of inter-relatedness with other complementary technologies find it difficult to obtain the information and skills needed for a new technology (Allen, 1998). Thus, countries with a small base of high technology and innovative capital goods are likely to experience lower rates of diffusion for emerging new technologies (Antonelli, 1986). To put things in context, wider and deeper adoptions of PCs, mobile devices and other ICT applications are likely to lead to faster diffusion of BD.

The environments in developing countries are associated with adverse conditions in terms of markets and infrastructures, which are likely to slow down the diffusion of new technological innovations such as BD. Likewise, under-developed infrastructures such as those related to weather forecasting and satellite imaging technologies hinder the use of BD in environmental monitoring and protection in these countries.

BD deployment confronts developing economies with a variety of challenges. The lack of resources, in workforce terms and other assets, undermines the ability to tackle the environmental issues that face the developing world. For instance, South Africa's Kruger National Park, which has an area of 20,000 km^2, has only 400 rangers (Everett, 2014). Technologies and processes such as platforms, tools and crowdsourcing models to enable mass collaboration of environmental monitoring are currently at the stage of infancy. Scalability of the systems and operationalization of services are often limited by the lack of resources (Finn *et al.*, 2014).

In these countries there is limited hardware, software and other technological applications to generate and distribute the relevant data and knowledge. Moreover, the lower quality of hardware, software and infrastructure may lead to a lower amount of information flow. For instance, many businesses design websites with features such as 'low graphics' and 'text-only' to accommodate the needs of users in developing countries.

Most developing countries lack the market and infrastructure to make a technology available to potential adopters. Manufacturers of new technological products often focus their efforts on large distributors, which tend to be located in developed countries. The environment in developing countries is associated with adverse conditions in terms of markets and infrastructures, which are likely to slow down the diffusion of new technological innovations such as BD. For instance, a large proportion of firms in developing countries may lack the readiness to adopt BD. Likewise, under-developed infrastructures, such as those related to weather forecasting and satellite imaging technologies, hinder the use of BD in agricultural activities in these countries.

1.7 Some Forces to Overcome the Adverse Economic, Political and Cultural Circumstances

1.7.1 Multinationals launching Big Data applications in developing countries

While manufacturers of new technological products often find developing countries less attractive, some researchers have suggested that multinationals exploit technological capabilities internationally by means of activities such as export, movement of production activities abroad and licensing, which have driven the globalization of technologies (Archibugi and Michie, 1997; Iammarino and Michie, 1998). Such forces have been shown to influence the diffusion of the Internet and e-commerce-related technologies, especially in developing economies (Kshetri, 2001; Kshetri and Dholakia, 2002).

Among the visible examples of multinational companies based in the industrialized world that have made BD solutions available in developing countries are IBM and Google. In 2014, IBM launched the US$100 million 'Project Lucy', which is a ten-year initiative to bring cognitive computing technologies to Africa. A key feature of the cognitive computing system is that it is not programmed. Instead the systems and software improve by learning. The systems extract insights from huge amounts of data from diverse sources. In this way, they are expected to discover responses to questions and provide insights by analysing BD.

Cognitive computing has a large number of potential uses. For instance, outside big cities in sub-Saharan African economies, mostly community health workers deliver health care. The cognitive system can collect a large amount of data about traditional and non-traditional diseases, which can be used by doctors, nurses and field workers in diagnosing diseases and identifying the best treatment. For instance, IBM Watson, which is a cognitive system, makes it possible to expand the analysis beyond a narrow set of variables (e.g. school data about student performance, teacher expertise, attendance levels or learning materials). Cognitive computing systems provide an approach that involves learning, discovering answers to complex questions and suggesting solutions by analysing a huge amount of data. Cognitive computing and BD thus can play major roles in addressing development challenges facing developing countries by turning data into insights that can be readily put to use. As an example, using cognitive computing it may be possible to understand how contaminated water, a cholera epidemic and low levels of school attendance are related. It is also possible to understand the links between children's performance in the class and cultural traditions such as the childcare responsibility placed on older siblings in a family (forbes.com, 2014). Likewise, cognitive computing can help understand food price patterns and diseases unique to Africa and other regions (Wayua, 2014).

In 2013, Google announced a US$3 million grant to three anti-trafficking organizations (Polaris Project, Liberty Asia, and La Strada International) to fight human trafficking using BD. The organizations will analyse their internal data and match these with data from other sources such as trafficking emergency hotlines. The goal is to build a clearer picture of how and where the human-trafficking-related crimes occur in order to develop a more timely and effective response. The insights are likely to help develop appropriate intervention mechanisms involving law enforcement and victims' rights groups (Warner, 2013).

In 2012, Google provided a US$5 million grant to the World Wildlife Fund to use drones in combination with other technologies to track poachers and illicit wildlife trades in Namibia (unep.org, 2013). It combines imagery from drones with real-time location information about poachers, armed ranger patrols and electronically tagged rhinos in order to deploy rangers more effectively (Welz, 2013).

Google has also put effort into initiatives to fight against the Zika virus. In March 2016, it contributed US$1 million to support UNICEF's efforts in Latin America to combat Zika. The company was also reported to be providing help to build a mapping platform to help predict Zika outbreaks. The platform analyses data from different sources, including weather and travel patterns (Schnirring, 2016).

1.7.2 The roles of international development agencies

International development agencies such as the UN are also acting as key forces in providing support to facilitate BD diffusion in developing economies. For instance, BD has been in the centre of attention of development agencies. In August 2014, the UN Secretary-General named an Independent Expert Advisory Group on the Data Revolution for Sustainable Development. The group will provide inputs to shape the vision for the Post-2015 Development Agenda (un.org, 2014). ITU helps developing countries in their efforts to collect and disseminate data. Such supports are provided for the production of statistics related to ICT infrastructure, access and use (itu.int, 2016). Financial assistance from international organizations has enabled some developing countries to develop BD capability. In September 2015, the World Bank gave US$50 million to the Kenyan Bureau of Statistics in order to help the Bureau to accumulate more data (Mohammad, 2015).

1.8 Agriculture, Health and Environment: Intricate Relationship

The issues of agriculture, health and the environment are intricately intertwined with each other. For instance, air pollution in China is estimated to contribute to about 1.6 million deaths per year, which is 17% of all deaths in the country (Rohde and Muller, 2015). Likewise, during the 2015 Indonesian fires, air quality indexes in the many provinces such as Central Kalimantan, South Sumatra, Jambi and Riau reached hazardous levels (Siswo, 2015). It was estimated that fire and haze affected the health of over 120,000 people (Tanoto, 2016). Following the death of a 15-month-old infant, Latifa Ramadani, from a respiratory infection, a senior politician, Fahira Idris, asked local health authorities in the provinces of Sumatra and Kalimantan to perform additional checks on all babies and toddlers (mongabay.com, 2015).

According to the World Bank, over 1.1 billion people worldwide live off the electric grid and lack access to reliable power. An additional 2.9 billion people rely on wood or other biomass for cooking and heating. Due to the resulting indoor and outdoor air pollution, 4.3 million people are estimated to die each year (worldbank.org, 2015b). BD is helping some of these poor people to get a loan to buy solar panels (see Chapter 3).

Likewise, agriculture is an environmentally sensitive industry. Agricultural productivity is tightly linked to various characteristics of the environment. Returning to the example of the 2015 Indonesian fires, Indonesian farmers were expecting a poor harvest because plants received insufficient sunlight required for normal photosynthesis. As of November 2015, the haze had killed at least 10 people and about 504,000 had become sick in Borneo and Sumatra. Analysts believed that the actual number of deaths was much higher than this figure (voanews.com, 2015).

On the other hand, mega agricultural projects such as those undertaken by TH Milk in Vietnam (see Chapter 5) are likely to leave a significant ecological footprint. Other agricultural practices can also affect environmental quality. For instance, about 70% of the world's fresh water is used for agriculture (IBM, 2015). Thus, finding a better way to manage how water is used is likely to have a big impact on the supply of fresh water.

A related point is that some data sources have multiple uses and implications. For instance, data from sensors installed in orbiting Earth-observing satellites can monitor environmental risk factors that are likely to lead to malaria epidemics and increased mortality. Such sensors can monitor and measure landscape-level environmental indicators, such as the size and configuration of coastal habitats and vegetation cover and how they change over time. These sensors can also provide information about soil characteristics such as texture, organic matter and fertility, which can be used for precise prescriptions.

1.9 Discussion and Concluding Comments

BD is likely to be of tremendous benefit to developing countries. BD allows researchers, policy makers and developmental agencies to analyse diverse challenges that poor people and poor countries face. If properly and creatively used, BD can improve the welfare of farmers and rural communities. It is probably fair to say that some signs of BD-led transformation in economic and social life are already visible in developing countries.

Nonetheless it would be unreasonable to expect that BD will be panacea or magic bullet to solve all the developmental issues. Key social, political and economic challenges stand in the way of successful deployment of BD. Without strong political commitment, the potential of BD to improve agricultural, environmental and health-care conditions cannot be fulfilled. Likewise, the inescapable fact is that the values or cultures in many developing countries lack compatibility with BD.

It is important to recognize the prominent roles that government agencies, international development and donor agencies, NGOs, education institutions and private sector organizations play in the deployment of BD in developing economies. Funding for some of the technologies has come from companies' philanthropic and environmental programmes.

The emergence of high-profile BD firms based in the developing world, such as Alibaba, offers a very encouraging sign that locally developed BD solutions may effectively address various developmental challenges. Cases like Alibaba are, however, extreme and rare in the developing world. Most BD projects undertaken in developing countries are more similar and closer to the Agrilife platform than they are to Alibaba's ODPS. In many cases, firms based in the developing world have launched their own versions of what are considered to be BD deployments. However, most are in their early phase of development and growth, and their long-term results are yet to be confirmed.

The above discussion suggests that the biggest impact is likely to occur when BD is used to promote transparency and reduce corruption. Environmentalists and others have put forward convincing arguments that are based on hard data. Actors engaged in illegitimate conduct find it difficult to defend themselves against arguments that are firmly supported by data and analysis. For instance, activists' actions were crucial in pressuring the Peruvian government to impose sanctions against United Cacao, which allegedly deforested about 7000 ha of rainforest in the Peruvian Amazon (see Chapter 3).

References

alibabagroup.com (2015) Ant Financial unveils China's first credit-scoring system using online data. Available at: http://www.alibabagroup.com/en/news/article?news=p150128 (accessed 15 February 2016).

Allen, D. (1998) New telecommunications services: network externalities and critical mass. *Telecommunications Policy* 257–271.

Antonelli, C. (1986) The international diffusion of new information technologies. *Research Policy* 3,139–147.

Archibugi, D. and Michie, J. (1997) Technological globalisation or national systems of innovation? *Futures* 29(2), 121–137.

Arthur, L. (2013) What is Big Data? Available at: http://www.forbes.com/sites/lisaarthur/2013/08/15/what-is-big-data/ (accessed 18 August 2014).

Balding, C. (2015) Big Data means better data for China. Available at: http://www.bloombergview.com/articles/2015-11-09/big-data-means-better-economic-data-for-china (accessed 15 February 2016).
Bays, J. (2014) Harnessing big data to address the world's problems. Available at: http://voices.mckinseyonsociety.com/harnessing-big-data-to-address-the-worlds-problems/ (accessed 18 August 2014).
bigdata-startups.com (2013) How Big Data can help the developing world beat poverty. Available at: http://www.bigdata-startups.com/big-data-developing-world-beat-poverty/ (accessed 18 August 2014).
Bowker G.C. (1996) The history of information infrastructures: the case of the international classification of diseases. *Information Processing & Management* 32(1), 49–61.
Boyd, D. and Crawford, K. (2012) Critical questions for Big Data: provocations for a cultural, technological, and scholarly phenomenon. *Information, Communication & Society* 15(5), 662–679.
Buente, W. and Robbin, A. (2008) Trends in internet information behavior, 2000–2004. *Journal of the American Society for Information Science and Technology* 59(11), 1743–1760.
Byford, S. (2013) Facebook's drive into developing nations scores 100 million users. Available at: http://www.theverge.com/2013/7/21/4544326/facebook-for-every-phone-has-100-million-users (accessed 18 August 2014).
capacity.org (2013) Agrilife platform. Available at: http://www.capacity.org/capacity/opencms/en/topics/gender-and-social-inclusion/agrilife-web-platform-kenya.html (accessed 15 February 2016).
Carew, J. (2013) World war water. Available at: http://www.itweb.co.za/?id=64253:World-War-Water (accessed 18 August 2014).
Caulderwood, K. (2014) Cheap phones, big data and good business. Available at: http://www.ibtimes.com/cheap-phones-big-data-good-business-1567731 (accessed 15 February 2016).
Cheng, J.H.-W. (2014) UNDP China. Big Data for development in China. Available at: http://www.cn.undp.org/content/dam/china/docs/Publications/UNDP%20Working%20Paper_Big%20Data%20for%20Development%20in%20China_Nov%202014.pdf (accessed 7 April 2016).
Chunara, R., Andrews, J. and Brownstein, J. (2012) Social and news media enable estimation of epidemiological patterns early in the 2010 Haitian cholera outbreak. *American Journal of Tropical Medicine and Hygiene* 86, 39–45. Available at: http://www.ajtmh.org/content/86/1/39.abstract (accessed 18 August 2014).
cisco.com (2014) Cisco Visual Networking Index: global mobile data traffic forecast update, 2015–2020. Available at: http://www.cisco.com/c/en/us/solutions/collateral/service-provider/visual-networking-index-vni/white_paper_c11-520862.html (accessed 18 August 2014).
Couto, L. (2015) Brazil's Big Data and analytics market will top $800M. Available at: https://icrunchdatanews.com/brazil-big-data-analytics-market-800m (accessed 15 February 2016).
DiMaggio, P., and Hargittai, E. (2001) From the 'digital divide' to 'digital inequality': studying Internet use as penetration increases. Princeton University Center for Arts and Cultural Policy Studies, Working Paper #15. Available at: http://www.princeton.edu/~artspol/workpap/WP15%20-%20DiMaggio%2BHargittai.pdf (accessed 18 August 2014).
DiMaggio, P., Hargittai, E., Celeste, C. and Shafer, S. (2004) From unequal access to differentiated use?: a literature review and agenda for research on digital inequality. In: Neckerman, K. (ed.), *Social Inequality*. Sage, New York, pp. 355–400.
Dutton, S. (2011) What Justin Bieber proves about the human face of Big Data. Available at: http://www.business2community.com/big-data/what-justin-bieber-proves-about-the-human-face-of-big-data-01321898 (accessed 15 February 2016).
environmentalleader.com (2015) As oil prices plunge, big oil turns to Big Data. Available at: http://www.environmentalleader.com/2015/09/10/as-oil-prices-plunge-big-oil-turns-to-big-data/ (accessed 15 February 2016).

eu-africa-cc.org (2014) 'Big Data' comes to Africa. Available at: http://eu-africa-cc.org/index.php/fr/news/95-ict/448-big-data-comes-to-africa (accessed 5 February 2015).
Everett, C. (2014) Out of Africa: the digital tech taking on the rhino poachers. Available at: http://diginomica.com/2014/11/06/africa-digital-tech-taking-rhino-poachers/#.VF0MoWdINmc (accessed 15 February 2016).
Fengler, W. (2013) Big Data and development: 'The second half of the chess board'. Available at: https://blogs.worldbank.org/africacan/big-data-and-development-the-second-half-of-the-chess-board (accessed 18 August 2014).
Fengler, W. and Kharas, H. (2015) Personalising data for development. Available at: http://blogs.ft.com/beyond-brics/2015/09/23/personalising-data-for-development/ (accessed 15 February 2016).
fin4ag.org (2014) Agrilife Platform. Available at: http://fin4ag.org/en/session/agrilife-platform.html (accessed 15 February 2016).
Finel, B.I. and Lord, K.M. (1999) The surprising logic of transparency. *International Studies Quarterly* 43, 315–339.
Finn, R., Donovan, A., Wadhwa, K., Bigagli, L. and García, J.M. (2014) Big data roadmap and cross-disciplinary community for addressing societal externalities. European Union.
Firth, N. (2013) How open data empowers citizens of poorer nations. Available at: http://www.newscientist.com/article/mg22029434.400-how-open-data-empowers-citizens-of-poorer-nations.html#.VTaxVfDSlEg (accessed 15 February 2016).
forbes.com (2014) Could Big Data and cognitive computing solve Africa's greatest challenges? Available at: http://www.forbes.com/sites/ibm/2014/11/20/could-big-data-and-cognitive-computing-solve-africas-greatest-challenges/ (accessed 15 February 2016).
G-Analytix (2013) Credit information sharing: unlocking access to affordable credit. Alternative data to drive financial inclusion, The 2nd Regional Credit Information Sharing Conference, 24–25 September 2013, Nairobi, Kenya.
gartner.com (2013) Big Data. Available at: http://www.gartner.com/it-glossary/big-data/ (accessed 18 August 2014).
GSM Association (2012) GSMA announces new global research that highlights significant growth opportunity for the mobile industry. Available at: http://www.gsma.com/newsroom/press-release/gsma-announces-new-global-research-that-highlights-significant-growth-opportunity-for-the-mobile-industry/ (accessed 7 April 2016).
GSM Association (2014) Understanding the Internet of Things (IoT). Available at: http://www.gsma.com/connectedliving/wp-content/uploads/2014/08/cl_iot_wp_07_14.pdf (accessed 7 April 2016).
Harari, N.Y. (2015) Industrial farming is one of the worst crimes in history. Available at: http://www.theguardian.com/books/2015/sep/25/industrial-farming-one-worst-crimes-history-ethical-question (accessed 15 February 2016).
Hawkins, R. (2003) Looking beyond the dot com bubble: exploring the form and function of business models in the electronic marketplace. In: Bouwman, H., Preissl, B. and Steinfield, C. (eds) *E-Life After the Dot-com Bust*. Physica-Verlag, Heidelberg, Germany.
Heald, D. (2006) Varieties of transparency. In: Hood, C. and Heald, D. (eds) *Transparency: the Key to Better Governance?* Oxford University Press, Oxford, UK, pp. 23–45.
Hilbert, M. (2014) Technological information inequality as an incessantly moving target: the redistribution of information and communication capacities between 1986 and 2010. *Journal of the Association for Information Science and Technology* 65(4), 821–835.
hsph.harvard.edu (2014) Big Data for social good. Available at: http://www.hsph.harvard.edu/ess/bigdata.html (accessed 18 August 2014).
Iammarino, S. and Michie, J. (1998) The scope of technological globalisation. *International Journal of the Economics of Business* 5(3), 335–353.

IBM (2015) Precision agriculture: using predictive weather analytics to feed future generations. Available at: http://www.research.ibm.com/articles/precision_agriculture.shtml (accessed 15 February 2016).
IPCC [The Intergovernmental Panel on Climate Change] (2015) The IPCC special report on managing the risks of extreme events and disasters to advance climate change adaptation. World Meteorological Organization, Geneva, Switzerland. Available at: http://www.ipcc-wg2.gov/SREX/ (accessed 7 April 2016).
itnewsafrica.com (2013) Cloud taking big data analytics to new heights. Available at: http://www.itnewsafrica.com/2013/07/cloud-taking-big-data-analytics-to-new-heights/ (accessed 15 February 2016).
itu.int (2016) Capacity development. Available at: http://www.itu.int/en/ITU-D/Statistics/Pages/capacitydev/default.aspx (accessed 15 February 2016).
Khumalo, F. (2011) African firms begin to find value in Big Data. Available at: http://www.africasciencenews.org/en/index.php?option=com_content&view=article&id=1342:african-firms-begin-to-find-value-in-big-data&catid=45:hitech&Itemid=116 (accessed 16 February 2016).
Kim, E. (2014) A company spun out of Alibaba is now worth as much as $50 billion. Available at: http://www.businessinsider.com/ant-financial-closes-deal-that-gives-50-billion-valuation-2015-7 (accessed 15 February 2016).
Kshetri, N. (2001) Determinants of the locus of global e-commerce. *Electronic Markets* 11(4), 250–257.
Kshetri, N. (2009) Institutionalization of intellectual property rights in China. *European Management Journal* 27(3), 155–164.
Kshetri, N. and Dholakia, N. (2002) Determinants of the global diffusion of B2B e-commerce. *Electronic Markets* 12(2), 120–129.
Kumar, R. (2015) Use data, not nepotism, to deliver aid in Nepal. Available at: http://time.com/3845593/nepal-earthquake-response-data/ (accessed 15 February 2016).
Laney, D. (2001) 3D data management: controlling data volume, velocity and variety. Available at: http://blogs.gartner.com/doug-laney/files/2012/01/ad949-3D-Data-Management-Controlling-Data-Volume-Velocity-and-Variety.pdf (accessed 18 August 2014).
Laskowski, N. (2016) Delving into an enterprise IoT initiative? Read this first. Available at: http://searchcio.techtarget.com/feature/Delving-into-an-enterprise-IoT-initiative-Read-this-first (accessed 15 February 2016).
Lesser, A. (2015) Declining sensor costs open up new consumer applications. Available at: https://gigaom.com/2015/01/25/declining-sensor-costs-open-up-new-consumer-applications (accessed 7 April 2016).
Letouzé, E. (2012) Big data for development: what may determine success or failure? OECD Technology Foresight 2012, Paris, October 22. Available at: https://www.oecd.org/sti/ieconomy/Session_5_Letouz%C3%A9.pdf (accessed 7 April 2016).
Lewis, S. (2009) Remote sensing for natural disasters: facts and figures. Available at: http://www.scidev.net/global/earth-science/feature/remote-sensing-for-natural-disasters-facts-and-figures.html (accessed 15 February 2016).
Li, J., Zhang, Y., Wu, D. and Zhang, W. (2014) Winter Bridge: a global view of big data. Available at: https://www.nae.edu/Publications/Bridge/128772/129193.aspx (accessed 15 February 2016).
Li, X.X. (2014) Alibaba has big hopes for new big data processing service. Available at: http://english.caixin.com/2014-07-17/100705224.html (accessed 15 February 2016).
Lohr, S. (2013) Searching big data for 'digital smoke signals'. Available at: http://www.nytimes.com/2013/08/08/technology/development-groups-tap-big-data-to-direct-humanitarian-aid.html?_r=0 (accessed 18 August 2014).

Loras, S. (2015) Windfall for advertisers as Tencent opens third party data access. Available at: https://www.clickz.com/clickz/news/2410703/windfall-for-advertisers-as-tencent-opens-third-party-data-access (accessed 7 April 2016).
Lorenzetti, L. (2014) Alibaba's first public earnings reveal major revenue growth. Available at: http://fortune.com/2014/11/04/alibabas-first-public-earnings-reveal-major-revenue-growth/ (accessed 15 February 2016).
Lovett, G.M., Burns, D.A., Driscoll, C.T., Jenkins, J.C., Mitchell, M.J., *et al.* (2007) Who needs environmental monitoring? *Frontiers in Ecology and the Environment* 5, 253–260.
Madsen, A.K. (2013) Web-Visions: repurposing digital traces to organize social attention. The Doctoral School of Organisation and Management Studies, Copenhagen Business School. Available at: http://openarchive.cbs.dk/bitstream/handle/10398/8746/Anders_Koed_Madsen.pdf?sequence=1 (accessed 15 February 2016).
Mark, M. (2014) Nigerian gold mining: farmers choose death by lead poisoning over poverty. Available at: http://www.theguardian.com/global-development/2014/mar/17/nigeria-gold-mining-farmers-lead-poisoning-poverty (accessed 15 February 2016).
Markusen, J.R. and Venables, A.J. (1999) Foreign direct investment as a catalyst for industrial development. *European Economic Review* 43(2), 335–356.
Mayer-Schönberger, V. and Cukier, K. (2013) Big Data: a revolution that will transform how we live, work and think. Houghton Mifflin Harcourt, Boston, USA.
McLellan, C. (2013) M2M and Internet of Things: a guide. Available at: http://www.zdnet.com/article/m2m-and-the-internet-of-things-a-guide/ (accessed 15 February 2016).
Meier, P. (2012) How the UN used social media in response to Typhoon Pablo (updated). Available at: http://irevolution.net/2012/12/08/digital-response-typhoon-pablo/ (accessed 15 February 2016).
mhealthinfo.org (2011) Malaria surveillance & mapping. Available at: http://www.mhealthinfo.org/project/malaria-surveillance-mapping (accessed 18 August 2014).
Mims, C. (2012) Facebook's plan to find its next billion users: convince them the internet and Facebook are the same. Available at: http://qz.com/5180/facebooks-plan-to-find-its-next-billion-users-convince-them-the-internet-and-facebook-are-the-same/ (accessed 18 August 2014).
Mohammad, O. (2015) Reliable data is the answer to Africa's $1 trillion agriculture opportunity. Available at: http://qz.com/501379/reliable-data-is-the-answer-to-africas-1-trillion-agriculture-opportunity/ (accessed 15 February 2016).
mongabay.com (2015) Indonesian healthcare in focus as haze worsens; NASA data show Papua ablaze. Available at: http://news.mongabay.com/2015/10/indonesian-healthcare-in-focus-as-haze-worsens-nasa-data-show-papua-ablaze/ (accessed 15 February 2016).
O'Neil, H.M., Pouder, R.W. and Buchholtz, A.K. (1998) Patterns in the diffusion of strategies across organizations: insights from innovation diffusion literature. *The Academy of Management Review* 23(1), 98–114.
oilandgasbigdata.com (2015) Big data tools a recent phenomenon in GCC oil and gas firms. Available at: http://www.oilandgasbigdata.com/news/gcc-oil-and-gas-firms-use-big-data-tools-to-boost-output (accessed 15 February 2016).
Oluoch-Kosura, W. (2010) Institutional innovations for smallholder farmers' competitiveness in Africa. *African Journal of Agricultural and Resource Economics* 5(1), 227–242.
Ozores, P. (2014) Big data name of the game, says Brazil bank. Available at: http://www.bnamericas.com/news/banking/big-data-name-of-the-game-says-brazil-bank (accessed 15 February 2016).
Pokhriyal, N., Dong, W. and Govindraj, V. (2015) Big Data for improved diagnosis of poverty: a case study of Senegal. Available at: http://www.brookings.edu/blogs/africa-in-focus/posts/2015/06/02-big-data-poverty-senegal (accessed 15 February 2016).
Robinson, L. (2009) A taste for the necessary: a Bourdieuian approach to digital inequality. *Information, Communication & Society* 12(4), 488–507.

Rogers, E.M. (1995) *Diffusion of Innovations*, 4th edn. Free Press, New York, USA.
Rohde, R.A. and Muller, R.A. (2015) Air pollution in China: Mapping of concentrations and sources. *PLoS ONE* 10(8), e0135749.
sas.com (2013) Big Data: what it is and why it matters. Available at: https://www.sas.com/en_us/insights/big-data/what-is-big-data.html (accessed 18 August 2014).
Schnirring, L. (2016) Google aids Zika response; GBS cases show virus persistence in urine. Available at: http://www.cidrap.umn.edu/news-perspective/2016/03/google-aids-zika-response-gbs-cases-show-virus-persistence-urine (accessed 7 April 2016).
Schwarzmann, P. (2015) Alibaba, Mobile, India and you: Mary Meeker and what's trending now. Available at: https://blog.equinix.com/2015/06/alibaba-mobile-india-and-you-mary-meeker-and-whats-trending-now/ (accessed 15 February 2016).
Shamah, D. (2015) Israeli big data teaches farmers a cup of joe means better crops. Available at: http://www.timesofisrael.com/israeli-big-data-teaches-farmers-a-cup-of-joe-means-better-crops/ (accessed 15 February 2016).
Siswo, S. (2015) Nearly 1,000 hotspots detected in Sumatra as haze thickens. Available at: http://www.channelnewsasia.com/news/asiapacific/nearly-1-000-hotspots/2125114.html (accessed 15 February 2016).
SSE [Shanghai Stock Exchange] (2013) Statistical Yearbook of the Shanghai Stock Exchange. Available at: www.sse.com.cn/researchpublications/publication/yearly/c/tjnj_2013.pdf (accessed 16 February 2016).
SZSE [Shenzhen Stock Exchange] (2013) Statistical Yearbook of the Shenzhen Stock Exchange. Available at: www.szse.cn/main/files/2013/05/28/101380619096.pdf (accessed 4 May 2016).
Swedberg, C. (2015) Chinese RFID adoption takes many forms. Available at: http://www.rfidjournal.com/articles/view?13386 (accessed 15 February 2016).
Talbot, D. (2013) Big Data from cheap phones. Available at: http://www.technologyreview.com/featuredstory/513721/big-data-from-cheap-phones/ (accessed 15 February 2016).
Tanoto, A. (2016) How can Indonesia extinguish its forest fires for good? Available at: http://www.weforum.org/agenda/2016/01/how-can-indonesia-extinguish-its-forest-fires-for-good (accessed 15 February 2016).
Taylor, L. (2013) Surveil the rich, observe the poor: Big Data at the Internet Governance Forum 2013. Available at: http://linnettaylor.wordpress.com/2013/10/25/surveil-the-rich-observe-the-poor-big-data-at-the-internet-governance-forum-2013/ (accessed 18 August 2014).
telecomasia.net (2015) China unveils guidelines for big data. Available at: http://www.telecomasia.net/content/china-unveils-guidelines-big-data (accessed 15 February 2016).
The World Bank (2010) Getting the numbers right: making statistical systems a real plus for results. The World Bank: IBRD Results. Available at: http://documents.worldbank.org/curated/en/2010/04/20379774/getting-numbers-right-making-statistical-systems-real-plus-results (accessed 7 April 2016).
The World Bank Group (2014) Country and lending groups. Available at: http://data.worldbank.org/about/country-and-lending-groups#Low_income (accessed 18 August 2015).
tradearabia.com (2015) Huawei launches centre for smarter energy solutions in Saudi. Available at: http://www.tradearabia.com/news/IT_289908.html (accessed 15 February 2016).
UN Global Pulse (2012) Big data for development: opportunities and challenges. Available at: http://www.unglobalpulse.org/projects/BigDataforDevelopment (accessed 18 August 2014).
UN Global Pulse (2013a) Monitoring perceptions of crisis-related stress using social media data (2011) UN Global Pulse. Available at: http://www.unglobalpulse.org/projects/twitter-and-perceptions-crisis-related-stress (accessed 18 August 2014).
UN Global Pulse (2013b) Landscaping study: digital signals & access to finance in Kenya. UN Global Pulse. Available at: http://www.unglobalpulse.org/Kenyan-access-finance (accessed 18 August 2014).

un.org (2014) Data revolution advisory group named by UN Secretary-General. Available at: http://www.un.org/apps/news/story.asp?NewsID=48594#.VNGIlSzSnS4 (accessed 15 February 2016).

unctad.org (2016) Least developed countries (LDCs). Available at: http://unctad.org/en/Pages/ALDC/Least%20Developed%20Countries/LDCs.aspx (accessed 15 February 2016).

unep.org (2013) Thematic focus: climate change, ecosystem management, environmental governance. A new eye in the sky: eco-drones. Available at: http://www.unep.org/pdf/UNEP-GEAS_MAY_2013.pdf (accessed 7 April 2016).

voanews.com (2015) Scientists warn of health damage from Indonesia's haze fires. Available at: http://www.voanews.com/content/scientists-warn-of-health-damage-from-indonesia-haze-fires/3055261.html (accessed 15 February 2016).

Wang, S.S., Purnell, N. and Bhattacharya, S. (2015) Nepal aid workers helped by drones, crowdsourcing. Available at: http://www.wsj.com/articles/nepal-aid-workers-helped-by-drones-crowdsourcing-1430483540 (accessed 15 February 2016).

wantchinatimes.com (2015a) Opportunities coming in China's big data sector. Available at: http://www.wantchinatimes.com/news/content?id=20150922000084&cid=1102 (accessed 15 February 2016).

wantchinatimes.com (2015b) Chengdu to set up big data agency. Available at: http://www.wantchinatimes.com/news-subclass-cnt.aspx?id=20150904000043&cid=1102 (accessed 16 February 2016).

Warner, B. (2013) Google turns to Big Data to unmask human traffickers. Available at: http://www.bloomberg.com/bw/articles/2013-04-10/google-turns-to-big-data-to-unmask-human-traffickers (accessed 15 February 2016).

Wayua, C. (2014) How Project Lucy is helping unlock the possibilities of Africa. Available at: http://asmarterplanet.com/blog/2014/11/project-lucy.html (accessed 15 February 2016).

WEF [World Economic Forurm] (2012) Big data, big impact: new possibilities for international development. World Economic Forum. Available at: http://www3.weforum.org/docs/WEF_TC_MFS_BigDataBigImpact_Briefing_2012.pdf (accessed 7 April 2016).

Welz, A. (2013) The war on African poaching: is militarization fated to fail? Available at: http://e360.yale.edu/feature/the_war_on_african_poaching_is_militarization_fated_to_fail/2679/ (accessed 15 February 2016).

Weslowski, A., Eagle, N. and Noor, A.M. (2013) The impact of biases in mobile phone ownership on estimates of human mobility. *Journal of the Royal Society Interface* 10(81), 20120986.

worldbank.org (2015a) What areas need the most assistance in reducing poverty? Bangladesh's new poverty maps may have answers. Available at: http://www.worldbank.org/en/news/feature/2014/09/30/poverty-maps (accessed 15 February 2016).

worldbank.org (2015b) Overview. Available at: http://www.worldbank.org/en/topic/energy/overview (accessed 15 February 2016).

worldbank.org (2016) Country and lending groups. Available at: http://data.worldbank.org/about/country-and-lending-groups (accessed 15 February 2016).

xinhuanet.com (2015) What's being said on Facebook about China. Available at: http://news.xinhuanet.com/english/2015-08/26/c_134558545.htm (accessed 15 February 2016).

2 Big Data Ecosystem in Developing Countries

Abstract

Organizations in the developing world face various challenges and barriers in the adoption of BD. This chapter examines the context dependence in BD models and compares the relative effectiveness of various data sources in different contexts. Some key barriers to utilization of BD are discussed. It also introduces the concept of a vicious circle of BD in the developing world. This chapter looks at some encouraging and favourable signs in order to deploy BD in key economic and social activities. It argues that the Internet of Things can be a key component of BD for diverse activities. This chapter also presents guidelines for creating a virtuous circle of effective BD deployment in the developing world.

2.1 Introduction

Data unavailability and the low quality of available data hinder the efforts of developing countries to successfully utilize BD in addressing key challenges facing them. For example, consider the data-related efforts of the eight Millennium Development Goals (MDGs) aimed at addressing extreme poverty in many dimensions, which the United Nations (UN) Member States agreed to try to achieve by 2015. The MDGs provided an incentive to invest in data-gathering initiatives. A UN expert panel found that after over a decade's worth of efforts, the vast majority of required data were still missing. For instance, as of October 2014, a look at the data availability in the MDG database, which covered 55 core indicators for 157 developing countries, indicated that there was not a single five-year period for which more than 70% of the needed data was available. Moreover, a huge portion of the data was simply estimated data (Donnan, 2014).

Unsurprisingly, most organizations in the developing world have not yet taken advantage of BD due to various challenges and barriers. It was reported that many Gulf Cooperation Council (GCC)-based oil and gas companies have collected a huge amount of data from various sources. However, they lack the skills and capacity needed to analyse the data and obtain meaningful insights (oilandgasbigdata.com, 2015). Two key problems related to BD implementations have been observed in these economies. Firstly, the limited data that is publicly available in the region performs poorly in usability. Data portals are not regularly updated and available data are of questionable quality and uncertain reliability. The governments lack the necessary technology and systems to share the available data with companies and stakeholders. Secondly, there has been the lack of localization of analytical tools for Arabic content. In the Middle Eastern economies, most of the content is in Arabic. Consequently, most BD service providers operating in the region are largely unequipped and unprepared to provide accurate BD and business intelligence solutions (oilandgasbigdata.com, 2015). This problem is not unique to Arab economies. Out of more than 6000 spoken languages, just ten languages account for more than 80% of the content on the World Wide Web (Leetaru, 2015).

Similar problems have been reported in other economies. For instance, the Open Data Task Force of the Philippines received support from Microsoft and local telecom companies. It is, however, facing a number of barriers. The lack of digital literacy and coordination among government agencies has been a key problem. Moreover, datasets provided by various ministries are incompatible (internetsociety.org, 2015).

Likewise, the World Bank's study indicated that many countries in the Latin American and Caribbean region lack a strategic vision required for the overall management of the statistical system (The World Bank, 2010). In some cases, short-sighted policies and practices have adversely affected the development of data ecosystems. For instance, in the 1980s, African meteorological agencies were encouraged to sell data in order to be more sustainable and effective. This was a short-sighted policy because the agencies' services unsurprisingly focused on more profitable clients such as those in the airline industry, and ignored more critical issues. For example, access to data for non-commercial purposes such as malaria research was constrained due to poor collaboration and high data fees (Thomson *et al.*, 2011).

A further problem is that the available data are often of poor quality. A major cause that underlies poor data quality is the lack of analytical capacity in developing countries. Due to poor data analytics, there is often no demand for high-quality data. This situation creates a vicious circle of poor analysis and the lack of demand for high-quality data (Carletto *et al.*, 2015).

Despite the above-noted challenges, there are a number of encouraging trends that seem likely to have a positive impact on the developing world's BD ecosystem. For instance, by 2025, half of Africa's 1 billion population will have Internet access and the continent will have 360 million smartphones (reuters.com, 2015). In 2014, 82% of Kenyans owned mobile phones and 61% of the owners used them for mobile banking or activities involving money transfers (Hormats, 2015). Instead of the web, the Unstructured Supplementary Service Data, which is a simple, text-based data-transfer protocol, is more popular among African mobile phone networks. It is used for a wide range of purposes, from day-to-day transactions to tax payments, and from insurance to savings (Mirani, 2014). Less appreciated, but no less important, is the role of these transactions in enriching the BD ecosystem.

New technological advances can make it feasible to access alternative sources of information for various decision-making purposes. For instance, in the future it may be possible to use satellite imagery to assess the size of a farmer's plot or roof type. This information can be cross referenced to a household's receipt of remittances (Chen and Faz, 2015).

Regarding the high data costs, there are some encouraging developments. For instance, due to increased competition in the Latin American mobile broadband market, broadband data charges dropped by 52% during 2011–2014 (Almazán and Sitbon, 2014). The rapidly declining costs of mobile phones has been equally encouraging. For instance, it was reported that in February 2016, an Indian company launched the world's cheapest smartphone, which was priced at US$4 (aljazeera.com, 2016).

2.2 Context Dependence in Big Data Models

BD models are context dependent, which means that various aspects of the context are important in different settings. We present some examples to illustrate this. The study, 'Impact of human mobility on the emergence of dengue epidemics in Pakistan', published in the *Proceedings of the National Academy of Sciences* (Wesolowski *et al.*, 2015), estimated the mobility of over 30 million mobile phone subscribers during the 2013 dengue outbreak using anonymized call data. Compared to estimates by traditional climate-based vulnerability models alone, adding the estimated movements of infected travellers provided a 'chronologically and geographically more nuanced picture of transmission' and a markedly different risk pattern. For instance, in southern Pakistan, a low instance of dengue was attributed to low numbers of infected travellers visiting the area. On the other hand, on the Afghan border, low infection rates had more to do with temperature (Oldgard, 2015).

As another example, a study conducted in Brazil, India and the USA showed that satellite data performed well in capturing temperature information, whereas the weather stations were a superior source of precipitation data. The authors of the study recommended combining satellite data for temperature with ground-station data for precipitation (Mendelsohn *et al.*, 2007).

These examples underscore the context-dependent nature of the BD models and the need for a careful choice of important data and sources. Since different types of data may perform differently in various contexts, it is important to have access to diverse sources of data.

2.3 Barriers, Challenges and Obstacles in Using Big Data

The lack of good data often hampers the effectiveness of policy making and implementation. Observers have noted that most reports from government agencies and development institutions often include disclaimers stating that 'severe data limitations' hampered the quality of the report (Fengler and Kharas, 2015).

The lack of information has been a main barrier to developing and implementing effective health-care systems, environmental monitoring tools and agricultural information systems and making strategic business decisions. For instance, while there is a rising prevalence of diabetes in Indonesia, there are no data available to measure the effects beyond intermediate outcomes such as the number of people trained, the percentage of health centres providing education, or the development of training material and guidelines (e.g. training's impact on detection rate and outcomes and screening's impact on complications) (Soewondo *et al.*, 2013).

A steep learning curve and high costs may prevent many organizations based in the developing world from implementing BD. In Africa, businesses face challenges and constraints such as the lack of access to relevant technology, expensive connectivity and shortage of human resources to tackle technical problems. This may contribute to an increase in the risk of BD being 'ring-fenced' as an information technology (IT) issue and separated from other key organizational functions. It is hard to explain the value of BD to business stakeholders and development actors and make them understand (Van Der Poll, 2015).

Thus while BD holds promise to significantly improve economic, social and environmental well-being in developing countries, the reality seems to diverge significantly from this ideal. For several reasons the situation is not as optimistic as some experts believe. Developing economies face a number of challenges that may limit their capability to utilize BD effectively. The above examples, which discussed the inability of government agencies in the Philippines and the oil and gas industry in the GCC economies to utilize BD, suggest that this lack of capacity needs to be addressed. They include the lack of data, poor quality data, and the shortage of BD skills and capacity needed to analyse data and obtain meaningful insights. In this section, we provide a brief overview of some of the key barriers.

2.3.1 Low degree of digitization

A UN panel of independent experts from academia and business noted that the world is divided into two classes: data 'haves' and data 'have nots' (undatarevolution.org, 2015). A low degree of digitization is among the biggest barriers. Quite simply, a large proportion of the population in developing countries still lacks a digital footprint to benefit from BD. Among the main concerns is the low penetration rate of information communication technology (ICT) products in many of the least developed parts of the world. The lack of widespread mobile access has been a major problem. For instance, many rural areas in Liberia completely lack mobile phone services (Shacklett, 2015). It is reported that people in rural areas of Brazil sometimes need to climb trees in order to get a signal for mobile phones (Levy, 2014).

According to the International Telecommunications Union, there were 3.2 billion people worldwide using the Internet in 2015, of which 2 billion were from developing countries. There were 91.8 mobile phone subscriptions per 100 inhabitants in developing countries in 2015 (ITU, 2015a). However, as shown in Table 2.1, there is still a significant gap between rich and poor nations. As Table 2.2 shows, many people in least developed countries (LDCs) still lack access to a mobile phone.

Table 2.1. Key ICT indicators for countries with various levels of economic development.

	Fixed-telephone subscriptions	Mobile telephone subscriptions	Active mobile broadband subscriptions	Fixed broadband subscriptions	Households with a computer	Households with Internet access	Individuals using the Internet
Developed	39	120.6	86.7	29	80.8	81.3	82.2
Developing	9.4	91.8	39.1	7.1	32.9	34.1	35.3
Least developed countries			12.1	0.5		6.7	9.5
World	14.5	96.8	47.2	10.8	45.4	46.4	43.4

Source: ITU (2015a,b).

Table 2.2. Countries with lowest penetration rates of ICTs (2014, %).

Country	Mobile phone penetration	Individuals using Internet	Fixed broadband subscriptions	Individuals using computer
Eritrea	6.4	0.99	0.003	
North Korea	11.2	0.00	–	
Cuba	22.5	30.0	0.069	29.2 (2013)
Burundi	30.5	1.38	0.016	
Central African Republic	31.4	4.03	0.01 (2012)	

Source: ITU (2015a).

A farmer living in poverty in Eritrea, which had just 6% penetration of mobile phones, is unlikely to create any digital footprint. Countries such as Eritrea are thus not in a position to benefit from BD's potential to improve people's living standards and the quality of life.

Likewise, being able to accurately count the number of children is the first step for realizing the benefit of BD in health care. Some countries have a notoriously poor record, even in registering the children born. Estimates suggest that only 44% of children under 5 years of age in sub-Saharan African (SSA) economies have been registered. The proportions are even lower in rural areas. In Eastern and Southern Africa, the proportion is reported to be 38% and it is estimated to be as low as 3% in Somalia (unicef.org, 2016). Many people living in slums in countries such as India and Nigeria cannot provide birth certificates or utility bills required by banks. Financial institutions have imposed these oppressively burdensome requirements in order to prevent money laundering (economist.com, 2014a,b).

Most developing countries lack the infrastructures and capability to handle data and information. For instance, according to the 13th Global Information Technology Report, in 2012 the international data bandwidth for the top 20 countries averaged 465.7 kilobits per second (KBPS) per Internet user, compared to 159.1 KBPS in 2010. The bottom 20 countries averaged 1.6 KBPS per Internet user in 2012 compared to 0.7 in 2010 (Orcutt, 2014). Infrastructural challenges are thus the most daunting in most developing countries. In the examples discussed in Chapter 1, to protect rhinos in Africa, the key challenges are connectivity and battery life. Sending a video is a bandwidth-intensive task and most satellites are not equipped to deal with high bandwidth in real time. Likewise, batteries of most global-positioning system (GPS) packs attached to the animals do not last more than 9 months (Higginbotham, 2015).

Another way to measure digitization is to consider Booz & Company's Digitization Index (BCDI), which is based on 23 indicators such as access, affordability, reliability, speed and usability of digital services/applications, and users' skills. For instance, the BCDI score of emerging economies was 27 compared to 54 in developed countries. Booz & Company has described most emerging economies as being in the constrained or emerging stages of digitization, whereas developed economies are in the transitional or advanced stage (El-Darwiche *et al.*, 2012). These countries have limited hardware, software and other technological applications to generate and distribute relevant data and knowledge (UNDP, 2011).

Moreover, the lower quality of hardware, software and infrastructure may lead to a reduced amount of information flow in developing countries. For instance, many businesses design websites using features such as 'low graphics' and 'text only' to accommodate the needs of users in developing countries.

2.3.2 Costs associated with participating in the digital economy

High costs associated with creating and acquiring data add to the problems of data unavailability and low-quality data. These include the prices of data charged by data owners, prices of BD services charged by BD analytics firms for organizations, and the costs of mobile phones, voice calls and data plans for individual users. For instance, getting data from Kenya's national meteorological services was reported to be too costly for researchers (Waweru *et al.*, 2011).

For organizations interested in using the Internet of Things (IoT), high costs of sensors and related components serve as a barrier. For instance, for the IoT as a source of BD, budget constraints often force companies to sacrifice a desired level of accuracy and go for a more affordable sensor (asirobots.com, 2015). Such constraints are even more evident for most potential users in the developing world.

Prohibitively high costs and unavailability of mobile phones and other ICT devices render BD useless and irrelevant in many LDCs. For instance, consider Eritrea, which is the world's least connected country. By many measures, Eritrea is technologically less advanced than North Korea. It was reported that, in 2014, a customer in Eritrea needed to pay US$13.29 to the local authorities in order to get permission to apply for a mobile phone. Then, to get a connection, US$33.60 needed to be paid to the government-controlled Eritrea Telecommunication Services (EriTel), which is the only phone company in the country. At least US$3.65 was needed to be paid to add credits to the SIM card every time. Note that the country's per-capita income was about US$500 (Winter, 2014). High costs thus discourage individuals and businesses in Eritrea from engaging in activities that will lead to the creation of data and make data-driven decisions.

High data costs are also a major obstacle for consumers in other countries to engage in activities that generate data. Consider South Africa. Consumers with an income of R3000 (US$225) a month, which is significantly above the national minimum wage, needed to work around 18 hours in order to afford a 500MB data plan. This means that even if consumers can afford smartphones, they are often forced to use them like 'dumb' phones (Thomas, 2015).

As a further example that illustrates barriers that high costs impose to BD projects, consider a blood-bank monitoring system in Kenya designed by a US engineer. The project involved recruiting nurses across the country to send text messages about their hospitals' current blood-supply levels to a central database. The project was highly successful in the beginning as the nurses sent data every hour. After about a month, almost all the nurses stopped sending the texts. It was found that the high price of a text message was the main reason why the nurses stopped sending the required information (Shaw, 2014).

In some cases, the lack of healthy competition has rendered BD expensive and unprofitable. For instance, it was reported that due primarily to Alibaba's high advertising rates, most vendors on Taobao were making losses. According to an article published in the Chinese language newspaper *Enterprise Observer* in August 2013, over 80% of sellers on Taobao did not make a profit. It was also reported that thousands of shops on Taobao close down every day (Kshetri, 2016).

There have been only a few programmes and initiatives that have been effective in pulling policy and regulatory levers. There has been a lack of feedback loops and other systems to improve data quality (Fengler and Kharas, 2015). Solar lighting products such as those offered by SSA-based GreenWize Energy are more costly for consumers due to high transaction fees in addition to the instalments they pay for the products. For instance, Safaricom's M-PESA is reported to charge both the sender and the receiver, which can add up to Kshs 195 (US$1.20) to transfer Kshs 10,000 (US$98). The fees are even higher to send money to other operators (Wadongo, 2015).

2.3.3 Data usability

According to the International Data Corporation, in 2013, 22% of digital information was a candidate for analysis and 5% was actually analysed (Michal, 2014). Likewise, according to IBM, 90% of all data from connected devices such as smartphones and tablets is never analysed (Camhi, 2015). The figures for the developing world are likely to be less than the world's average values. This means that only a vanishingly small fraction of data is actually analysed in developing countries. Furthermore, most of the datasets are fragmented and do not communicate with other datasets.

2.3.4 Poor data quality

Poor data quality is one of the huge obstacles to the utilization of BD in improving agriculture, health care and environmental conditions. Addressing this challenge may be no small feat. In 2014, researchers of the Center for Global Development and the African Population and Health Research Center expressed concerns that too little reliable data on Africa was available (Donnan, 2014). It is also reported that most African countries use more than five-decade-old accounting methodologies to generate vital and key statistics such as those related to gross domestic product (Bhushan, 2012).

Prior researchers have noted that official statistics in SSA economies 'systematically exaggerate development progress'. These researchers have also noted that governments often misreported data on key indicators such as vaccination rates to foreign donors (Sandefur and Glassman, 2014).

While problems related to unavailability and questionable quality of data are common to most developing countries, such problems are more acute in SSA countries (Carletto *et al.*, 2015). Of 44 SSA countries rated by the Food and Agriculture Organization (FAO), only two countries had high standards of data collection; the standards were low in 21 countries (FAO, 2008). Studies have also noted that the poorest countries, which rely the most on agriculture, tend to have the lowest quality data. Moreover, the poorest countries are not able to direct more resources to improve the quality of data and statistics (African Development Bank, 2004).

There has been a proliferation of data sources in Africa. However, compelling evidence exists of manipulation, misreporting and misrepresentation of data from some sources. For instance, a comparison of maize yield estimates for Malawi for 2006–2007 from the three available sources (a routine data system from the Ministry of Agriculture; the National Census of Agriculture and Livestock conducted by the National Statistical Office; and the FAO) indicated that there were significant inter-source differences. Likewise, the estimates of the total number of farm households in Malawi varied: the Malawi Ministry of Agriculture estimated

3.4 million whereas the Malawi National Statistical Office estimate was 2.47 million.

There has been an overall lack of institutionalization of data-based decisions (Staff, 2014). A further challenge is that there is a general lack of documentation describing the data collection procedure (Carletto *et al.*, 2015). Many developing countries do not disseminate data in a timely manner. For instance, Tanzania produced the national and regional reports from the 2003 Agricultural Census Sample Survey in the 2006–2007 fiscal year (Carletto *et al.*, 2015).

Many of the innovations involving BD use multiple data sources and involve transferring data to third parties (Lenard and Rubin, 2013). A study of the UK-based trade group Direct Marketing Association indicated that over US$150 billion in marketing services could be generated using individual-level data as a key component, and over 70% of such services would require the exchange of data among firms in the value delivery network (Deighton and Peter, 2013).

Organizations based in the developing world are not positioned to benefit from such approaches. They experience great difficulty in exchanging existing data and information. For instance, in most SSA countries the use of standard codes across ministries is not common. The upshot of these tendencies is that there are agency-specific data silos without an effective national data architecture. One way to address this problem is to use systematic geo-referencing of household and plot-level information. By linking socioeconomic and farm-level variables collected from household surveys with information from remote sensing and other spatial data sources, it may be possible to gain a more comprehensive understanding of farm outputs and other variables (Carletto *et al.*, 2015).

There are also issues related to questionable representativeness, accuracy and generalizability. This is especially the case for BD generated by social media. In developing countries, which have limited Internet access, there are concerns about bias. Data from Twitter is likely to over-represent urban elites (unocha.org, 2013). Some critics also worry that by putting too much faith in BD and an emphasis on the authoritativeness of numbers, policy makers and development agencies may miss many essential messages and lessons that can be learned by working directly with local communities (Makri, 2015).

2.3.5 Low degree of value chain integration and disconnection between data users and producers

The lack of sound business models has prevented efforts to capture value from data. Part of the problem is that the data are captured by disparate companies in various parts of the value chain such as seed companies, equipment manufacturers, traders and software developers. In the industrialized world, strategic partnerships, mergers, acquisitions and reorganizations have taken place in order to capture value from critical data points, which has reshaped the industry structure (Goedde *et al.*, 2015). The lack of such initiatives in the developing world has hampered the ability of firms to capture value from data.

A related point is that the databases of different agencies exhibit a silo structure characterized by the lack of inter-agency communication and interaction.

An agency often wants to minimize its dependence on other agencies. These agencies thus lack the ability to leverage the existing knowledge base of others and thus lack a holistic view of the economy and the society.

A further challenge that needs to be addressed is the disconnection between users and producers of data. There has been significant debate about the potential causes of the rise in malaria observed during the last 30 years in the Kenyan highlands. Analysts disagree as to whether the rise is associated with local temperature changes or whether the changes are related to global climate change processes (Waweru *et al.*, 2011). A study showed a long-term trend of temperature rise at Kericho, in the Kenyan highlands. Furthermore, the trend was linked partly with temperatures of the sea surface and land surface in the tropics (Omumbo *et al.*, 2011). The reason why it took about a decade to establish a robust analysis of Kericho's climate was arguably related to a disconnection between the users and producers of climate information (Thomson *et al.*, 2011).

Most studies relied heavily on interpolated data that was intended for regional or global-scale analyses. They used only a small fraction of the stations that were maintained by National Meteorological and Hydrological Services. Moreover, short-time data that lacked quality control was used. Researchers had limited access to high-quality data from Kericho meteorological stations (Waweru *et al.*, 2011).

In most SSA economies, agricultural data collection efforts have exhibited institutional isolation. There is little inter-sectoral coordination. For instance, in many countries the ministries of agriculture databases are not linked with data from the national statistical offices or other ministries (e.g. labour, education and health). There are virtually no efforts to combine, share and exchange datasets from two or more agencies in order to gain insights into key developmental indicators. Collaboration, coordination and communication are lacking on this front (Carletto *et al.*, 2015).

In Tanzania, three institutions collect education data: (i) the Ministry of Education collects data on indicators such as school enrolment, infrastructure and teaching staff; (ii) the National Examination Council of Tanzania (NECTA) collects data related to the outcomes of primary and secondary school standardized tests; and (iii) the National Bureau of Statistics' census data include the location of landmarks such as markets, religious sites and schools. These agencies have taken a myopic approach in the management of different sets of data that live in departmental silos and agency boundaries. The NECTA publishes test results on a per-school level. The Ministry of Education creates pivot tables that summarize the data, which lack usability. The census geodata, on the other hand, has not been released (schoolofdata.org, 2013).

2.3.6 Interoperability and standardization issues

The lack of maturity in BD standards has been a significant challenge in implementing BD technologies. In China, for instance, the lack of standards has been a major obstacle to wide application of BD. It was reported that BD projects in China are carried out on an ad hoc basis.

The challenges related to interoperability and standardization issues are especially evident in the IoT industry. Many vendors are building 'silos' that do not easily inter-connect or share information (mckinsey.com, 2015). The IoT-related standards are currently fragmented among the relevant, new technologies to ensure the interoperability of communication protocols (itu.int, 2015). As an example, consider the health-care sector. Health-care organizations face the challenge of integrating data from consumer-based sensors such as Internet-based blood pressure monitoring systems and weight scales into the overall IT architecture. These systems present data exchange challenges; for example, home devices may not have the same level of accuracy and need to be recalibrated (Robert, 2014). Such challenges are likely to be even more acute and obvious in developing countries.

2.3.7 Big Data skills deficit

One study found that 15% of profit increases from BD were related to the availability of data and analytics experts (Bughin, 2016). Accurate and actionable data require considerable technical skills to handle data mining, analytical methodology and database systems. One major concern is the lack of broad skills, knowledge, expertise and experience required to work in BD projects in developing countries. Even industrialized countries such as those in EU economies have reported a huge skills shortage for data-related workforces (Kroes, 2013). Data scientists are both in short supply and expensive to employ in developing economies (WEF, 2012).

More specifically, BD is as much about analytics as it is about the data. The improvement in analytical capacities (e.g. statistical machine learning and algorithms) is the key to understanding the patterns and trends in data (scidev.net, 2014). Developing countries need to deal with a talent deficit in this area. The BD labour market in these economies faces challenges on two fronts. Firstly, there are insufficient BD engineers and scientists that are able to perform analytics. Secondly, many analytics consultants tend to lack capabilities to understand, interpret and put the data to work. Some estimates suggest that India will soon experience a shortage of 1 million data consultants. India's analytics professionals are reportedly paid 50% more than other IT workers (Rai, 2014).

The lack of a BD workforce with a high level strategic thinking capability has been a particular challenge. For instance, China has a rich endowment of BD human resources thanks to an abundant supply of engineers. The country, however, lacks experts at the executive level (Swanson, 2015). Likewise, the lack of strategic leadership and the lack of ideas of where to start the implementation of solutions have been noted as the main reasons why Colombian companies have not taken advantage of BD (Beroes Ríos, 2016). Similar points can be made about other developing countries.

BD skill deficits are related to a broader problem of low educational quality, achievement and standards. For instance, the inability of Vietnamese universities to train the next generation of highly skilled workers has been a roadblock in the development of a BD-related workforce (Hoagland, 2010). Likewise, according to

UNESCO only 6% of Africa's young people are enrolled in higher educational institutions compared to the global average of 26% (Kajunju and Crozier, 2015). A large number of organizations in Africa have had limited experience in data cleansing or standardization. There is thus a general lack of skills in advanced techniques and technologies required for BD (africanbusinessreview.co.za, 2014).

2.3.8 Values and cultures

A concern is that the values and cultures in many developing countries may not support BD projects. For instance, it is argued that health-care providers, system administrators and other relevant personnel in these countries lack training in various aspects of data science (Wyber *et al.*, 2015). The upshot of this issue is that there is a lack of organizational culture that demands high-quality data. Studies conducted in SSA economies have indicated that this culture is associated with and facilitated by poor data analytical skills (Carletto *et al.*, 2015). For instance, factors such as the lack of numerical literacy among managers, preference to the 'artistic side' and a high level of emphasis on short-term instead of long-term results hinder efforts to utilize BD (Whitler, 2013).

According to a worldwide survey conducted by the data storage company EMC in 2013, culture was found to be among the greatest barriers to deploying BD solutions. For instance, 73% of Colombian respondents said that culture acted as the major obstacle to the implementation of BD in their organizations. This included the lack of a culture of information, and managers' propensity to make decisions on the basis of personal preference rather than measurement and evidence (Santos, 2013).

Another issue among some organizations and groups is an unwillingness to share data. For instance, while universities and research centres constitute a key source of data and knowledge, it is argued that scientists working in these institutes are against making relevant data accessible due to security, privacy and other concerns. They often use reasoning against data sharing, such as: 'I don't want to share it', 'it's mine' or 'it's government property' (Patel, 2013). Likewise, in China many government departments are reported to be reluctant to disclose data. Moreover, information is scattered among different government departments. When the government of Nanjing city in China was planning to launch a smart transportation programme, it found that relevant information was spread across the public security, traffic management, transportation, housing, environmental protection and planning departments (news.xinhuanet.com, 2013). The databases of different agencies exhibit departmental silos characterized by bureaucratic and hierarchical administrative structures and a lack of inter-agency communication and interaction. An agency often wants to minimize its dependence on other agencies. These agencies do not have the ability to leverage the existing knowledge base of others and thus lack a holistic view of the economy and the society.

The implementation of BD projects may also require an organizational culture that fosters cross-functional collaboration. We illustrate this with an example of the global fast food restaurant chain McDonald's. In order to foster more data-driven decision making, McDonald's created multidisciplinary teams to 'discover, develop and deploy' new solutions. The discovery phase involved stimulating new ideas and incubating them. Necessary skill sets involved operations, IT, analytics and engineering. In the development phase, additional skills in the areas of human resources, training and finance were needed to develop new projects. In the deployment phase, other departments such as marketing and design needed to be involved (datafloq.com, 2015). Thus effective utilization of BD required organizational capability to handle cooperation across different units and departments. Organizations in many developing countries may lack capabilities to organize and manage such multidisciplinary teams.

2.4 Some Encouraging and Favourable Signs

Several encouraging and favourable signs have been noted. Despite the current disappointing state of BD among most developing countries, they are experiencing exponential growth rates in the creation and use of data. For instance, according to the Cisco Global Cloud Index, which forecasts the growth of global data centres and cloudbased IP traffic (cisco.com, 2014), the highest cloud workload growth rates during 2013 to 2018 are expected to be in the Asia Pacific (45% compound annual growth rate [CAGR]), Middle East and Africa (39% CAGR) and Latin America (34% CAGR) regions. Data centre traffic in the Middle East and Africa is expected to reach 366 exabytes per year by 2018 compared to 68 exabytes per year in 2013. Note that data centre traffic is the sum of data centre-to-user traffic, data centre-to-data centre traffic, and traffic within data centres (allafrica.com, 2014).

With the proliferation of low-cost satellites, it is becoming increasingly easy and affordable to get data and information in order to gain a better understanding of various economic, social and environmental indicators. Many of them rotate around 250 miles above the Earth's surface. It is expected that in the near future these satellites will have the capability to scan most of the Earth's surface between 40 and 70 times a day (computervisiononline.com, 2015). The Japanese heavy machinery maker IHI has announced a plan to launch low-cost satellites that can be used in farming and disaster prevention. For instance, the satellites can measure the temperature and nutritional levels of soil in Africa. This information can help improve crop yields and identify mining reserves in Africa. Other potential uses include improving surveillance operations for natural disasters such as tsunamis and typhoons, and monitoring forests in emerging countries (asia.nikkei.com, 2013).

Some ambitious, high-profile projects planned in the developing world deserve a mention. The radio telescope project Square Kilometre Array (SKA) is expected to facilitate the use of BD in SSA. The SKA is planned to be built in South Africa and Australia from 2018 (ska.ac.za). SKA's satellite dishes will cover Australia, New Zealand and eight SSA countries. After its completion, the SKA is expected to be the world's single largest source of data. It is likely to help the host countries develop data-processing skills and enhance the BD ecosystem (economist.com, 2014a).

On the bright side, global technology giants are making efforts to improve the BD ecosystem in developing countries. Google has announced a plan to develop high-speed wireless networks in developing countries using high-altitude balloons that can transmit signals across a large area. The goal is to connect an additional 1 billion people to the Internet in Africa, Southeast Asia and other regions. In March 2013, Google started a trial in Cape Town, South Africa, using three antenna mast towers at Stellenbosch University's campus to transmit to ten local schools (Garside, 2013). In June 2014, Google announced a plan to spend a substantial amount of money on satellites. The project's starting phase will involve 180 small, high-capacity satellites that will orbit the Earth at lower altitudes than traditional satellites. The projected cost of the project is in the US$1 billion to US$3 billion range (Barr and Pasztor, 2014).

2.5 Big Data-Related Entrepreneurship and Some Notable Big Data Companies Operating in the Developing World

Most of the top BD companies are from the industrialized world, especially the US. Neelie Kroes, the former European Commissioner for the Digital Agenda, noted that of the top 20 global BD companies, 17 are from the USA and 2 from Europe (Kroes, 2013). Another study suggested that of the 15 most powerful BD companies, 14 were US-based and 1 was based in Europe (Korolov, 2013). It is argued that the highest performance computers are unaffordable even to a member state of the EU (Kroes, 2013). Developing competitive indigenous companies in the BD area is not an easy task for developing countries.

However, against this backdrop of the developed world's dominance in the global BD industry, an abundance of BD-related entrepreneurship in developing countries has been an encouraging trend. This is important because Western firms often consider developing countries to be less attractive markets. Firms based in the developing world are rapidly emerging as providers of products, services, software and solutions related to BD (Kshetri, 2011). A study conducted by India's National Association of Software and Services Companies and CRISIL Global Research & Analytics estimated that the Indian BD industry was valued at US$200 million in 2012, and was expected to increase to US$1 billion in 2015 (Srikanth, 2013). Some developing economies have set forth an ambitious agenda on the BD front. For instance, China's goal has been to create ten global leading enterprises in the BD industry and 500 firms focusing on BD applications, services and manufacturing by 2020 (telecomasia.net, 2015).

The following sections describe some of the BD companies based in the developing world.

2.5.1 Alibaba

As noted in Chapter 1, one company based in the developing world cashing in on the BD trend is Alibaba. The company uses BD to improve risk management and control. In early 2016, Alibaba announced a plan to launch a BD cloud platform in China consisting of all activities in the 'data development chain'. The services that will be provided include data services and visualization products to help organizations in data processing and analysis, as well as capabilities for machine learning (Gilchrist, 2016).

2.5.2 Mediatrac

Indonesia's Mediatrac provides BD analytics for companies. Mediatrac was founded in 2003 as a media monitoring agency. Since 2010, it decided to focus only on BD analytics. Mediatrac has developed databases that are unique to the Indonesian market.

The firm is reported to have demographic and consumption-related data from over 60 million households in Indonesia. It also has an archive of contents from media such as newspapers, magazines, blogs and social media (Freischlad, 2015a). It can combine its datasets with client data to give more meaningful and relevant insights. Mediatrac clients include the World Bank, Nestlé, Telkom Indonesia, Kalbe, Indosat and Bank Mandiri. Mediatrac also organizes the Big Data Week event in Indonesia, which helps to attract big companies and share knowledge with local entrepreneurs (Freischlad, 2015a).

In July 2014, Mediatrac announced the formation of a partnership with the South Korean marketing firm Yello Digital Marketing (YDM) and the Palo-Alto-based software company Cloudera. Mediatrac is expected to use YDM's affiliates in Southeast Asia to enter into new markets. Cloudera is expected to provide Mediatrac with the tools and resources needed to develop and market Cloudera's BD software in Indonesia. Mediatrac and Cloudera are also expected to establish a BD centre in Indonesia (Freischlad, 2015b).

Collective Intelligence Agriculture (CI-Agriculture), a subsidiary of Mediatrac, has developed precision farming techniques that have been adapted to the Indonesian context. In 2014, CI-Agriculture began its first trial on a rice paddy near Jakarta at the foot of Mount Gede. CI-Agriculture experimented with drones and weather sensors over a period of 4 months. During the planting season, soil conditions were monitored and aerial photographs were created. CI-Agriculture also learned about local farming practices and supply chains (Freischlad, 2015a). It has developed agricultural management systems that utilize BD to analyse data related to weather and soil conditions, as well as satellite imagery and drones. Based on the trial, CI-Agriculture decided to focus on three products (fareasternagriculture.com, 2015):

1. Crop Accurate: Using sensor systems, drones and remote sensing, farmers collect data that can be used by the smart farming systems. It analyses the soil condition, weather and growth progress and gives advice regarding the best time to plant, fertilize and use pest control. The technology is scalable, which means that it is possible to gradually increase the area covered by sensors. Agricultural data are collected and analysed on a regular basis to predict crop yields. At the end of each season, the smart farming system analyses the data and provides recommendations to improve farming activities during the next season.

2. Agritrack: The Agritrack system is a supply chain solution that links farmers with distributors, markets and end customers. Each party of the supply chain provides real-time data via an app. Real-time information on key indicators such as commodity prices is provided that can help predict prices and demand.

3. Crop Insurance: Insurance is provided to farmers, which is based on calculations and schemes on smart farming technology, sensor systems and analysis of other categories of data (fareasternagriculture.com, 2015). Insurance models are based on an analysis of weather data for up to 10 years (Freischlad, 2015a).

As of mid-2015, CI-Agriculture had been testing the three products in a pilot project in South Sumatra. The company worked with 1500 maize farmers in 1300 ha. CI-Agriculture's future plan is to offer the software on a subscription-based model to farmers, end users, researchers and government agencies (Freischlad, 2015a).

2.5.3 Nedbank

Nedbank is among the largest banks in South Africa. In July 2015, Nedbank became the first South African bank to offer a data analytics tool, Market Edge, which records customers' shopping behaviour. The tool offers behavioural insights mined through BD on a platform that provides information about customers' spending patterns, income segmentation, gender and age demographics. Businesses can look at consumers' transaction histories, which can be used to improve product development and maximize engagement, conversions and loyalty. Market Edge has been made available to Nedbank's card-accepting businesses (Mungadze, 2015).

2.6 The Internet of Things as a Key Component of Big Data

The IoT holds great promise and potential for developing countries. While the technology is not new, IoT components such as sensors, which were prohibitively expensive in the past, are more affordable now.

Sensors are already being deployed at different levels of sophistication in developing countries. The convergence of a number of trends such as innovations in low-cost devices and sensors, scalable network connectivity, and maturity of cloud and BD models have facilitated the evolution of IoT-based value-add services (Hartani, 2015). Thanks to advances in wireless networking technology and standardization of communications protocols, data collection from sensors is becoming increasingly easy. Collected data can be stored and analysed via cloud computing at a large scale and at declining cost (Chui *et al.*, 2010).

A study by McKinsey suggested that about 40% of the IoT's worldwide market value will be generated in developing economies by 2020 (Bolton, 2015). In fact, developing economies have fewer legacy issues to grapple with and thus arguably have the potential to leapfrog the industrialized world in some areas of IoT applications (Bughin *et al.*, 2015). This observation is especially pertinent to the development of BD ecosystems in developing countries, because analysts have noted that data created by industrial equipment such as electrical tools, hand tools, drones, office equipment heaters, generators, wind turbines, jet engines and magnetic resonance imaging (MRI) machines (also called industrial Internet), have a higher potential business value compared with the same amount of data associated with social media and the consumer Internet (Rfidjournal.com, 2016).

One estimate suggested that by introducing IoT- and BD-based analytics to track, monitor and manage operations equipment and other assets, productivity of industrial processes can be increased by as much as 30%. For example, one water utility company installed smart meters and sensors on pipes, treatment facilities and other operational assets with analytics leveraged to predict leaks and adverse weather events and other critical situations. The company expected to save on scheduled repair and overall maintenance cost (Hartani, 2015).

Some developing countries are emerging as global leaders in some sectors of the IoT. For instance, in 2014 China had over 150 radio-frequency identification (RFID) companies, which accounted for 85% of the global manufacture capacity of RFID tags (He, 2015).

It is estimated that manufacturing, transportation, smart city and consumer applications currently account for more than 50% of IoT activities. By 2020, IoT is likely to be pervasive across all economic sectors and processes (ITU, 2015b). Some of the key areas of IoT deployment in developing economies are likely to be mining, oil and gas drilling, construction and manufacturing (Bughin *et al.*, 2015). Nonetheless, economic sectors associated with agriculture, health care and the environment are likely to undergo significant transformation and restructuring. Some examples are provided that are relevant to the topics of this book.

2.6.1 Health care

The IoT has the potential to transform a number of industries. For instance, by adding RFID tags to medication containers, producers, consumers and regulators can be better informed about the drug supply chain. The tags can also be embedded into the medication. The IoT devices and processes may reduce drug development costs and make drugs safer, which can help drug companies and health-care providers reduce risks and losses (Harpham, 2015). Likewise, preventive maintenance can be made more efficient by collecting information from medical equipment such as MRI scanners, ultrasound systems and computed tomography scanners (John, 2014).

2.6.2 Environmental security and resource conservation

A major IoT-led transformation is also likely to occur in environmental protection and resources conservation. For instance, the IoT is likely to play a key role in protecting rhinos, elephants and other endangered species in Africa. An initiative in South Africa, called Project RAPID (real-time anti-poaching intelligence device), which is supported by the International Humane Society, entails monitoring rhinoceroses' heart rates using sensors, and combining the information with satellite signals. Information is transmitted to the anti-poaching team, which monitors the activities using video streaming. The plan is to monitor hundreds of square miles of terrain. When the monitor indicates an increase in the heart rate or signals other types of distress, the anti-poaching team gets a notification. The team can then check a video camera that is installed on the rhinoceros' secondary horn. If the animal is wounded, a helicopter is sent to the location with the help of the GPS coordinates (Higginbotham, 2015).

2.6.3 Agriculture

In the agricultural sector, the power of the IoT can be helpful in deploying effective and inexpensive alternatives to pesticides. For instance, wireless sensor networks are being used to monitor pest counts. Semios, the Canadian-based (Vancouver) developer of precision crop management solutions for the agricultural industry, has developed camera-equipped traps to monitor pest activity. The equipment is placed throughout a field, about one per hectare. A central hub delivers this information and weather data to SemiosNET software, which records the data and manages the devices. Semios analysts monitor crops in real time. If the pest population is detected to be too high in a given area, remotely controlled dispensers (about two per hectare) spray pheromones (naturally occurring odourless substances excreted externally by a fertile body, which conveys a signal that triggers responses from the opposite sex). Pheromones manipulate insects' communication pathways and confuse them so that males cannot find females. The pheromone treatments are reported to be non-toxic and cost less than traditional pesticides (Meschino, 2014). Semios described its business model as delivery of a service through IoT. The use of pesticides thus can be minimized or even avoided completely (Mohammad, 2013). As of 2013, Semios was planning its expansion into Latin America.

2.7 Creating a Virtuous Circle of Effective Big Data Deployment

We noted above the existence of a vicious circle of poor practices involving BD in developing countries. In the absence of appropriate measures, the elements of the vicious circle reinforce each other and lead to poor utilization of data for developmental activities, which results in wider gaps between developed and developing countries. The existence of a vicious circle underlines the importance for intervention on one or more of the key variables. Where should we start to break the vicious circle of poor data practices and to facilitate the utilization of BD in key development projects and initiatives?

In Figure 2.1 we present various elements of the BD ecosystem and suggest some possible mechanisms in the formation of a virtuous circle of effective BD deployment. The availability of high-quality data and qualified data professionals may also act as an incentive to attract new actors in the BD sector. New actors may also have more incentives to build new datasets because it is possible to create a higher value of newly created data by combining with existing datasets. Overall, new and existing actors can enrich and strengthen the BD ecosystem.

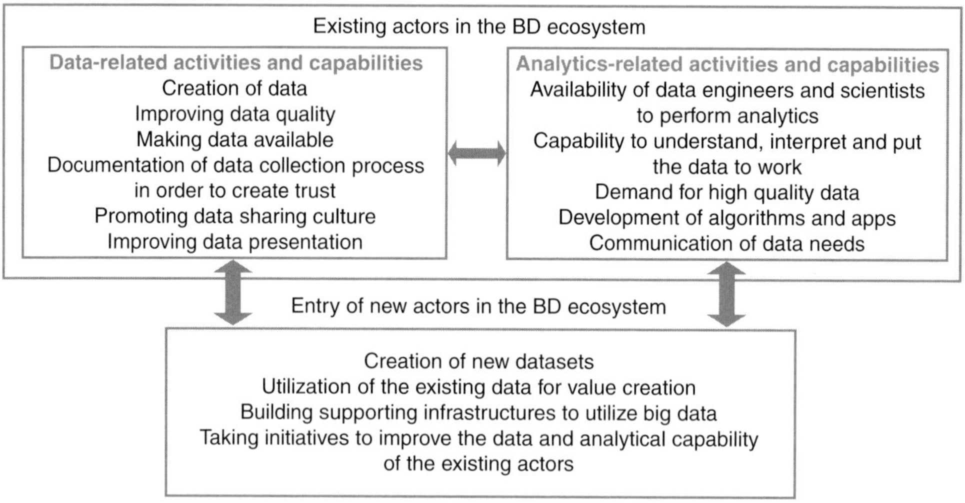

Fig. 2.1. Creating a virtuous circle of effective BD utilization in agriculture, health and environmental security.

2.7.1 Existing actors in the Big Data ecosystem

Data-related activities and capabilities

IMPROVING DATA QUALITY. Perhaps the greatest barrier in utilizing the existing data for key development activities centres on the lack of standardized identifying variables, which means that data files are often isolated. Currently, the potential of the data to inform and guide policy is limited. Various measures need to be developed to improve data quality.

Countries with better developed data infrastructures have addressed this problem by using standard identification for geographic regions, or by adding internationally accepted measures of locations (e.g. latitude and longitude) (Carletto *et al.*, 2015). By adding common identifying traits in each file, data from different agencies and institutions can be easily merged. In this way, different datasets can talk and communicate with each other.

Efforts of various international agencies in improving data quality deserve appreciation. For instance, the Department of International Development is supporting work to generate better data on Tanzania's schools and open the data. The organization is also ensuring that Tanzania's government fulfils the President's commitment to the Open Government Partnership principles. Some progress has already been made. As of the end of 2014, GPS locations of the country's 20,000 schools have been identified and new coding systems have been developed to help link information to a master list (Attfield, 2014).

CREATION OF DATA. New data sources have a higher value addition in developing economies compared to industrial economies. For instance, economists have demonstrated the informational value of luminosity (measured with the intensity of night-time lights visible from space), especially for countries that have low-quality statistical systems and/or those countries that have no recent population or economic censuses (UN Global Pulse, 2015).

Various new initiatives and programmes to create new data have been launched during the last decade. For one thing, markets without strong identification systems cannot capitalize on the opportunity provided by digital data. In this regard, some governments are improving the digitization of national identification. An example is India's Unique Identification Authority that can be used to cross-reference databases and link data on an individual. The possibility to combine and cross-reference data from sources that are otherwise unconnected can provide more powerful insights.

Likewise, mobile phones make it possible for parents to register their child's birth. It allows governments to plan public health interventions such as immunization and vaccination schedules, education and other public services in a better way. In October 2015, Tanzania started a nationwide campaign to help parents register their children's births by mobile phone. The plan is to roll out the new system across the country over the next 5 years. Using the system, a health worker can send the baby's name, gender, birth date and other details by phone to a central database. A birth certificate is then issued free of charge. The Registration, Insolvency and Trusteeship Agency, UNICEF and the telecommunications company Tigo have teamed up in this project (aljazeera.com, 2015). The Uganda Registration Services Bureau has collaborated with Uganda Telecom and UNICEF to launch a mobile Vital Records System (VRS) (Uganda Telecom, 2010). The VRS allows the use of mobile phones and the Internet to register births and deaths.

MAKING DATA AVAILABLE TO INTERESTED PARTIES. In order to improve access for diverse stakeholders, data and tools can be made available online. Open data initiatives can play an important sociopolitical role. Governments can increase transparency by making information available to the public. For instance, the US Government's launch of the website Data.gov in 2009, which makes statistical information collected by over 50 federal agencies available to the public, is considered to be an important transparency measure (Etzioni, 2010). Among developing countries, Kenya and Ethiopia present some good examples of ways to make the existing data available to interested parties in order to create applications and increase transparency.

Among developing economies, Kenya is probably the most spectacular example of making data available to the public and facilitating the use of BD. In 2011, Kenya launched an open data portal (ODP) with the help of the World Bank. The project received support at the highest levels of the government. The data in the ODP includes a full digital edition of the 2009 census, government expenditure for 12 years, household income surveys, and data about the location of schools and health facilities.

Ethiopia's National Meteorology Agency (NMA) has redesigned its website to make the presentation better. Users can easily locate the products and services offered by the NMA (Dinkul *et al.*, 2011). Ethiopia has generated and made available 30-year time series data on rainfall and temperature. The data consist of ten daily timescales for every 10-km grid for the country. The rainfall dataset draws on data from over 600 rain gauge stations, which have been merged with 30 satellite-derived rainfall estimates. For temperature, data from over 300 stations have been combined with data from the Moderate Resolution Imaging Spectroradiometer (MODIS) satellite land-surface temperature (LST). The MODIS LST supplies daily, 8-day and monthly global temperature data.

In the past, spatial gaps existed in the data due to a sparse station network. There were also temporal gaps as a result of interrupted observations or lost data because of communication and other problems. These spatial and temporal gaps have been addressed. For instance, national climate observations were cleaned and combined with satellite proxies (Dinkul *et al.*, 2011).

PROMOTING A DATA-SHARING CULTURE. It is important to emphasize the importance of promoting a data-sharing culture. Measures need to be taken to institutionalize practices promoting high-quality data as well as practices related to data governance and data sharing. For instance, a system that encourages the flow of information from scientists to policy makers, as well as a feedback loop that encourages policy makers to send back information to scientists, is needed.

The widespread interests in BD-related activities have promoted ideas related to data sharing, such as data philanthropy and data liberation. The idea of data philanthropy emerged at the World Economic Forum in Davos in 2011. Data philanthropy is likely to play a key role in the meaningful and productive utilization of BD in developing countries (Pawelke and Tatevossian, 2013).

The basic idea behind data philanthropy is simple: it involves a partnership in which businesses share data for public benefits. Data philanthropy is described as the 'next movement in charitable giving and corporate citizenship' (Coren, 2011). Data donated by corporations and governments can be used to track diseases, avoid economic crises and aid development. Data sharing thus can be considered to be an alternative method of philanthropy for corporations.

While a huge amount of data is held by businesses, they are reluctant to distribute it even anonymously due primarily to privacy concerns (Coren, 2011). It is thus important for national governments and international agencies to work closely with businesses such as Twitter and Facebook and encourage them to engage in data philanthropy.

DOCUMENTATION OF DATA COLLECTION PROCESS. As noted above, the general lack of documentation of data collection procedures hinders the use of data. It is important to discuss details regarding the data collection methods and processes as well as objectives and evaluation criteria. Documentation of the data collection process helps to create trust in the data.

Analytics-related activities and capabilities

The lack of data analytics-related capabilities is perhaps the most serious shortcoming of most developing economies. Developing economies must develop academic and training programmes that produce data engineers and scientists with capabilities to understand, interpret and put the data to work and to perform analytics. They also need to develop algorithms and apps. Data engineers and scientists can also enrich the BD ecosystem by demanding high-quality data and clearly communicating their data needs.

Some initiatives have been aimed at improving analytics-related capabilities. In 2015, IBM announced a plan to expand its Africa Technical Academy and Africa University Program and invest US$60 million by 2017 to bridge the skills gap for technical talent in Africa. The goal of the programme is to provide IT professionals with advanced skills in analytics, cloud and BD technologies. The training and certification programmes are expected to benefit 1000 faculty members and 35,000 students in 80 universities in more than 20 African countries by 2017. In Kenya, for instance, IBM has partnered with the Kenya Education Network in order to deliver advanced hands-on certification courses to faculty members and students in 50 universities (Kajunju and Crozier, 2015).

It is also important to address data usability issues. As noted above, the lack of local contents is a major challenge. China has launched local and national initiatives to support research on IoT and apps that are likely to lead to adaptation of the technology to local conditions and circumstances (itu.int, 2015).

2.7.2 Entry of new actors in the Big Data ecosystem

A rich BD ecosystem can play an important role in attracting organizations that can create and capture value using data and further enrich the BD ecosystem via various mechanisms. For instance, consider the city of Nairobi in Kenya. The Intelligent Community Forum (ICF) listed Nairobi as among the world's 21 most intelligent cities in 2014 and 2015. It was the only African city to be included in the ICF's list. The ICF cited M-Shwari and other mobile money-related innovations in its justification to include Nairobi in the list (intelligentcommunity.org, 2015). Multinationals such as Huawei, Intel, Microsoft, SAP, Oracle, Google and Samsung, as well as local technology corporations, partner with universities to teach practical skills to students through their university programmes (Macharia, 2015).

Many examples of companies that have recognized BD as highly valuable and beneficial can be cited. They utilize the existing data for value creation. In Kenya's case, a fairly developed mobile-payment system has resulted in a virtuous circle of BD deployment that has enhanced the overall outcome of BD efforts. For instance, the founder of solar energy technology company M-KOPA noted that the reason why he chose Kenya to launch its solar package concerned the quality of the payment system. Thanks to Kenya's better mobile money infrastructure, it is easier for M-KOPA to collect its payments. On the other hand, it is more difficult for customers in Tanzania and Uganda to pay to use M-KOPA. Due to the payment difficulty, customers in Tanzania and Uganda are reported to pay in larger quantities (the average payment is of 11–12 days' worth) compared to Kenya (about a week's worth of payments). This means that due to the lack of mobile money infrastructure, consumers in Tanzania and Uganda experience a higher burden.

Another example is Kenya's Century Microfinance Bank, which uses the Agrilife platform to lend to individual Agrilife farmers. The bank obtains a loan guarantee from farmer cooperatives and other aggregators (Grossman and Tarazi,

2014). Century started giving loans via Agrilife in August 2013. By December 2013, Century's outstanding loan portfolio increased from KSH 25.2 million (US$246,000) to KSH 88.6 million (US$864,000). In this way, data provided by the Agrilife platform helped Century increase its loan portfolio by 250% in 4 months with minimal additional investments and costs (Grossman and Tarazi, 2014). The point is that it is possible to improve the long-term sustainability of BD projects by creating data and information that key partners and stakeholders find valuable.

As a further example, consider Kenya's M-Shwari, which is offered jointly by Safaricom and the Commercial Bank of Africa. M-Shwari is a bank account that combines savings and loans. Mobile phone data of individuals who seek credit are analysed to set an initial credit limit. For a client using M-Shwari, subsequent savings and credit behaviours drive the credit limits. For instance, a customer's loan limit is determined by the amount of savings of the customer (Wahito, 2015). In July 2014 the Commercial Bank of Africa reported that its M-Shwari unit's loan–loss ratio was below the industry average of 5% (Business Daily Africa, 2014). M-Shwari was reported to charge 7.5% interest for each loan (Wadongo, 2015).

By drastically eliminating the time it would have taken for customers to sign up or apply in person, M-Shwari added about 1 million accounts in its first 3 months (Kendall and Voorhies, 2014). As of February 2015, M-Shwari had 9 million customers, who saved US$1.47 billion (Popper, 2015).

New actors may also create new datasets, build supporting infrastructures to utilize BD and take initiatives to improve the data and analytical capability. We can illustrate this point with another example from Kenya: Nairobi-based Gro Ventures. Gro Ventures collects, aggregates and processes data in order to provide an understanding of a number of economic and environmental issues such as weather patterns, trade flows, pricing dynamics and production of crops (Okafor, 2014). It has teamed up with non-profit organizations, social enterprises and developmental agencies in the field of agriculture focusing on Africa. The company has developed proprietary algorithms, which provide data analytics related to agriculture markets (Megaw, 2016).

The company also formed a strategic relationship with the African Risk Capacity Agency in the African Union to use data, which was not made accessible previously. As of 2013, Gro Ventures was reported to have comprehensive and granular data on 35 of the 54 African countries. The founder of Gro Ventures claimed that the company had near real-time data on a 10 km × 10 km basis. Prices are updated daily and weather data are updated every 10 days.

Gro Ventures also collects data on its own. The company's plan is to partner with enterprises that deliver agricultural services to farmers. It will pay for the farmers' airtime or give farmers extra airtime in return for primary data (Byme, 2013).

2.8 Discussion and Concluding Comments

BD, artificial intelligence (AI) and improving computing power have opened up tremendous opportunities for firms based in the developing world. AI can play a key role in improving economic and social well-being of the developing world, especially with sufficiently large datasets and computing power and adaptable algorithms, which change behaviour based on the information available at the time they are run (Schmidt and Cohen, 2015).

The barriers and hurdles that must be overcome in order to participate in the BD economy include the lack of high-quality and relevant datasets, insufficient computing power and poor analytics tools. High data-acquisition costs further exacerbate and perpetuate these problems.

Strong BD ecosystems are likely to have beneficial socioeconomic and environmental outcomes. For instance, agriculture employs about 41% of Indonesia's workforce. However, most of the farmers live on a subsistence level due to low-technology farming practices. BD applications such as CI-Agriculture have the potential to help them escape from the low productivity trajectory.

Likewise, there has been an interest in promoting women's entrepreneurship in recent years. A 2014 report published by the World Bank Group and The ONE Campaign found that about half of African agricultural workers are women. However, women's farm productivity is significantly lower than that of men's. For instance, women farmers produce 13% less than men in Uganda and 25% less in Malawi (worldbank.org, 2014). Very little is known, however, about the factors contributing to low productivity of women farmers. Some say that if telephone companies operating in developing countries disaggregate their customers by gender and analyse their behaviours, it can provide a better understanding of their needs (mobileworldlive.com, 2015). The insights and ideas generated from an analysis of their mobile phone usage behaviours can help promote women's entrepreneurship and empower women.

Among the key outcomes of digitization is the formalization of the informal economic sector. The so-called legalists' view of informal economy is that informality is a rational response to over-regulation by the government (de Soto, 1990). Entrepreneurs who run informal businesses exercise their 'power' to operate informally due to unreasonable bureaucratic controls (Carr and Chen, 2002). Due to digitization of economic activities, government bureaucrats are likely to be better able to exercise their control over informal businesses. Thus digitization typically results in a diminished power of informal businesses vis-a-vis the government bureaucrats. A key benefit for financial products such as M-Shwari is that they offer economic incentives for formalizing the informal economy. It is estimated that about US$2.3 billion in informal savings exist in Kenya. As noted above, M-Shwari has helped to move some of the money into a formal system (Yeoman, 2015).

Explicit attempts need to be made to break various barriers and develop a virtuous circle that can enable developing countries to escape from the vicious circle of poor data practices. One way to develop a virtuous circle of effective BD deployment could be public–private partnerships (PPPs). A PPP involves arrangements and cooperative relationships between public and private sectors, under which the latter undertakes actions that have been traditionally performed by the former (Savas, 2000). A PPP is especially well-suited for areas that require diverse types of expertise and knowledge to address complex problems. Prior research suggests that the public and private sectors' different strengths, expertise and experience could lead to complementary roles in meeting developmental and social needs (Linder, 1999). Private and public sectors engaged in PPPs have different objectives, agendas and interests. For example, one goal of the public sector is to employ private sector's capital and technology and share risks with the latter to provide the delivery of public services or goods. By winning the public sector's support, the private sector can increase profitability. For instance, in the agricultural sector, while data collection standards are low in most SSA countries, some are considered to have high standards in data collection (FAO, 2008). Government agencies are the main sources for key data. They can make data and statistics related to agricultural activities available to private lenders in order to assess the lending risks. In return, the private lenders make low interest loans available to smallholder farmers.

The enormous market potential of BD has stimulated entrepreneurial activities in this sector. BD markets of many developing countries have already attracted leading global companies, as well as local entrepreneurial technology companies. Entrepreneurial activities of indigenous as well as foreign BD companies have greatly benefited the local BD ecosystem.

International developmental agencies have emphasized the importance of increasing funding and investment to strengthen national statistical capacity. Exploring new data sources (e.g. those coming from citizens) and harnessing advanced technologies (e.g. visualization) will help to make the data understandable and 'liberate' the data to benefit from the analytical creativity of users, thus holding policy makers responsible and accountable (UN Global Pulse, 2015).

Developing a good BD ecosystem requires a multipronged approach. This chapter highlights the importance of using the various measures and techniques that contribute towards higher data quality. In order to enrich the BD ecosystem, governments and international agencies need to make serious efforts and spend more resources in bolstering data capabilities of developing countries. Measures and initiatives need to be taken to create more data, relevant data and higher quality data. In many cases, geospatial, terrestrial and climate- and weather-related data and information such as soil texture, soil moisture, soil depth, soil carbon levels, soil bulk density, soil water holding capacity, crop yields, and leaf analyses are clearly less controversial and more beneficial than personal data.

References

africanbusinessreview.co.za (2014) Big Data in Africa: IBM dissects a developing trend in a developing market. Available at: http://www.africanbusinessreview.co.za/technology/1783/Big-Data-in-Africa:-IBM-Dissects-a-Developing-Trend-in-a-Developing-Market (accessed 15 February 2016).

African Development Bank (2004) The Marrakech Action Plan for Statistics: Better Data for Better Results: An Action Plan for Improving Development Statistics. 2nd International Roundtable on Managing for Development Results, 4–5 February 2004, Marrakech, Morocco.

aljazeera.com (2015) Tanzania rolls out birth registration by mobile phone. Available at: http://www.aljazeera.com/news/2015/10/tanzania-rolls-birth-registration-mobile-phone-151014134550042.html (accessed 8 April 2016).

aljazeera.com (2016) Indian company launches smartphone for less than $4. Available at: http://www.aljazeera.com/news/2016/02/indian-company-launches-smartphone-4-160218130245036.html (accessed 7 April 2016).

allafrica.com (2014) Namibia: 'Katiti' mobile airtime distribution service launched in Namibia. Available at: http://allafrica.com/stories/201411041022.html (accessed 16 February 2016).

Almazán, M. and Sitbon, E. (2014) Smartphones & mobile money: the next generation of digital financial inclusion, GSMA discussion paper. Available at: http://www.gsma.com/mobilefordevelopment/wp-content/uploads/2014/07/2014_MMU_Smartphones-and-Mobile-Money-The-Next-Generation-of-Digital-Financial-Inclusion_Web.pdf (accessed 7 April 2016).

asia.nikkei.com (2013) IHI to make low-cost, ultracompact satellites. Available at: http://asia.nikkei.com/Tech-Science/Tech/IHI-to-make-low-cost,-ultracompact-satellites (accessed 16 February 2016).

asirobots.com (2015) More affordable sensors lead to greater opportunities for automation. Available at: http://www.asirobots.com/more-affordable-sensors-lead-to-greater-opportunities-for-automation/ (accessed 7 April 2016).

Attfield, I. (2014) Data revolution at 19,000 feet. Available at: https://dfid.blog.gov.uk/2014/11/19/data-revolution-at-15000-feet/ (accessed 16 February 2016).

Barr, A. and Pasztor, A. (2014) Google invests in satellites to spread internet access. Available at: http://www.wsj.com/articles/google-invests-in-satellites-to-spread-internet-access-1401666287 (accessed 16 February 2016).

Beroes Ríos, M.A. (2016) En Colombia apuestan por una mejor utilización del Big Data. Available at: http://www.cioal.com/2016/02/01/en-colombia-apuestan-por-una-mejor-utilizacion-del-big-data/ (accessed 16 February 2016).

Bhushan, A. (2012) Big data. USAID Frontiers in Development. Available at: https://www.usaid.gov/sites/default/files/documents/1868/AniketBhushan.pdf (accessed 7 April 2016).

Bolton, D. (2015) Developing countries will drive the growth of the Internet of Things. Available at: http://arc.applause.com/2015/12/02/internet-of-things-growth-developing-countries/ (accessed 16 February 2016).

Bughin, J (2016) Big data: getting a better read on performance, McKinsey Quarterly. Available at: http://www.mckinsey.com/industries/high-tech/our-insights/big-data-getting-a-better-read-on-performance?cid=other-eml-alt-mkq-mck-oth-1602 (accessed 29 February 2016).

Bughin, J., Chui, M. and Manyika, J. (2015) An executive's guide to the Internet of Things. The rate of adoption is accelerating. Here are six things you need to know. Available at: http://www.mckinsey.com/Insights/Business_Technology/An_executives_guide_to_the_Internet_of_Things?cid=digital-eml-alt-mip-mck-oth-1508 (accessed 16 February 2016).

Business Daily Africa (2014) CBA aims for 10 million M-Shwari accounts by Christmas. *Business Daily Africa*. Available at: http://www.businessdailyafrica.com/Corporate-News/-/539550/2380584/-/vv2a2mz/-/index.html (accessed 7 April 2016).

Byme, C. (2013) Data-driven lending could help African farmers feed the world. Available at: http://www.fastcolabs.com/3019953/data-driven-lending-could-help-african-farmers-feed-the-world (accessed 16 February 2016).

Camhi, J. (2015) How IBM's $3 billion investment will drive IoT growth. Available at: http://www.businessinsider.com/how-ibms-3-billion-investment-will-drive-iot-growth-2015-4 (accessed 15 February 2016).

Carletto, G., Jolliffe, D. and Banerjee, R. (2015) From tragedy to renaissance: improving agricultural data for better policies. Policy Research Working Paper 7150, *The World Bank Group*, Development Research Group Poverty and Inequality Team.

Carr, M. and Chen, A.M. (2002) Globalization and the informal economy: how global trade and investment impact on the working poor. Working Paper on the Informal Economy No. 1, 2002. International Labour Office, Employment Sector, Geneva, Switzerland.

Chen, G. and Faz, X. (2015) The potential of digital data: how far can it advance financial inclusion? Focus Note. CGAP, Washington, DC, USA. Available at: http://www.cgap.org/sites/default/files/Focus-Note-The-Potential-of-Digital-Data-Jan-2015.pdf (accessed 7 April 2016).
Chui, M., Löffler, M. and Roberts, R. (2010) The Internet of Things, McKinsey. Available at: http://www.mckinsey.com/industries/high-tech/our-insights/the-internet-of-things (accessed 7 April 2016).
cisco.com (2014) Cisco Global Cloud Index: forecast and methodology, 2014–2019 White Paper. Availableat:http://www.cisco.com/c/en/us/solutions/collateral/service-provider/global-cloud-index-gci/Cloud_Index_White_Paper.html (accessed 16 February 2016).
computervisiononline.com (2015) Low cost satellite imagery meets big data. Available at: http://www.computervisiononline.com/blog/low-cost-satellite-imagery-meets-big-data, Omidyar Network (accessed 16 February 2016).
Coren, M.J. (2011) Data philanthropy: open data for world-changing solutions. Available at: http://www.fastcoexist.com/1678963/data-philanthropy-open-data-for-world-changing-solutions (accessed 18 August 2014).
datafloq.com (2015) From Big Data to Big Mac; how McDonalds leverages Big Data. Available at: https://datafloq.com/read/from-big-data-to-big-mac-how-mcdonalds-leverages-b/403 (accessed 16 February 2016).
de Soto, H. (1990) *The Other Path: The Invisible Revolution in the Third World.* Harper Collins Press, New York, USA.
Deighton, J. and Peter, A.J. (2013) The value of data: consequences for insight, innovation & efficiency in the US economy. The Data Driven Marketing Institute. Available at: http://ddminstitute.thedma.org/#valueofdata (accessed 15 February 2016).
Dinku, T., Asefa, K., Hilemariam, K., Grimes, D. and Connor, S. (2011) Improving availability, access and use of climate information. Available at: http://public.wmo.int/en/bulletin/improving-availability-access-and-use-climate-information (accessed 1 August 2016).
Donnan, S. (2014) Inequality and why the world's poor are being left behind by Big Data. Available at:http://blogs.ft.com/beyond-brics/2014/11/06/inequality-and-why-the-worlds-poor-are-being-left-behind-by-big-data/ (accessed 29 February 2016).
economist.com (2014a) Scientific research in Africa is gathering momentum. Available at: http://www.economist.com/news/middle-east-and-africa/21611112-scientific-research-africa-gathering-momentum-rise (accessed 16 February 2016).
economist.com (2014b) A phoneful of dollars: the world's poor need the stability and security that banks have traditionally offered, but increasingly they do not need banks to provide it. Available at: http://www.economist.com/news/briefing/21632441-worlds-poor-need-stability-and-security-banks-have-traditionally-offered (accessed 15 February 2016).
El-Darwiche, B., Sharma, A., Singh, M. and Samad, R.A. (2012) Digitization in emerging economies: Unleashing opportunities at the bottom of the pyramid. Available at: http://www.strategyand.pwc.com/media/file/Strategyand_Digitization-in-Emerging-Economies.pdf (accessed 7 April 2016).
Etzioni, A. (2010) Is transparency the best disinfectant? *Journal of Political Philosophy* 18(4), 389–404.
FAO [Food and Agricultural Organization of the United Nations] (2008) *The Agricultural Bulletin Board on Data Collection, Dissemination and Quality of Statistics.* FAO, Rome, Italy.
fareasternagriculture.com (2015) Bringing big data to farming in Indonesia. Available at: http://www.fareasternagriculture.com/technology/machinery-a-equipment/bringing-big-data-to-farming-in-indonesia (accessed 16 February 2016).
Fengler, W. and Kharas, H. (2015) Personalising data for development. Available at: http://blogs.ft.com/beyond-brics/2015/09/23/personalising-data-for-development/ (accessed 29 February 2016).

Freischlad, N. (2015a) Indonesia's nerdiest company joins Yello Mobile and Cloudera in multi-million dollar partnership. Available at: https://www.techinasia.com/mediatrac-strategic-partnership-cloudera-yello-mobile/ (accessed 16 February 2016).
Freischlad, N. (2015b) Drones over the rice paddy: Ci-Agriculture brings smart tech to the field. Available at: https://www.techinasia.com/ci-agriculture-precision-farming-indonesia/ (accessed 7 April 2016).
Garside, J. (2013) Google to bring net access to Africa using blimps, masts and satellites. Available at: http://www.theguardian.com/technology/2013/may/28/google-africa-blimps-net-access (accessed 16 February 2016).
Gilchrist, A. (2016) Alibaba launches Big Data cloud platform in China. Available at: http://betanews.com/2016/01/25/alibaba-launches-big-data-cloud-platform-in-china/ (accessed 7 April 2016).
Goedde, L., Horii, M. and Sanghvi, S. (2015) Pursuing the global opportunity in food and agribusiness. Available at: http://www.mckinsey.com/insights/food_agriculture/pursuing_the_global_opportunity_in_food_and_agribusiness (accessed 15 February 2016).
Grossman, J. and Tarazi, M. (2014) Serving smallholder farmers: recent developments in digital finance (Focus Note). *CGAP*, 94, June.
Harpham, B. (2015) How the Internet of Things is changing healthcare and transportation. Available at: http://www.cio.com/article/2981481/healthcare/how-the-internet-of-things-is-changing-healthcare-and-transportation.html (accessed 16 February 2016).
Hartani, R. (2015) Into the Internet of Things Era: the African context. *Africa Telecom & IT*, 6(2), 47–48.
He, X. (2015) IDTechEx: China's RFID market value will reach $4.3 billion by 2025, 21 May. Available at: http://www.idtechex.com/research/articles/idtechex-chinas-rfid-market-value-will-reach-4-3-billion-by-2025-00007854.asp (accessed 16 February 2016).
Higginbotham, S. (2015) How the Internet of things is protecting endangered rhinos. Available at: http://fortune.com/2015/08/11/chobe-angels-women-safari-guides/ (accessed 16 February 2016).
Hoagland, K. (2010) Communiqué: Vietnam: avoiding the 'middle income trap'. Available at: http://ash.harvard.edu/news/communiqu%C3%A9-vietnam-avoiding-%E2%80%98middle-income-trap%E2%80%99 (accessed 15 February 2016).
Hormats, R. (2015) Kenya, open for business. Available at: http://foreignpolicy.com/2015/07/24/kenya-open-for-business-obama-africa-china/ (accessed 15 February 2016).
intelligentcommunity.org (2015) Community. Available at: http://www.intelligentcommunity.org/index.php?src=news&refno=1598&category=Community&prid=1598 (accessed 16 February 2016).
internetsociety.org (2015) Big Data in the Philippines: challenges and opportunities. Available at: http://www.internetsociety.org/articles/big-data-philippines-challenges-and-opportunities (accessed 15 February 2016).
ITU (2015a) Key ICT indicators for developed and developing countries and the world. Available at: www.itu.int/en/ITU-D/Statistics/.../ITU_Key_2005-2013_ICT_data.xls (accessed 7 April 2016).
ITU (2015b) *Measuring the Information Society Report*. International Telecommunication Union, Geneva, Switzerland.
itu.int (2015) The Internet of Things. Available at: http://www.itu.int/itunews/manager/display.asp?lang=en&year=2005&issue=09&ipage=things (accessed 29 February 2016).
John, G. (2014) Reshaping a global healthcare strategy. *CIO* 27(9), 26–26.
Kajunju, A. and Crozier, J. (2015) Closing Africa's skills gap and fostering innovation through technology. Available at: http://www.huffingtonpost.com/amini-kajunju/closing-africas-skills-ga_b_8180370.html (accessed 15 February 2016).
Kendall, J. and Voorhies, R. (2014) The mobile-finance revolution. *Foreign Affairs* 93(2), 9–13.

Korolov, M. (2013) 15 most powerful Big Data companies, Available at: http://www.networkworld.com/slideshow/114134/15-most-powerful-big-data-companies.html#slide1 (accessed 18 August 2014).

Kroes, N. (2013) Speech: Big Data for Europe, European Commission. Available at: http://europa.eu/rapid/press-release_SPEECH-13-893_en.htm (accessed 18 August 2014).

Kshetri N. (2011) Cloud computing in the global south: drivers, effects and policy measures. *Third World Quarterly* 32(6), 995–1012.

Kshetri, N. (2016) Big Data's role in expanding access to financial services in China. *International Journal of Information Management* 36 (3), 297–308.

Leetaru, K. (2015) Do Big Data results depend on what data we look at? Available at: http://www.forbes.com/sites/kalevleetaru/2015/10/05/do-big-data-results-depend-on-what-data-we-look-at/ (accessed 16 February 2016).

Lenard, T.M. and Rubin, P.H. (2013) The big data revolution: privacy considerations. Available at: http://www.techpolicyinstitute.org (accessed 15 February 2016).

Levy, S. (2014) Google's balloon internet experiment, one year later. Available at: http://www.wired.com/2014/06/google-balloons-year-later/ (accessed 15 February 2016).

Linder, H.S. (1999) Coming to terms with the public–private partnership: a grammar of multiple meanings. *American Behavioral Scientist* 43(1), 35–51.

Macharia, K. (2015) Why Nairobi is ranked the 'smartest city' in Africa, Available at: http://www.capitalfm.co.ke/business/2015/02/why-nairobi-is-ranked-the-smartest-city-in-africa/ (accessed 16 February 2016).

Makri, A. (2015) Is big data the gold dust of medical aid? Available at: http://www.scidev.net/global/data/scidev-net-at-large/big-data-the-gold-dust-of-medical-aid.html (accessed 16 February 2016).

Megaw, N. (2016) Smart Africa: Big-data tools transform business. Available at: http://www.ft.com/cms/s/0/6a55808c-c0ef-11e5-846f-79b0e3d20eaf.html (accessed 16 February 2016).

Mendelsohn, R., Kurukulasuriya, P., Basist, A., Kogan, F. and Williams, C.C. (2007) Analysis with satellite versus weather station data. *Climatic Change* 81(1), 71–83.

Meschino, C. (2014) Congratulations to SemiosBIO, #3 in 2013's most innovative companies in B.C. Available at: http://semios.com/category/press/ (accessed 16 February 2016).

mckinsey.com (2015) The Internet of Things: five critical questions. Available at: http://www.mckinsey.com/Insights/High_Tech_Telecoms_Internet/The_Internet_of_Things_Five_critical_questions?cid=digital-eml-alt-mip-mck-oth-1508 (accessed 16 February 2016).

Michal, L. (2014) What's the next big thing in big data? Bigger data. *Fortune* 169(8), 233–238.

Mirani, L. (2014) How to manage all your financial affairs from a $20 mobile phone. Available at: http://qz.com/218988/how-to-manage-all-your-financial-affairs-from-a-20-mobile-phone/ (accessed 15 February 2016).

mobileworldlive.com (2015) Big data could unlock mobile service success amongst women. Available at: http://www.mobileworldlive.com/m360-2015-africa/big-data-could-unlock-mobile-service-success-amongst-women/ (accessed 16 February 2016).

Mohammed, J. (2014) Surprise: Agriculture is doing more with IoT innovation than most other industries. Available at: http://venturebeat.com/2014/12/07/surprise-agriculture-is-doing-more-with-iot-innovation-than-most-other-industries/ (accessed 16 February 2016).

Mungadze, S. (2015) Nedbank rolls out SA's first big data service. Available at: http://www.bdlive.co.za/business/financial/2015/07/16/nedbank-rolls-out-sas-first-big-data-service (accessed 16 February 2016).

news.xinhuanet.com (2013) Xinhua insight: China aids big data development amid challenges. Available at: http://news.xinhuanet.com/english/indepth/2013-10/21/c_132817622.htm (accessed 7 April 2016).

oilandgasbigdata.com (2015) Big data tools a recent phenomenon in GCC oil and gas firms. Available at: http://www.oiland/gasbigdata.com/news/gcc-oil-and-gas-firms-use-big-data-tools-to-boost-output (accessed 16 February 2016).
Okafor, E. (2014) Gro Ventures. Available at: http://www.afrika.no/Detailed/25373.html (accessed 16 February 2016).
Oldgard, M. (2015) Defeating epidemic diseases with big data. Available at: https://www.digitalnewsasia.com/insights/defeating-epidemic-diseases-with-big-data (accessed 15 February 2016).
Omumbo, J.A., Waweru, M.S., Omumbo, A.J., Lyon, B., Thomson, C.M. and Connor J.S. (2011) Raised temperatures over the Kericho tea estates: revisiting the climate in the East African highlands malaria debate. *Malaria Journal* 10:12.
Orcutt, M. (2014) Poorer countries stand to miss out on the big data boom. Available at: http://www.technologyreview.com/view/526941/poorer-countries-stand-to-miss-out-on-the-big-data-boom/ (accessed 16 February 2016).
Patel, P. (2013) Feeding the world with big data. Available at: http://spectrum.ieee.org/computing/networks/feeding-the-world-with-big-data (accessed 18 August 2014).
Pawelke, A. and Tatevossian, R.A. (2013) Data philanthropy: where are we now? Available at: http://www.unglobalpulse.org/data-philanthropy-where-are-we-now (accessed 18 August 2014).
Popper, B. (2015) Can mobile banking revolutionize the lives of the poor? Available at: http://www.theverge.com/2015/2/4/7966043/bill-gates-future-of-banking-and-mobile-money (accessed 16 February 2016).
Rai, S. (2014) India's high demand for big data workers contrasts with scarcity of skilled talent. Available at: http://www.techrepublic.com/article/indias-high-demand-for-big-data-workers-contrasts-with-scarcity-of-skilled-talent/ (accessed 16 February 2016).
reuters.com (2015) Africa Business: With iCow and M-Farm, smartphones reboot African agriculture. Available at: http://www.reuters.com/article/2015/03/16/africa-farming-idUSL5N0WB34920150316 (accessed 15 February 2016).
rfidjournal.com (2016) RFID frequently asked question. Available at: https://www.rfidjournal.com/faq/show?84 (accessed 16 February 2016).
Robert, L.M. (2014) Internet of Things. *Computerworld* 48(7), 12–16.
Sandefur, J. and Glassman, A. (2014) The political economy of bad data: evidence from african survey & administrative statistics. Available at: http://www.cgdev.org/publication/political-economy-bad-data-evidence-african-survey-administrative-statistics-working?callout=3-3 (accessed 15 February 2016).
Santos, M. (2013) La situación del Big Data en Colombia. Available at: http://www.enter.co/chips-bits/enterprise/la-situacion-del-big-data-en-colombia/ (accessed 16 February 2016).
Savas, E.S. (2000) *Privatization and Public-Private Partnerships*, Seven Bridges Press, New York.
Schmidt, E. and Cohen, J. (2015) Technology: inventive artificial intelligence will make all of us better. Available at: http://time.com/4154126/technology-essay-eric-schmidt-jared-cohen/ (accessed 7 April 2016).
schoolofdata.org (2013) A deep dive into fuzzy matching in Tanzania. Available at: http://schoolofdata.org/2013/12/06/a-deep-dive-into-fuzzy-matching-in-tanzania/ (accessed 15 February 2016).
scidev.net (2014) Big data for development: facts and figures. Available at: http://www.scidev.net/global/data/feature/big-data-for-development-facts-and-figures.html (accessed 16 February 2016).
Shacklett, M. (2015) Fighting Ebola with a holistic vision of big data. Available at: http://www.techrepublic.com/article/fighting-ebola-with-a-holistic-vision-of-big-data/ (accessed 7 April 2016).

Shaw, J. (2014) Why 'Big Data' is a big deal. Available at: http://harvardmagazine.com/2014/03/why-big-data-is-a-big-deal (accessed 16 February 2016).

ska.ac.za (2016) Media releases and statements. Available at: http://www.ska.ac.za/media-releases/ (accessed 16 February 2016).

Soewondo, P., Ferrario, A., Levenus, T.D. (2013) Challenges in diabetes management in Indonesia: a literature review. *Globalization & Health* 9(1), 1–34.

Srikanth, R.P. (2013) The Big Data opportunity for Indian IT service providers. Available at: http://www.informationweek.in/informationweek/news-analysis/277187/opportunity-indian-service-provider (accessed 18 August 2014).

Staff, M. (2014) Big Data in Africa: IBM dissects a developing trend in a developing market. Available at:http://www.africanbusinessreview.co.za/technology/1783/Big-Data-in-Africa:-IBM-Dissects-a-Developing-Trend-in-a-Developing-Market (accessed 15 February 2016).

Swanson, A. (2015) How Baidu, Tencent and Alibaba are leading the way in China's big data revolution. Available at: http://www.scmp.com/tech/innovation/article/1852141/how-baidu-tencent-and-alibaba-are-leading-way-chinas-big-data (accessed 16 February 2016).

telecomasia.net (2015) China unveils guidelines for big data. Available at: http://www.telecomasia.net/content/china-unveils-guidelines-big-data (accessed 16 February 2016).

The World Bank (2010) Getting the numbers right: making statistical systems a real plus for results. The World Bank: IBRD Results. Available at: http://documents.worldbank.org/curated/en/2010/04/20379774/getting-numbers-right-making-statistical-systems-real-plus-results (accessed 8 April 2016).

Thomas, S. (2015) Getting the next billion online: why emerging markets need a lighter internet [Tech4Africa]. Available at: http://memeburn.com/2015/10/getting-the-next-billion-online-why-emerging-markets-need-a-lighter-internet-tech4africa/ (accessed 15 February 2016).

Thomson, C.M., Connor, J.S., Zebiak, E.S., Jancloes, M. and Mihretie, A. (2011) Africa needs climate data to fight disease, *Nature*, 471, 440–442. Available at: http://www.nature.com/nature/journal/v471/n7339/full/471440a.html (accessed 28 April 2016).

undatarevolution.org (2015) A world that counts: mobilising the data revolution for sustainable development. Report of the UN Secretary-General's Independent Expert Advisory Group on a Data Revolution for Sustainable Development. Available at: http://www.undatarevolution.org/wp-content/uploads/2014/11/A-World-That-Counts.pdf (accessed 8 April 2016).

UNDP (2011) Africa Adaptation Programme: capacity building experiences improving access, understanding and application of climate data and information. Discussion Paper Series 2. Available at: http://www.undp.org/content/undp/en/home/librarypage/environment-energy/climate_change/capacity_development/africa_adaptationprogrammecapacitybuildingexperiences.html (accessed 8 April 2016).

UN Global Pulse (2015) A 'data revolution' for the MDGs/SDGs? Pulse Lab Jakarta. Available at: http://www.unescap.org/sites/default/files/UNESCAP%20Laos%20presentation.pdf (accessed 7 April 2016).

unicef.org (2016) Birth registration. Available at: http://www.unicef.org/esaro/5480_birth_registration.html (accessed 15 February 2016).

Uganda Telecom (2010) About mobile vital records system. Available at: http://www.mobilevrs.co.ug/home.php (accessed 28 April 2016).

unocha.org (2013) Big data and humanitarianism: 5 things you need to know. Available at: http://www.unocha.org/top-stories/all-stories/five-things-big-data-and-humanitarianism (accessed 15 February 2016).

Van Der Poll, A. (2015) Embracing big data in Africa: approach with caution. Available at: http://www.bizcommunity.com/Article/410/16/136096.html (accessed 15 February 2016).

Wadongo, E. (2015) Why competition in mobile innovation is good for consumers. Available at: http://venturesafrica.com/why-competition-in-mobile-innovation-is-good-for-consumers/ (accessed 15 February 2016).

Wahito, M. (2015) Safaricom, KCB launch banking product. Available at: http://www.capitalfm.co.ke/business/2015/03/safaricom-kcb-launch-banking-product/ (accessed 8 April 2016).

Waweru, M.S., Omumbo, A.J., Lyon, B., Thomson, C.M. and Connor J.S. (2011) Revisiting the East African malaria debate. Available at: http://www.wmo.int/pages/publications/bulletinarchive/archive/60_1_en/60_1_Waweru_en.html (accessed 15 February 2016).

WEF (2012) Big Data, big impact: new possibilities for international development. World Economic Forum. Available at: http://www3.weforum.org/docs/WEF_TC_MFS_BigDataBigImpact_Briefing_2012.pdf (accessed 8 April 2016).

Wesolowski, A., Qureshi, T., Boni, M.F., Sundsøy, P.R., Johansson, M.A., Rasheed, S.B., Engø-Monsen, K. and Buckee, C.O. (2015) Impact of human mobility on the emergence of dengue epidemics in Pakistan. *Proceedings of the National Academy of Sciences of the United States of America* 112(38), 11887–11892.

Whitler, K.A. (2013) What can marketers do to manage and leverage Big Data? Available at: http://www.forbes.com/sites/kimberlywhitler/2013/03/07/what-can-marketers-do-to-manage-and-leverage-big-data/ (accessed 16 February 2016).

Winter, C. (2014) Eritrea's Communications Disconnect. Available at: http://www.bloomberg.com/bw/articles/2014-06-26/eritrea-worlds-least-connected-country-tech-wise (accessed 15 February 2016).

worldbank.org (2014) Gender gap holds back Africa's women farmers: new report identifies policy interventions to narrow and eliminate gender inequality. Available at: http://www.worldbank.org/en/news/press-release/2014/03/18/gender-gap-holds-back-africas-women-farmers-new-report-identifies-policy-interventions-to-narrow-and-eliminate-gender-inequality (accessed 16 February 2016).

Wyber, R., Vaillancourt, S., Perry, W., Mannava, P., Folaranmi, T. and Celi, L.A. (2015) Big data in global health: improving health in low- and middle-income countries. *Bulletin of the World Health Organization* 93(3), 203–208.

Yeoman, K. (2014) M-PESA helps world's poorest go to the bank using mobile phones. Available at: http://www.csmonitor.com/World/Making-a-difference/Change-Agent/2014/0106/M-Pesa-helps-world-s-poorest-go-to-the-bank-using-mobile-phones (accessed 16 February 2016).

3 Big Data in Environmental Protection and Resources Conservation

Abstract

BD holds great promise for environmental monitoring, protection and planning in developing economies. Various actors involved in environmental monitoring and protection activities are increasingly relying on vast amounts and diverse types of data in order to tackle a wide range of environmental issues. This chapter seeks to deepen our understanding of facilitators and inhibitors of diffusion and effective utilization of BD in environmental monitoring and protection in these economies. It also introduces various data sources in the context of environmental monitoring, protection and natural resources conservation. In this chapter, a variety of examples are presented of environmental projects undertaken in developing countries that utilize BD. It also analyses how various characteristics of BD are applicable in the context of environmental monitoring, protection and conservation strategies. It covers issues of foreign and local BD technologies in environmental monitoring and protection. It also highlights the role of BD in promoting transparency by fighting environmental crimes and injustices.

3.1 Introduction

Environment-related concern is of special importance to developing economies, which account for a significant and growing proportion of the world's greenhouse gas emissions. During the period 1850–2010, developing economies' share in greenhouse gas emissions was 48%, which is estimated to reach 51% by 2020 (pbl.nl, 2013). BD has offered promising opportunities to improve environmental monitoring and protection and conservation of resources in these economies.

The increasing use of BD in environmental monitoring and protection is reflected in a sizable and rapidly growing market for environmental technologies in developing countries. The Chinese market of products involving environmental monitoring technology was estimated at RMB1 billion (about US$160 million) in

2006, which increased to RMB4.9 billion (about US$800 million) in 2013 (prweb.com, 2014).

There is some evidence that BD-related tools have made it easier to detect and quantify challenges such as deforestation, desertification and climate change, which were not possible until few years ago (Anderson, 2014). For instance, the Global Forest Watch (GFW) is a platform launched by the World Resources Institute for mapping BD related to forests in near real time. It updates data and images every few weeks, and daily in the case of fire alerts. Using BD, cloud and crowdsourcing, it helps to study changes in tree cover with the help of indicators related to deforestation, harvesting of tree plantations, fire damage and forest die-off from disease and pests. Analysts, policy makers, conservationists and others can use it to track progress on efforts to conserve forests (Butler, 2015).

In order to fight against the slaughter of elephants for ivory, non-governmental organizations (NGOs) working in the Democratic Republic of the Congo use satellite imagery and predictive analytics to assist park rangers in Garamba National Park (Gunther, 2015). Low data storage costs, powerful clouds, the availability of Internet connectivity in remote places and free access to remote sensing data (e.g. US government satellites) are key driving forces that are likely to change the way NGOs such as the GFW work.

Machine learning and artificial intelligence have become an important component in unlocking the potential of BD (Senior, 2014). Alphabet Inc.'s chairman Eric Schmidt and Google Idea's director Jared Cohen predict that the next generation of artificial intelligence (AI) will have the same level of economic and social impact as the technological revolutions associated with the Internet and mobile phones, which have fundamentally changed the way individuals and organizations communicate and interact with the world (Schmidt and Cohen, 2015/2016).

One encouraging trend is that machine learning and AI have already made remarkable inroads into environmental projects in the developing world. The Beijing Municipal Environmental Protection Bureau and IBM signed a 10-year, US$160 billion deal known as Green Horizon, which provides a high-profile example of the deployment of machine learning and AI.

Green Horizon relies on real-time data from optical sensors, weather satellites and meteorological data, other structured databases, the cloud, BD analytics and the Internet of Things (IoT) in order to gain deeper insights into the type, source, dispersion and levels of the city's pollutant emissions. The system also makes optimizations and adjustments to better utilize renewable energy sources. In addition, cognitive computing analyses and learns from real-time data and information (Greengard, 2014). According to IBM, the system uses 'adaptive machine learning', which constantly learns the way to improve a forecast for different time horizons and different locations of a city using different models.

The IBM Green Horizon initiative was first launched in July 2014 to help the Chinese government achieve its environmental targets over a 10-year period. The targets included: (i) reducing fine air pollution particulate matter (PM2.5; tiny particles that are smaller than 2.5 micrometres, i.e. less than one-hundredth of the thickness of a human hair) concentration by up to 25% by 2017; (ii) increasing the proportion of renewable energy to 15% by 2020; and (iii) achieving a 45% reduction in carbon intensity by 2020 (IBM.com, 2014).

Using climate modelling technologies, it is possible for the Beijing municipal government to predict 72 hours in advance the location where harmful pollutants are likely to spread. IBM researchers have been tasked to expand the system's capability to provide medium- and long-term forecasts as far as 10 days ahead (Knight, 2015). Such a prediction can help the city to perform a scenario analysis that looks at the effects of various short-term policy options such as traffic restrictions, mandatory installation of filtering systems and relocation of facilities. It can also provide relevant information to residents so that they can avoid specific areas in the city. Relevant information can also be posted on electronic freeway signs. The traffic can be diverted to less-congested and less-polluted areas. It is also possible to work with factories to plan and synchronize production cycles (Shumway, 2014).

IBM's China Research Laboratory has led the effort. It is utilizing the expertise, knowledge, experience and resources of IBM's 12 global research labs and partnering with government, academia and the private sector. In December 2015, IBM announced four more partnerships to deploy Green Horizon: two in China (Baoding, Zhangjiakou), one in India (Delhi) and one in South Africa (Johannesburg) (Howard, 2015).

An accurate and effective forecasting of the availability of renewable energies can help a more sustainable power generation and supply. For instance, weather modelling and cloud imaging tools can be used to more accurately predict the performance of solar and wind farms in advance. This information can be used to maximize and store electrical output (Shumway, 2014).

A project implemented in Zhangbei in Hebei Province, known as the Zhangbei Demonstration Project, which is China's largest renewable energy project, utilizes BD to integrate wind energy into the grid. IBM's renewable energy forecasting system combines data related to cloud movements, wind speed, temperature and direction, which can be used by utility firms to forecast clean energy power production up to one week in advance (verdantix.com, 2015). Some impressive accomplishments in energy conservation have been made. It is reported that the deployment of IBM's supply and demand management system reportedly led to a reduction of energy waste from 30% to 20% (chinatechnews.com, 2014). By the end of 2014, the plant had integrated 10% more alternative energy from its wind farm into the grid. The Zhangbei Project's energy forecasting system is reported to have a 90% predictive accuracy (Shumway, 2014).

A key application of BD in the near future is likely to be in the development of smart cities in developing economies, which is a result of global trends in energy supply and consumption and environmental sustainability (Bartoli *et al.*, 2011). China has plans for building 103 smart cities, districts and towns (dorsey.com, 2013). Likewise, India's Prime Minister, Narendra Modi, has announced plans to build 100 smart cities (Tolan, 2014).

There are already some encouraging results and observations. For instance, in China's Zhenjiang city, buses report their positions and operating characteristics to a control centre. The results are improved efficiency and reduced fuel use and emissions. The city has reported a reduction of 6700 tons of carbon dioxide annually (Johnson, 2014). It is also expected to save US$2.7 million in fuel costs annually (Holliman, 2015). Likewise, in March China's state-owned Aerospace

Science and Industry Corp announced that the southern city of Shenzhen started tracking vehicles in the city using a radio-frequency identification (RFID)-based smart traffic tracking system (Anderson, 2016).

Finally, increasing digitization has promoted behaviours that are environmental friendly. In Kenya, for instance, there are companies such as M-KOPA and GreenWize Energy, which offer solar lighting products to poor households. M-KOPA sells its solar package for a down payment of about US$30. It is worth US$200, which includes US$25 in interest; the users can pay a daily instalment of US$0.50 for one year and then own an 8-watt solar panel, two LED lights, a USB phone charger and a portable solar-powered radio. Most people in Africa are reported to spend US$0.50 daily on kerosene. As of November 2015, M-KOPA's 85,000 customers had paid their loans in full (Odengo, 2015). Each solar panel has a SIM card powered by Safaricom. People can use M-PESA to pay bills. Sensors have enabled this 'pay-as-you-go' model to serve remote communities. A customer can pay the fee using a mobile phone. If a customer fails to make a payment, the system can be shut off remotely. The power can be switched back on after the customer pays the instalments (Popper, 2015). M-KOPA solar panels can be used to power services such as lighting, mobile phone charging and radios. Remote sensors also monitor changes in demand. Solar power companies can send engineers to repair the system if there is an unusual drop in demand. Likewise, solar panels can be added to the grid if the system reaches full capacity (GE Look Ahead, 2015).

3.2 Various Data Sources in the Context of Environmental Monitoring and Protection

A wide range of techniques and diverse types of datasets are being used to tackle environmental issues in developing countries.

3.2.1 The Internet of Things

According to the *World Water Development Report 2012*, inadequate water supply, sanitation and poor hygiene lead to about 3.5 million deaths annually, the majority of which occur in developing countries (UN Water, 2014). The IoT can be used in environmental applications such as monitoring of water supply and quality. For instance, sensors can monitor pollutants in a town or a river and pinpoint the source of an anomalous situation.

One example is Vietnam's Da Nang, which is a major port city on the South China Sea coast next to the Han River. Da Nang Water Company (DAWCO) uses BD to provide real-time analysis and monitoring of the city's water supply (Pretz, 2014). The goal is to manage the system better by detecting leaks and accurately forecasting future demand. In the past, DAWCO needed to collect water samples manually. The BD project involves installing sensors throughout each stage of its water treatment process. Managers can track the water's turbidity, salinity, pH, chlorine and conductivity levels in real time. They receive alerts and notifications when these readings indicate sudden changes (Wheatley, 2013).

Da Nang teamed up with Intel to construct a modern green data centre. The Da Nang People Committee introduced over 135 e-government services, which include school admissions to property registration. Sensors also monitor water levels in the Han River, which has a high flood risk associated with sea level rise and other factors (Rajan, 2013).

Da Nang uses BD for predicting and preventing congestion on roads, and to coordinate responses in the case of adverse weather or road accidents (Dubow, 2014). The data are aggregated from multiple sources. Sensors embedded in roads, highways and on buses detect anomalies and control traffic flow (Mallya, 2014). The system also gives the Department of Transport access to real-time information for its fleet of buses. From the city's traffic control centre, city officials can monitor traffic and control the traffic light system. If there is traffic congestion caused by an accident, traffic lights can be adjusted, which allows time for cars affected by the jam to pass through. These data are accessible to passengers through video screens at bus stations or via mobile apps. Users can see details such as the location of a bus, speed and predicted time of a trip. The plan in the future is to alert citizens to how crowded a bus is likely to be when it arrives. The Vietnamese government wants to discourage the country's growing middle class from buying cars. One way to do so is to make the public transport system more reliable and efficient (Woody, 2013).

Da Nang's transport grid was established based on people's movement pattern and the city's growth pattern. It was reported that the majority of IBM's customers for Smarter Cities technology are in developing countries such as China, India, Indonesia and Vietnam. In China, IBM is reportedly focusing on smaller cities with populations of about 1 million. The traffic problems are more difficult to solve in large cities such as Shanghai and Beijing (Woody, 2013).

The failure to deploy appropriate IoT devices and sensors are found to be the cause of some of the worst environmental disasters of human origin in developing countries. For instance, consider the 2008 Royal Dutch Shell oil spill in Bodo, Nigeria. It was estimated that 500,000 barrels of oil had leaked, which damaged 600,000 ha of mangrove swamp. It was reported that the pipeline did not have leak detection systems or flow rate meters, which are industry standard in the industrialized world. Shell argued that it could not use systems such as flow monitoring or acoustic sensors due to sabotage and theft (Mustoe, 2014).

3.2.2 Social networking websites

Perpetrators of illegal wildlife trade are reported to use social media platforms such as WeChat to conduct business. Tencent utilizes BD to help catch ivory smuggling criminal syndicates. As of December 2015, Tencent had closed 622 private accounts that were allegedly operated by illegal wildlife traders (allafrica, 2015).

3.2.3 Remote sensing technologies

Remote sensing technologies such as satellite imagery have become important data sources in environmental protection. As noted in Chapter 1, remote sensors can be used to monitor and measure landscape level environmental indicators, such as the size and configuration of coastal habitats and vegetation cover and how they change over time. For instance, the GFW and other agencies use satellite data made available by the US government and other sources (Gunther, 2015).

China's Ministry of Environmental Protection is planning to improve a satellite-based remote sensor network. The plan is guided by the goals of the 13th Five-Year Plan (2016–2020). Satellites, drones and remote sensors are used to locate pollution sources. For instance, polluted areas were located in the Tengger Desert in northern China and scattered straw burnings were identified. Since the beginning of 2014, Hebei province teamed up with the ministry's Satellite Environment Center to monitor the city's pollution (foreignaffairs.co.nz, 2015).

3.3 Characteristics of Big Data in the Context of Environmental Monitoring and Protection

Massive amounts of data generated by social media, mobile phones, satellite and other digital communication tools are a true form of BD, which are being increasingly used in environmental monitoring and protection in developing countries. The following discussion will examine how the various characteristics or dimensions of BD discussed in Chapter 1 are related to environmental monitoring and protection in developing countries (Table 3.1).

Table 3.1. Relevance of Big Data dimensions in environmental monitoring and protection

Characteristic	Some examples in the context of environmental monitoring and protection
Volume	GCM data consists of over 66,000 files with about 6 TB of data
Velocity	Kruger National Park's gunshot detection system involves analysing the data sent by the sensors at the Incident Review Center, sending a text message to Kruger's ranger operations centre and taking actions quickly
Variety	The World Resources Institute's Global Forest Watch combines structured data such as past data on forest changes and unstructured data such as near real-time satellite monitoring, and crowdsourced stories in order to help decision makers on the community level (Kahn, 2014)
Variability	High rates of data flow during peak poaching seasons/periods When drones are deployed, they are used as an additional source of data
Complexity	Scientists at CIAT analysed data from an annual rice survey, a harvest monitoring dataset, and results from experiments on rice sowing data and historical weather data

GCM, Global Circulation Models; TB, terabytes.

3.3.1 Volume

Environmental monitoring activities and processes such as environmental sensors and remote monitoring are moving online (Bilbao-Osorio *et al.*, 2014). The data for the Global Circulation Models (GCM), which are important tools for representing future climate conditions, come from the CGIAR Research Program on Climate Change, Agriculture and Food Security. The data are stored in Amazon S3. It consists of over 66,000 files with about 6 TB of data (amazon.com, 2014). As a further example, in an attempt to provide insights into respiratory disease, scientists are combining huge amounts of air quality data from polluted areas and matching them with health care datasets (hsph.harvard.edu, 2012).

3.3.2 Velocity

BD provides the possibility for real-time feedback, which can lead to important environmental outcomes. A number of BD initiatives in environmental monitoring and protection have focused on velocity of data. For instance, real-time monitoring of illegal resource extraction provides valuable information, which can be acted upon quickly to reduce the harm poachers and other criminals can cause to the environment. Eco-drones can be used to capture images and monitor disaster events or illegal resource extraction in real time, and collect meteorological data (CielMap, 2012). Brazil's Sao Paulo environmental police use drones to monitor deforestation in the Amazon, and to track poachers and illegal mining operations (Cohen, 2011).

In an attempt to facilitate surveillance, early warning and detection, in October 2014, South Africa National Parks (SANParks) started a two-year project to build an Intensive Protection Zone in the south of the Kruger National Park, where 60% of the park's rhino population lives. Boundary fences have been fitted with motion sensors to track movement and send GPS coordinates to an operations centre. Rangers will be deployed by truck or helicopter in the case of a security breach. In the Park's 220-mile border with Mozambique, a gunshot detection system, known as ShotSpottehas, has been developed and implemented since May 2013 (Everett, 2014).

As another example, Intel's credit card-sized Galileo motherboards with 3G communication and storage have been attached to critically endangered black and white rhinos in Africa. The project is a partnership between Intel South Africa and the cloud company, Dimension Data. The Galileo board is an ankle collar with a rhino-proof case. A RFID chip is placed on a rhino's horn, and Vodafone has provided the connectivity. Anti-poaching teams are contacted if the two pieces are disconnected. In the next phase, the project team hopes to monitor rhinos' heart rate and other vital indicators, so that poachers can be caught before they kill the animals (Gilpin, 2014).

3.3.3 Variety

As an example of the use of a variety of data in environmental monitoring and protection, the World Resources Institute's GFW combines structured data (e.g.

past data on forest changes) and unstructured data (e.g. near real-time satellite monitoring) with crowdsourced stories in order to help decision makers at the community level (Welz, 2013). The Great Elephant Census attempts to count African elephants in order to help local authorities manage conservation efforts and fight illegal poaching. The census utilizes techniques such as imaging drones and automated image recognition to collect data (Korte, 2014).

3.3.4 Variability

Multiple data sources are often used to track and monitor the environment. Variability in data flow may arise as a result of variation in the amount of data as well as variation in the number and nature of data stores. For instance, drones are becoming a vital tool for saving wildlife and protecting resources by monitoring activities such as poaching and illegal resources extraction in Africa, Asia and South America (unep.org, 2013). Drones are often deployed only during certain time periods (e.g. time of the day, season, etc.). When drones are deployed, they are used as an additional source of data. As another example, high rates of data flow may take place during times of peak poaching activity. For instance, poachers are often more active at night than during the day (rhinorage.org, 2016). Likewise, more poaching activities are likely to occur during the days around a full moon, when it is easy for poachers to see their prey, than on the days around a new moon (Snitch, 2015).

3.3.5 Complexity

Matching and linking data from multiple sources such as open portals, social media, government agencies, NGOs and corporations can provide a whole picture of the environmental challenges facing the developing world and the opportunities available to address them. As an example, Danish and South African researchers have developed a technique to calculate the difference between the potential amount of carbon that vegetation can store in the absence of disturbances and the amount of carbon currently stored in vegetation. The researchers based their analysis on a satellite-derived map of carbon stored in vegetation. Combining it with data on environmental factors that affect plant growth, such as climate and soil, they modelled the maximum amount of carbon that could be stored in vegetation across tropical Africa. By subtracting the actual amount of carbon currently stored in vegetation from this, they could thus determine locations in Africa where carbon-stocking projects would be profitable (Troelsen, 2013).

As another example, Rio de Janeiro, Brazil, has implemented a new data-driven operations plan, which involves a 'command centre' receiving data and information from 30 different agencies related to traffic, public transport, utility services, emergency services and weather feeds, as well as information sent in by employees and the public by phone, Internet and radio. Data and information from sensors, video feeds and other sources are used to predict weather and other problems. It was reported that the emergency response time had improved by 30% since the launch of the operations (technologyreview.com, 2014).

As a further example, consider BVRio, based in Rio de Janeiro. According to Chatham House, annual illegal timber imports into countries that process wood products (e.g. China, Thailand and Vietnam) as well as to markets of such products (e.g. the US, UK, France, the Netherlands, Japan, South Korea and India) are worth US$17 billion (Leahy, 2015). BVRio announced plans to open *Responsible Timber Exchange*, which uses BD to assess potential sellers' compliance with US and European restrictions on illegal wood imports. BVRio's database will use official documentation such as logging permits and sawmill operating licences, and the legal records of forest owners, loggers and the forest engineers involved in a shipment to assess the risk of irregularities. Other categories of data include the average volumes of a given species of tree normally cut under a standard permit and satellite images. In the future it will also employ field checks (Leahy, 2015).

3.4 Foreign and Local Big Data Technologies in Environmental Monitoring and Protection

3.4.1 Role of foreign multinational corporations

Firms in the BD sector based in the developed world have made inroads into the developing world markets. Various mechanisms of technology globalization discussed in Chapter 1 are relevant in the diffusion of BD-related technologies in environmental monitoring and protection activities in developing economies. In the 'Green Horizon' example discussed in the Introduction, it is clear that IBM's advanced technologies are key components of Beijing's environmental initiatives. Likewise, the BD firm C3 Energy, which provides software and monitoring system for businesses' energy consumption, has expanded its business to China (reuters.com, 2014). C3 Energy's system records the amount of energy consumed by businesses in various processes and compares the pattern with buildings and businesses in the same area. By preparing a detailed profile of the business, it also suggests ways to reduce energy consumption (e.g. by upgrading equipment) (bbc.com, 2013).

Microsoft researchers in Beijing have developed a model to measure real-time and fine-grained air quality information, which is based on historical and real-time data from its monitor stations, as well as data obtained from other sources such as temperature, humidity, wind speed, weather, traffic flow, human mobility and structure of road networks. The project is called Urban Air, which is an interactive map that allows users to see air quality levels in 72 cities in China as of November 2015. The model uses BD and machine learning (Soper, 2015).

Another company is Wireless Energy Management Systems (WEMS), which offers its products in China and South Africa. WEMS provides a range of wireless sensors and controllers to monitor and adjust a building's energy usage. They can be used to reduce lighting if it is bright outside and reduce temperature levels if it is warm. The system can be monitored remotely (bbc.com, 2013).

Some Chinese companies are aggressively pursuing foreign BD firms. For instance, Alibaba and Baidu are reportedly looking for BD-related promising innovations in Israel (Ackerman, 2015).

Finally, local and foreign firms are teaming up to generate BD solutions. For instance, AliCloud supports Philips with cloud computing services to store and process the data of Philips' connected products and solutions in China. In October 2014, Smart Air Purifier was launched in China, which was Philips' first connected product supported by AliCloud. In particular, people living in big cities and those affected by allergies or respiratory conditions are concerned about their homes' air quality. People can use the Philips Smart Air Purifier to monitor air quality in their homes as well as the reported city air quality index data such as the PM2.5 index. The Smart Air Purifier can be operated from anywhere at any time. It sends alerts to users' mobile devices in real time when the indoor air quality reaches unhealthy levels or when the filter needs replacement (newscenter.philips.com, 2014).

3.4.2 Big Data applications created in developing countries

An encouraging trend is that there has been an abundance of BD-related entrepreneurship in developing countries and creation of BD applications locally. Firms in these countries are rapidly emerging as providers of products, services, software and solutions related to BD (Kshetri, 2011).

As an example, Nigeria's satellite NigeriaSat is engaged in environmental monitoring activities such as tracking desertification and locust swarms. It was reported that, following the 2004 Indian Ocean tsunami, NigeriaSat contributed images to aid workers (Aron, 2013). As another example, Colombia-based CIAT teamed up with the Nature Conservancy, King's College London and Switzerland's University of Applied Sciences and Arts to develop the Terra-i system, which monitors deforestation on a near real-time basis (see Case 5, Appendix: Integrative Cases of Big Data Deployment in Agriculture, Environmental Security and Healthcare).

3.5 The Roles of Philanthropic and International Development Organizations

Prior research has suggested that philanthropic and international development organizations influence the global diffusion of information communication technologies (ICTs) in several ways (Kshetri, 2001). These organizations have also launched a number of initiatives to facilitate the use of BD in developing countries. UNESCO and Hewlett-Packard provide hardware and software infrastructure that clusters and integrates high-end computer networks, databases and scientific instruments. Burkina Faso's University of Ouagadougou has launched two projects that involve modelling the movement of pollutants in the Sourou River drainage basin and implementing a high-performance computing grid. The 'Brain Gain' initiative was started in 2003, and by 2009 successful pilot projects had been carried out in a number of African economies such as Algeria, Ghana, Nigeria, Senegal and Zimbabwe. By the end of 2011, 20 higher educational institutions in 16 countries had benefited from the project (Kshetri, 2011).

Some encouraging philanthropic activities involving data donation have emerged in environmental monitoring and protection. For instance, GFW (http://www.globalforestwatch.org/) is a network and a near real-time monitoring platform that provides information available on forests. As another example, Linked Brazilian Amazon rainforest data was produced by the Institute for Geoinformatics, University of Münster, Germany, and the National Institute for Space Research in Brazil, which can be used by anyone for non-commercial research (Kauppinen, 2012). Likewise, at the UN climate meeting's 16th session of the Conference of the Parties (COP 16) held in 2010, Google launched a satellite and mapping service called Google Earth Engine, which consists of an open application program interface, a computing platform and 25 years of satellite imagery available to researchers, scientists, organizations and government agencies. Google Earth Engine offers tools and parallel processing computing power to groups that can be used to analyse environmental conditions.

Governments, researchers and the private sector have identified various possible uses of data that are donated or made freely available. For instance, using Google's Earth Engine, the government of Mexico created a comprehensive, high-resolution map of Mexico's forests. The map incorporated 53,000 images provided by Landsat satellites to produce a mapping product of 6 GB. The map can be used by the government and NGOs in making decisions in diverse areas such as appropriate land use, sustainable agriculture and protection of rare species of flora and fauna (Fehrenbacher, 2011).

Microsoft cofounder Paul Allen's Great Elephant Census project was started with a US$7.3 million grant and a partnership with Botswana's NGO Elephants Without Borders. In February 2015, a team of over 50 researchers started surveying 21 countries and 600,000 km^2 of Africa. A main goal of the two-year survey is 'to give numbers to policy makers, which they rely on to make decisions' in order to protect the species (Sommers, 2014).

As a final example, in 2012 the French telecom company Orange, which is a dominant player in Ivory Coast's mobile telephony market, released to the research community 2.5 billion anonymized records involving 5 months of calls made by five million people in Ivory Coast (Talbot, 2013a). IBM researchers used the movement data collected from mobile phone users in Ivory Coast's largest city, Abidjan, to develop a new model for optimizing the urban transportation system. The model entails changing bus routes based on people's movements, which are tracked with mobile phone records. It is expected to reduce travel times by 10%. The transportation model used the data to track ridership behaviour consisting of 539 buses, 5000 minibuses and 11,000 shared taxis (Talbot, 2013b).

3.6 Big Data and Transparency: Fighting Environmental Crimes and Injustices

Environmentalists are presenting BD-based evidence in order to pressure politicians and corporations responsible for environmental damage, degradation and harm to be transparent and accountable in environmental management. We present two examples that illustrate cases where BD produced positive results.

3.6.1 The 2015 Indonesian fires

Consider the 2015 Indonesian fires, which arguably represent the 'worst man-made environmental disaster since the BP gulf oil spill' (neurope.eu, 2015). Thousands of fires were deliberately started to clear land for palm oil and paper plantations. During January to October of 2015, over 117,000 forest fires had been detected via satellite in Indonesia, most of which were suspected to have been started deliberately to clear land for farming (Phipps, 2015). Guido van der Werf of VU University Amsterdam's Faculty of Earth and Life Science estimated fire emissions to the atmosphere based on satellite imagery of the fires and of vegetation (van der Werf, 2015). Based on this, he estimated that in 2015, Indonesian fires had emitted roughly 1713 million metric tons (about 1888 tons) of equivalents of carbon dioxide as of 9 November. These estimates come from data collected by satellites that can sense fires. Some examples include Germany's TET-1 and NASA'S MODIS, which cover the whole world and transmit data 24/7. Active fires emit radiations that can be picked up by the satellites on bands that are dedicated for this purpose. From this information, scientists can calculate the size, temperature and number of fires. Researchers can also calculate the amount of emissions produced (Leu, 2015).

Indonesian (Fogarty, 2015) and foreign media (mongabay.com, 2015c) used the findings from the World Resources Institute, the Global Fire Emissions Database and other resources to pressure the Indonesian government to be more responsive to the tragedy, act on the issue and adopt better peatland management practices. The environmental-activist group Greenpeace collected and presented evidence in a clear and thorough fashion. It also released video footage taken from drones. The Greenpeace Indonesia drones found that land burned in the autumn of 2015 on the island of Borneo was turned into palm oil plantations after a few weeks (Coca, 2015). Greenpeace researchers examined about 112,000 fire hotspots recorded from 1 August to 26 October 2015, which showed that about 40% of the fires had taken place inside so-called mapped concessions, which is land granted by the government to companies for logging or plantation development (Maitar, 2015). Greenpeace researchers also found that Asia Pulp & Paper, the largest concession holder in Indonesia, was the company associated with most of the fires.

BD-based evidence is likely to be more convincing and likely to prompt policy changes. The pressures have produced some desirable outcomes. Indonesia's

Environment Minister emphasized the importance of revising the country's environmental laws. The country's Environment and Forestry Minister, Siti Nurbaya, noted that the 2009 Law on Environmental Protection and Management allowed farmers to burn up to 2 ha of land to clear space for farming. The law thus contributed to the nation-wide forest fires (Jakartaglobe, 2015).

In October 2015, Indonesian President Joko Widodo noted that he instructed the environment and forestry minister to stop issuing new permits on peatlands and immediately begin revitalization (mongabay.com, 2015d). Singapore issued legal notices to Asia Pulp & Paper and four other Indonesian companies whose concessions are full of fires causing air pollution across the region. According to Singapore's Transboundary Haze Pollution Act of 2014, foreign companies can be held responsible for polluting air and can be fined up to 2 million Singapore dollars (US$1.4 million) (mongabay.com, 2015b).

3.6.2 Deforestation of rainforests in the Peruvian Amazon

It was reported that the Cayman Islands-based and London Stock Exchange-listed company United Cacao, which promises to produce ethical, sustainable chocolate, had deforested about 7000 ha (17,300 acres) of mostly primary, closed-canopy rainforest in the Peruvian Amazon (mongabay.com, 2015a). In 2013, work on the cocoa plantation started near the town of Tamshiyacu. The company tried to defend itself by claiming that the land had been previously cleared. In an audio interview with Directors Talk Interviews, United Cacao's CEO, Dennis Melka, said: 'By the time the plantation companies actually get to the land, that land has been logged and clear-cut of all tropical hardwoods. It's simply not rainforest . . .' (Stone, 2015).

An analysis of satellite images, however, showed the contrary. The international campaigning organization Environmental Investigation Agency (EIA), using three-dimensional forest mapping data and satellite imaging data from GFW and other sources to create Peru's map of carbon density, argued that the areas deforested by the Melka Projects were mostly primary forest before the launch of the project. Before the deforestation by Melka Projects, Tamshiyacu's average carbon stock value was 122 metric tons (about 134 tons) of carbon per hectare. An EIA researcher argued that such high levels of carbon stock values are only found in primary tropical forest in that part of the Amazon basin (Collyns, 2015).

The Peruvian government claims that land in the country is classified based on a technical definition, known as 'best land use capacity', which only includes soil and climatic characteristics (Environmental Investigation Agency, 2015). This definition ignores the presence of standing trees in the evaluation of requests for land use change. Thanks to this loophole, about 20 million ha of Peru's 74 million ha of Amazon rainforest have not actually been classified as forest. This means that a significant part the Amazon rainforest is open to being reclassified and labelled as agricultural land (Collyns, 2015). There is, however, another law that recognizes standing trees as part of the national forest patrimony. This means that the use of forests is prohibited for agriculture or other activities if such activities negatively affect the vegetation cover or the sustainable use and conservation of forest resources (Ley No. 27308: Forestry and Wildlife Law (2011), El Peruano) (Environmental Investigation Agency, 2015).

In August 2014, Peru's Ministry of Environment initiated legal actions to suspend the Melka Group's operations in Tamshiyacu and Nueva Requena. In December 2014, Peru's Ministry of Agriculture ordered United Cacao to stop work on the plantation. The ministry gave United Cacao 90 working days to produce a soil study that confirmed the site's ability to handle a cocoa plantation (Cannon, 2015). However, as of mid-2015, no action has been able to stop the companies' operations (Collyns, 2015).

3.7 Discussion and Concluding Comments

The various initiatives discussed above, to some extent, have helped overcome the challenges and problems associated with resource constraints and realize BD opportunities.

Reducing the greenhouse effect associated with the developing world is also in the interest of industrialized countries. For this reason, BD projects involving environmental monitoring and protection in developing economies should be able to attract more philanthropic contributions in the forms of data, donations and other community contributions. While a huge amount of data is held by businesses, they are reluctant to distribute even anonymous data due primarily to privacy concerns (Coren, 2011). Environment-related data are likely to be less privacy invading compared to most other categories of data. It is thus important for national governments and international agencies to work closely with businesses that have large amounts of data and encourage them to engage in data philanthropy.

A related point is that the amount of greenhouse gases generated by the world's data centres is of the same amount as that generated by countries such as Argentina or the Netherlands. Moreover, by some estimates, these emissions will increase by 400% by 2020. A study by McKinsey indicated that BD use in smart power grids, efficient buildings, better logistics planning and other areas can eliminate carbon emissions five times as much as that generated by the IT industry (Bughin *et al.*, 2015).

Governments in developing countries lack data-gathering infrastructures. Most systems deployed in the developing world for environmental monitoring and protection have demonstrated a heavy dependence on the West. For instance, in the Kruger National Park's gunshot detection system, audio and location information is sent to an Incident Review Centre in California via a 3G network. The employees at the Incident Review Centre test whether the transmitted noise is gunfire and upload the data to the cloud, which sends a text message to Kruger's ranger operations centre. The audio file coordinates and a link to Google Maps are also sent with the text message (Everett, 2014).

An important implication that is drawn from recent deployment of BD in environmental monitoring and protection in developing economies is that techniques and tools developed in industrialized countries for other purposes have been adapted to the environmental condition in developing countries.

Most adaptations can be explained by the lack of resources and the nature of low quality ICT infrastructure. For instance, Galileo motherboards have a solar panel to recharge on their own (Gilpin, 2014).

According to Rainforest Action Network, Indonesia loses over a million hectares of forest each year. The Indonesian rainforests are home to many unique species of plants and animals (Ferguson, 2013), and NGOs and activists have come up with IoT-based solutions to protect these resources. In 2013, the US-based Rainforest Connection teamed up with the Zoological Society of London to install old Android mobile phones encased in solar panels in trees in the rainforest in Sumatra, Indonesia. Each phone can catch the sound of a chainsaw within 1 square mile of its location. The sound and location data are sent to the cloud, and rangers patrolling the forests get an alert (Gilpin, 2014). Some of the phones were used for 5 years before being deployed in the project (21stcentech.com, 2014). The system has also been deployed in various sites in Cameroon to monitor 10,000 ha of rainforest. It can detect audio signals associated with logging and poaching (e.g. a chainsaw's whine, a gunshot and the sound of a logging truck) and alert local authorities (Butler, 2014).

Satellite images are being used to monitor forests. Nonetheless, detecting new areas of deforestation from satellite images often takes many days. The old mobile phones have thus been an effective tool for taking quick actions against logging and poaching. According to Rainforest Connection's estimate, each mobile phone can protect 300 ha of endangered forest, which can prevent the release of 15,000 tons of CO_2 (Revell, 2014).

In the same vein, Diceros has developed integrated surveillance systems that are based on US and South African military and security industry technologies. The systems involve a high-definition radar, in-earth microphones capable of intercepting communications, long-range cameras and drones. They have been successfully deployed to monitor cattle thieves and smugglers in Africa's Lake Victoria region. Diceros is marketing the system for wildlife conservation. Diceros combines radars with other sensors such as unmanned aerial vehicles (UAVs) to cover broad areas. After an animal or person is detected with the radar or UAVs, sensors can be positioned to determine the nature of the threats and track them. Underground sensors can detect people walking with metallic weapons (Morgan, 2012).

Similarly, with the decline in military spending on drones, manufacturers of such aircrafts are looking for civilian applications (Welz, 2013). African economies are acquiring surveillance drones, which were mostly made in the US for military operations, to track poachers. In a similar fashion, the Kruger National Park's gunshot detection system is an adaptation of a technology developed for a different purpose. California-based SST developed it to alert police of gunfire in US neighbourhoods. It involves placing three camouflaged sensors per km^2 high up in trees compared to 10 to 12 per km^2 in noisier urban areas. Each sensor includes a microphone and a GPS. The sensors have been modified in order to make them capable of using solar power. By careful positioning, the origin of gunshots fired more than three km away can be detected (Everett, 2014).

Different characteristics of BD may have different degrees of relevance depending on the essence and nature of the environmental problem being considered and the purpose of the environmental project. For instance, fast data (velocity) is important for catching forest offenders such as poachers and sandalwood smugglers, which requires quick actions. On the other hand, volume and complexity are often more important in environmental projects involving the long-term protection of flora and fauna.

An encouraging trend is that an increasing amount of relevant data on environmental challenges facing the developing world is already available. Nonetheless, data analysis alone is not sufficient to protect the environment. Among the most important points for practical purposes are that policy makers need to create programmes and collaborate with businesses and NGOs to act on the data. This issue is especially important in countries such as Indonesia, Malaysia, Paraguay, Bolivia, Zambia and Angola, which are experiencing significant forest losses (Hansen *et al.*, 2013). Finally, for national governments in developing countries and international agencies such as the UN or the World Bank, it is critical to engage in new and more comprehensive collaboration with the private sector in order to facilitate the diffusion and effective use of BD.

In many developing countries poor enforcement of existing laws has seriously hampered measures to protect the environment. For instance, in both Indonesia and Peru, some businesses used loopholes in the law and lax enforcement to clear forests and peatlands in order to grow crops such as cocoa and oil palm, which led to severe environmental degradation and damage. Thanks to BD, activists have forcefully presented their case, which has led to at least some realization of the underlying issue and the importance of closing the legal loopholes.

References

21stcentech.com (2014) How old cell phones will save the forests of our world. Available at: http://www.21stcentech.com/cell-phones-save-forests-world/ (accessed 8 April 2016).

Ackerman, G. (2015) Chinese investors back Israel startups amid Silicon Valley froth. Available at: http://www.bloomberg.com/news/articles/2015-12-01/chinese-investors-pour-money-into-israeli-technology-startups (accessed 17 February 2016).

allafrica.com (2015) Africa: Chinese Internet giant Tencent to promote wildlife conservation in Kenya. Available at: http://allafrica.com/stories/201512160323.html (accessed 16 February 2016).

amazon.com (2014) Earth science on AWS with new CGIAR and Landsat public data sets. Available at: https://aws.amazon.com/blogs/aws/earth-science-data-sets-on-aws/ (accessed 16 February 2016).

Anderson, J. (2014) 5 overlooked deforestation hotspots. Available at: http://www.wri.org/blog/2014/03/5-overlooked-deforestation-hotspots (accessed 16 February 2016).

Anderson, M. (2016) China's car-tracking scheme could mean fuel-guzzling cars pay more to fill up. Available at: https://thestack.com/cloud/2016/03/09/chinas-car-tracking-scheme-could-mean-fuel-guzzling-cars-pay-more-to-fill-up/ (accessed 8 April 2016).

Aron, J. (2013) How Nigeria has been using its satellites. Available at: http://www.newscientist.com/article/dn24025-how-nigeria-has-been-using-its-satellites.html#.VMesgCzSnS4 (accessed 17 February 2016).

Bartoli, A., Hernández-Serrano, J., Soriano, M., Dohler, M., Kountouris, A. and Barthel, D. (2011) Security and privacy in your smart city. Available at: http://smartcitiescouncil.com/resources/security-and-privacy-your-smart-city (accessed 5 February 2015).

bbc.com (2013) Keen businesses should be seen to be clean and green. Available at: http://www.bbc.com/news/business-21922098 (accessed 16 February 2016).

Bilbao-Osorio, B., Dutta, S. and Lanvin, B. (2014) Rewards and risks of Big Data. The Global Information Technology Report. World Economic Forum, Geneva, Switzerland. Available at: http://www3.weforum.org/docs/WEF_GlobalInformationTechnology_Report_2014.pdf (accessed 8 April 2016).

Bughin, J., Chui, M. and Manyika, J. (2015) An executive's guide to the Internet of Things. Available at: http://www.mckinsey.com/Insights/Business_Technology/An_executives_guide_to_the_Internet_of_Things?cid=digital-eml-alt-mip-mck-oth-1508 (accessed 17 February 2016).

Butler, A.R. (2014) Discarded cell phones to help fight rainforest poachers, loggers in real-time. Availableat:http://news.mongabay.com/2014/06/discarded-cell-phones-to-help-fight-rainforest-poachers-loggers-in-real-time/ (accessed 8 April 2016).

Butler, A.R. (2015) Global forest loss reached 46 million acres in 2014. Available at: http://news.mongabay.com/2015/09/global-forest-loss-reached-46-million-acres-in-2014/ (accessed 16 February 2016).

Cannon, C.J. (2015) Court rules deforestation of Peruvian rainforest for chocolate was legal. Available at: http://news.mongabay.com/2015/04/court-rules-deforestation-of-peruvian-rainforest-for-chocolate-was-legal/ (accessed 17 February 2016).

chinatechnews.com (2014) Big data used by Beijing government to alleviate pollution. Available at: http://www.chinatechnews.com/2014/07/15/20725-big-data-used-by-beijing-government-to-alleviate-pollution (accessed 18 August 2014).

CielMap (2012) Low-cost unmanned aircraft systems for development projects: a quiet revolution. Presentation, Sciences Po Paris, 27 June. Available at: http://www.letudiant.fr/examen/sciences-po-les-concours-2012-des-iep-en-direct/concours-sciences-po-paris-2012-les-sujets-de-l-epreuve-d-histoire.html (accessed 1 August 2016).

Coca, N. (2015) Palm oil from freshly-burned land: coming to a grocery store near you. Available at: http://www.triplepundit.com/2015/11/palm-oil-freshly-burned-land-coming-grocery-store-near/ (accessed 17 February 2016).

Cohen, M.J. (2011) Brazilian eyes in the sky focus on the disappearing rainforest. *Scientific American*. Available at: http://www.scientificamerican.com/article.cfm?id=brazilian-eyes-in-the-sky-focus-on-2011-10 (accessed 18 August 2014).

Collyns, D. (2015) Head of London-listed company linked to illegal clearing of Peru rainforest. Available at: http://www.theguardian.com/environment/2015/apr/07/head-of-london-listed-company-linked-to-illegal-clearing-of-peru-rainforest (accessed 17 February 2016).

Coren, M.J. (2011) Data philanthropy: open data for world-changing solutions. Available at: http://www.fastcoexist.com/1678963/data-philanthropy-open-data-for-world-changing-solutions (accessed 18 August 2014).

dorsey.com (2013) China: smart cities. Available at: http://www.dorsey.com/eu_cleantech_china_smart_cities/ (accessed 16 February 2016).

Dubow, J. (2014) Big data and urban mobility, Workshop organized by The World Bank Group. 2 June 2014, Cairo, Egypt. Available at: http://www.worldbank.org/content/dam/Worldbank/Feature%20Story/mena/Egypt/Egypt-Doc/Big-Data-and-Urban-Mobility-v2.pdf (accessed 1 August 2016).

Environmental Investigation Agency (2015) Deforestation by definition: the Peruvian government fails to define forests as forests, while the Malaysian influence and palm oil expansion threaten the Amazon. Available at: http://eia-global.org/news-media/deforestation-by-definition (accessed 1 August 2016).

Everett, C. (2014) Out of Africa: the digital tech taking on the rhino poachers. Available at: http://diginomica.com/2014/11/06/africa-digital-tech-taking-rhino-poachers/#.VF0MoWdINmc (accessed 17 February 2016).

Fehrenbacher, K. (2011) Microsoft cloud to power environmental big data. Available at: https://gigaom.com/2011/12/01/microsoft-cloud-to-power-environmental-big-data/ (accessed 17 February 2016).

Ferguson, C. (2013) Old smartphones called in to save Indonesian forests. Available at: https://www.newscientist.com/article/mg21829205-600-old-smartphones-called-in-to-save-indonesian-forests/ (accessed 8 April 2016).

Fogarty, D. (2015) Indonesia's carbon emissions set to cross 2006 crisis. Available at: http://www.thejakartapost.com/news/2015/10/22/indonesias-carbon-emissions-set-cross-2006-crisis-level.html#sthash.rF90j0Yj.dpuf (accessed 17 February 2016).

foreignaffairs.co.nz (2015) China to use satellites, drones, sensors to monitor pollution. Available at: http://foreignaffairs.co.nz/2015/08/05/china-to-use-satellites-drones-sensors-to-monitor-pollution/ (accessed 16 February 2016).

GE Look Ahead (2015) Power to the people. Available at: http://gelookahead.economist.com/power-to-the-people/ (accessed 16 February 2016).

Gilpin, L. (2014) 10 big data projects that could help save the planet. Available at: http://www.techrepublic.com/article/10-big-data-projects-that-could-help-save-the-planet/ (accessed 16 February 2016).

Greengard, S. (2014) Analytics tools help China deal with air pollution. Available at: http://www.baselinemag.com/analytics-big-data/analytics-tools-help-china-deal-with-air-pollution.html (accessed 16 February 2016).

Gunther, M. (2015) Google-powered map helps fight deforestation. Available at: http://www.theguardian.com/sustainable-business/2015/mar/10/google-earth-engine-maps-forest-watch-deforestation-environment (accessed 16 February 2016).

Hansen, M.C., Potapov, P.V., Moore, R., Hancher, M., Turubanova, S.A., *et al.* (2013) High-resolution global maps of 21st-century forest cover change. Available at: http://www.sciencemag.org/content/342/6160/850 (accessed 16 February 2016).

Holliman, C. (2015) China's urban centers getting smarter. Available at: http://www.amchamchina.org/news/chinas-urban-centers-getting-smarter (accessed 16 February 2016).

Howard, A. (2015) How IBM is using big data to battle air pollution in cities. Available at: http://www.huffingtonpost.com/entry/ibm-big-data-air-pollution_56684e44e4b080eddf565510 (accessed 16 February 2016).

hsph.harvard.edu (2012) The promise of big data. Available at: http://www.hsph.harvard.edu/news/magazine/spr12-big-data-tb-health-costs/ (accessed 16 February 2016).

ibm.com (2014) IBM research launches project "Green Horizon" to help China deliver on ambitious energy and environmental goals. Available at: http://www-03.ibm.com/press/us/en/pressrelease/44202.wss (accessed 16 February 2016).

Jakartaglobe (2015) Environment Minister calls for law revisions, rejects task force as haze thickens over Jakarta. Available at: http://jakartaglobe.beritasatu.com/news/environment-minister-calls-law-revisions-rejects-task-force-haze-thickens-jakarta/ (accessed 17 February 2016).

Johnson, E. (2014) Alibaba, China Mobile push for more of world cloud computing market. Available at: http://www.thestreet.com/story/12735135/1/alibaba-china-mobile-push-for-more-of-world-cloud-computing-market.html (accessed 16 February 2016).

Kahn, B. (2014) UN highlights climate Big Data ahead of summit. Available at: http://www.climatecentral.org/news/un-climate-summit-big-data-17977 (accessed 4 May 2016).

Kauppinen, T. (2012) Linked Brazilian Amazon rainforest. Available at: http://linkedscience.org/data/linked-brazilian-amazon-rainforest/ (accessed 17 February 2016).

Knight, W. (2015) How artificial intelligence can fight air pollution in China. Available at: https://www.technologyreview.com/s/540806/how-artificial-intelligence-can-fight-air-pollution-in-china/ (accessed 16 February 2016).

Korte, T. (2014) Data innovation in Africa. Available at: http://www.huffingtonpost.com/travis-korte/data-innovation-in-africa_b_6276112.html (accessed 16 February 2016).
Kshetri, N. (2001) Determinants of the locus of global e-commerce. *Electronic Markets* 11(4), 250–257.
Kshetri, N. (2011) Cloud computing in the global south: drivers, effects and policy measures. *Third World Quarterly* 32(6), 995–1012.
Leahy, J. (2015) New timber exchange seeks to tackle illegal logging. Available at: http://www.ft.com/intl/cms/s/0/8361d0c6-9250-11e5-9e3e-eb48769cecab.html#axzz3sQ2fL1fR (accessed 16 February 2016).
Leu, C. (2015) Satellites expose just how bad Indonesia's fires are. Available at: http://www.wired.com/2015/11/satellites-expose-just-how-bad-indonesias-fires-are/ (accessed 17 February 2016).
Maitar, B. (2015) 4 ways to STOP Indonesia's forest fires. Available at: http://www.greenpeace.org/international/en/news/Blogs/makingwaves/4-ways-to-stop-indonesias-forest-fires/blog/54598/ (accessed 17 February 2016).
Mallya, P. (2014) Big Data: the invisible force reshaping our world. Available at: http://www.thestar.com.my/Tech/Tech-Opinion/2014/03/15/Big-Data-The-invisible-force-reshaping-our-world/ (accessed 16 February 2016).
mongabay.com (2015a) Company chops down rainforest to produce 'sustainable' chocolate. Available at: http://news.mongabay.com/2015/01/company-chops-down-rainforest-to-produce-sustainable-chocolate/ (accessed 17 February 2016).
mongabay.com (2015b) Singapore takes legal action against 5 Indonesian companies over haze. Available at: http://news.mongabay.com/2015/10/singapore-takes-legal-action-against-5-indonesian-companies-over-haze/ (accessed 17 February 2016).
mongabay.com (2015c) Carbon emissions from Indonesia's peat fires exceed emissions from entire US economy. Available at: http://www.eco-business.com/news/carbon-emissions-from-indonesias-peat-fires-exceed-emissions-from-entire-us-economy/ (accessed 17 February 2016).
mongabay.com (2015d) Jokowi pledges Indonesia peatland 'revitalization' to stop the burning. Available at: http://news.mongabay.com/2015/10/jokowi-pledges-greater-indonesia-peatland-revitalization-no-legal-breakthrough-yet/ (accessed 17 February 2016).
Morgan, S. (2012) Increased use of technology to combat current rhino poaching crisis in Southern Africa. 1st National Rhino Conservation Dialogue Presented. Available at: https://www.environment.gov.za/sites/default/files/docs/publications/submissionpaper_useoftechnology_rhinopoaching.pdf (accessed 8 April 2016).
Mustoe, H. (2014) Shell 'warned Nigeria pipeline could leak before spills'. Available at: http://www.bbc.com/news/business-29997074 (accessed 16 February 2016).
neurope.eu (2015) Indonesia's devastating forest fires are manmade. Available at: http://neurope.eu/article/indonesias-devastating-forest-fires-are-manmade/ (accessed 17 February 2016).
newscenter.philips.com (2014) Philips launches Smart Air Purifier in China as the first result of the new partnership with Alibaba in cloud-based applications for a smarter and healthier lifestyle. Available at: http://www.newscenter.philips.com/main/standard/news/press/2014/20141014-philips-launches-smart-air-purifier-in-china-as-the-first-result-of-the-new-partnership-with-alibaba.wpd#.Vkdh3L_i_m4 (accessed 17 February 2016).
Odengo, R. (2015) East Africa: M-Kopa's founder on bringing hundreds of solar jobs to East Africa and what he looks for in new hires. Available at: http://allafrica.com/stories/201511131483.html (accessed 16 February 2016).
pbl.nl (2013) Countries' contributions to climate change: effect of accounting for all greenhouse gases, recent trends, basic needs and technological progress. Available at: http://www.pbl.nl/en/publications/countries-contributions-to-climate-change (accessed 16 February 2016).

Phipps, C. (2015) Indonesia fires: Widodo visits haze-hit zone as country becomes worst polluter. Available at: http://www.theguardian.com/world/2015/oct/29/indonesia-fires-widodo-haze-zone-country-becomes-world-top-polluter (accessed 17 February 2016).

Popper, B. (2015) Can mobile banking revolutionize the lives of the poor? Available at: http://www.theverge.com/2015/2/4/7966043/bill-gates-future-of-banking-and-mobile-money (accessed 16 February 2016).

Pretz, K. (2014) An urban reality: smart cities. Available at: http://theinstitute.ieee.org/technology-focus/technology-topic/an-urban-reality-smart-cities (accessed 16 February 2016).

prweb.com (2014) China environmental monitoring instrument market and industry size, share, growth, opportunity, trends and forecast report 2013–2015. Available at: http://www.prweb.com/releases/2014/10/prweb12261166.htm (accessed 16 February 2016).

Rajan, N. (2013) Lessons in big data, from Vietnam. Available at: http://www.businesstoday.in/technology/news/lessons-in-big-data-vietnam-apac-big-data-and-cloud-summit/story/197954.html (accessed 16 February 2016).

reuters.com (2014) C3 Energy reports record midyear performance. Available at: http://www.reuters.com/article/2014/11/11/ca-c3-energy-idUSnBw116431a+100+BSW20141111 (accessed 16 February 2016).

Revell, T. (2014) A network of recycled phones is listening for illegal logging in the rainforest. Available at: http://motherboard.vice.com/read/a-network-of-recycled-phones-is-listening-for-illegal-logging-in-the-rainforest (accessed 8 April 2016).

rhinorage.org (2016) The rhino wars: the real situation and the solutions. Available at: http://www.rhinorage.org/Media-office-article.aspx?id=34 (accessed 16 February 2016).

Schmidt, E. and Cohen, J. (2015/2016) Technology: inventive artificial intelligence will make all of us better. Available at: http://time.com/4154126/technology-essay-eric-schmidt-jared-cohen/ (accessed 8 April 2016).

Senior, D. (2014) How artificial intelligence is the key to unlocking big data. Available at: http://www.techradar.com/us/news/world-of-tech/how-artificial-intelligence-is-the-key-to-unlocking-big-data-1265333 (accessed 16 February 2016).

Shumway, R. (2014) Randy Shumway: one solution for air pollution: big data. Available at: http://www.deseretnews.com/article/865617771/One-solution-for-air-pollution-Big-data.html?pg=all (accessed 16 February 2016).

Snitch, T. (2015) Satellites, mathematics and drones take down poachers in Africa. Available at: https://theconversation.com/satellites-mathematics-and-drones-take-down-poachers-in-africa-36638 (accessed 16 February 2016).

Sommers, K. (2014) How Paul Allen's $7 million and big data are combating Africa's elephant crisis. Available at: http://mashable.com/2014/10/31/paul-allen-great-elephant-census/#ho3MboPU08q7 (accessed 17 February 2016).

Soper, T. (2015) As pollution in Beijing reaches extreme levels, here's what Microsoft Research is doing to help. Available at: http://www.geekwire.com/2015/pollution-beijing-reaches-extreme-levels-heres-microsoft-research-help/ (accessed 17 February 2016).

Stone, A. (2015) Dennis Melka CEO United Cacao Ltd SEZC an interview on rain-forest destruction and environmental footprints. Available at: http://www.directorstalkinterviews.com/dennis-melka-ceo-of-united-cacao-interview-on-rain-forest-destruction-and-environmental-footprints/412660893 (accessed 17 February 2016).

Talbot, D. (2013a) African bus routes redrawn using cell-phone data. Available at: http://www.technologyreview.com/news/514211/african-bus-routes-redrawn-using-cell-phone-data/ (accessed 17 February 2016).

Talbot, D. (2013b) Big data from cheap phones. Available at: http://www.technologyreview.com/featuredstory/513721/big-data-from-cheap-phones/ (accessed 8 April 2016).

technologyreview.com (2014) A closer look at smart cities. Available at: http://www.technologyreview.com/news/532526/a-closer-look-at-smart-cities/(accessed 5 February 2015).

Tolan, C. (2014) Cities of the future? Indian PM pushes plan for 100 'smart cities'. Available at: http://www.cnn.com/2014/07/18/world/asia/india-modi-smart-cities/ (accessed 16 February 2016).

Troelsen, C. (2013) Big data project reveals where carbon-stocking projects in Africa provide the greatest benefits. Available at: http://scitech.au.dk/en/current-affairs/news/show/artikel/big-data-project-reveals-where-carbon-stocking-projects-in-africa-provide-the-greatest-benefits/ (accessed 16 February 2016).

unep.org (2013) Thematic focus: climate change, ecosystem management, environmental governance. A new eye in the sky: eco-drones. Available at: http://www.unep.org/pdf/UNEP-GEAS_MAY_2013.pdf (accessed 16 February 2016).

UN Water (2014) Water quality. Available at: http://www.unwater.org/topics/water-quality/en/ (accessed 20 April 2016).

van der Werf, G. (2015) Global Fire Emissions Database: updates. Available at: http://www.globalfiredata.org/updates.html (accessed 20 April 2016).

verdantix.com (2015) IBM expands 'Internet of Things' Green Horizons initiative beyond China. Available at: http://www.verdantix.com/index.php/blog/ibm-expands-internet-of-things-green-horizons-initiative-beyond-china (accessed 16 February 2016).

Welz, A. (2013) The war on African Poaching: is militarization fated to fail? Available at: http://e360.yale.edu/feature/the_war_on_african_poaching_is_militarization_fated_to_fail/2679/ (accessed 16 February 2016).

Wheatley, M. (2013) Vietnam's cities use big data to ward off traffic & pollution. Available at: http://siliconangle.com/blog/2013/08/16/vietnams-cities-use-big-data-to-ward-off-traffic-pollution/ (accessed 16 February 2016).

Woody, T. (2013) Vietnam taps big data to avoid China's traffic catastrophe. Available at: http://qz.com/115427/vietnam-taps-big-data-to-avoid-chinas-traffic-catastrophe/ (accessed 16 February 2016).

4 Big Data in Health-Care Delivery and Outcomes

Abstract

BD holds tremendous potential and brings high expectations to address a number of health-care challenges facing the developing world. A key focus of this chapter is to examine the role of BD in expanding access to health-care services. Special consideration is given to the applications of the Internet of Things in health care that are supported by BD analytics. The chapter gives an overview of foreign as well as locally developed BD-based health-care solutions. It also highlights the deployment of BD-based solutions to fight fake drugs. The role of BD in promoting transparency and accountability in the health-care sector is also evaluated.

4.1 Introduction

The health-care sector in developing countries, like many other areas, has a great potential to benefit from BD. In order to illustrate and explain the importance of BD in addressing key health-care challenges faced by the developing world, consider malaria. One estimate suggested that there were 124–283 million cases of malaria worldwide in 2013, which led to 367,000–755,000 deaths (WHO, 2014). Most malaria deaths can be attributed to the lack of access to effective antimalarial drugs (connectaschool.org, 2013).

Some estimates suggest that direct prevention policies such as mosquito nets would reduce malaria deaths by 50% by 2025 or about 300,000 lives annually (Lomborg, 2015).

Multiple BD applications are in various phases of development and deployment to address this problem. The US-based location intelligence software company aWhere's Mosquito Abatement Decision Information System (MADIS) uses a satellite-based surveillance system to identify areas that are likely to face severe attacks by mosquitoes. This information can be invaluable to providers and users of mosquito nets to make decisions regarding the appropriate locations of where supplies can best be used (Surdak and Agarwal, 2014). MADIS combines satellite data, weather models and mosquito biology in order to locate and analyse mosquito breeding sites with a high level of accuracy (Clapp, 2011).

There are competing and differing views on the use of BD in health care of the developing world. Consequently, vociferous debates and high-level policy discussions are ongoing in this area. One view is that BD is likely to be a risk and an expensive distraction in the health-care sectors of developing countries. Supporters of this view maintain that BD is likely to divert focus and resources away from interventions that are mostly needed. According to proponents of this approach, BD in health care is driven by high-income countries, which tend to focus on disease-specific outcomes. They also point out the risks associated with poor data governance. Databases are often owned by private companies, which are characterized by frequent occurrences of privacy violation and security breach. At the same time, there is no recourse for citizens. The opposite argument is that BD could be a major turning point to improve the health-care sector in the developing world. Policy makers can develop a 'demand-side' platform to identify the information that is most needed. Partnerships need to be formed with academia, industry, international organizations and the non-profit sector in order to develop innovative solutions (Rosemary *et al.*, 2015).

BD has enormous appeal and tremendous potential to address a number of health-care challenges facing the developing world. As noted earlier, machine learning and the next generation of artificial intelligence are likely to produce about the same level of transformation as brought about by the Internet and mobile phones. For instance, an adaptive learning system can analyse the entire histories of patients' medical records and provide doctors with relevant information, which may help prevent a medication's negative reaction (Schmidt and Cohen, 2015/2016).

In Africa, over 400,000 babies are born with HIV infections, which is partly due to the lack of knowledge about the disease and treatment options, as well as the stigma associated with HIV. In order to fight this, the South African non-governmental organization Mothers-2-Mothers combines the cloud and mobile technologies with a database to fight HIV/AIDS transmission from mothers to children. Mothers-2-Mothers digitizes patient records and shares them with doctors, nurses, mentor mothers and counsellors across its networks of over 700 sites. The records contain information on treatment plans and advanced reporting tools, which allows quick response times. Women in villages authenticate children's medication with text messages.

There is a promising future for preventing and treating serious diseases using BD. For instance, doctors' notes listing symptoms during patient check-ups can be cross-checked by the public health-care agencies to identify outbreaks, epidemics and pandemics. For an individual patient, a doctor can aggregate heart rate, blood pressure and other circulatory parameters such as skin blood flow, assessing the information with risk factors from the patient's medical history to reveal hidden trends. They can then plan appropriate treatment options without unnecessary testing, which can reduce the risk of misdiagnosis. Medical research is being combined into huge searchable databases, which makes it easier to assess and compare results. By looking at databases in relation to prescription dosages, environmental patterns and age-related trends, physicians can accurately pinpoint the most likely causes of a health problem such as drugs, weather and humidity, or animal migration patterns (Dutton, 2011).

4.2 Big Data Deployment in Delivering Health-Care Services in Developing Countries: Some Examples

BD is being deployed in a number of health-care initiatives ranging from fighting endemics and evaluating the impacts of humanitarian interventions to controlling fake medicines. For instance, during January to May 2015, Uganda experienced a typhoid outbreak. As of the first week of March 2015, about 2000 suspected cases had been reported (WHO, 2015a). Pulse Lab Kampala, the World Health Organization (WHO) and the Ministry of Health produced a series of data visualizations which helped to improve the early response to the disease. Visualizations of reports from health centres were produced at a regular interval. The interactive maps displayed the spread of the disease at district, sub-county and individual health facility levels, which helped to identify the clusters of infection. The process aided the efficient allocation of medicine, medical personnel and health centres. It also helped in targeting training areas (unglobalpulse.org, 2015).

BD has been effectively used to evaluate and measure the impacts of humanitarian aid and similar interventions. One example is the UN's analysis of social media posts to determine whether the Every Woman Every Child (EWEC) initiative accomplished the goal of effectively delivering the message to the target audience. Note that EWEC is the UN's strategy to deal with women's, children's and adolescents' health.

The UN trained a team to monitor and recognize relevant tweets. The EWEC team used the analytical tool Foresight, developed by the social media analysis consulting firm Crimson Hexagon, to analyse public tweets from September 2009 to July 2013. The team developed a taxonomy of relevant keywords such as 'maternal health', 'breastfeeding' and 'vaccination of children' to identify messages that are relevant to women's and children's health, and searched for these keywords (UN Global Pulse, 2014). An analysis of millions of social media posts over a two-year period regarding the extent and frequency with which relevant keywords were used indicated a significant shift towards an increased awareness of parental health (Kirkpatrick, 2013).

In the pre-BD era, the principal method used to measure the impact of humanitarian aid programmes such as the EWEC would be to conduct household surveys. It is thus important to compare the performance of BD with such surveys. In this regard, Table 4.1 illustrates how different BD dimensions can be applied in the context of EWEC's analysis of social media posts. Regarding the volume, despite problems such as the relative lack of randomness compared to household surveys, it is possible to inexpensively extract a huge amount of data from social media posts. Sometimes the final results from household surveys may

Table 4.1. Relevance of Big Data dimensions in Every Woman Every Child's (EWEC) analysis of social media posts

Characteristic	Explanation in the EWEC context
Volume	The EWEC team analysed about 14 million tweets
Velocity	Utilization of user-generated digital content and Crimson Hexagon's analytical tool led to faster analysis and decision making
Variety	The analysis involved structured data such as the dates of Twitter posts and unstructured data such as Twitter texts for the relevant keywords
Variability	There was a sharp increase in tweets containing the keywords identified by the EWEC team during key events such as World AIDS Day, Mother's Day, International Women's Day and Millennium Development Goals summits
Complexity	Combining the tweet data with data from other sources (e.g. Facebook posts) might offer further insights and understanding of the EWEC initiatives and validate the results

take years to publish, since key processes such as visiting households for data collection and entering data into a computer system are extremely time consuming and expensive. Finally, such surveys are not effective in collecting and analysing unstructured data.

A similar use of BD has been in providing real-time information on important social and economic indicators. For instance, sentiment analysis can provide insights into a community's attitude towards certain key issues. For example, a UNICEF study showed that it is possible to track attitudes towards immunization by analysing parents' social media posts (UNICEF, 2013).

Another notable use of BD has been in the design of an effective method and system for efficient distribution and management of life-saving medicines that have limited supplies. One example is the WHO pilot programme in Tanzania called SMS for Life (http://www.rollbackmalaria.org/commodity-access/sms-for-life/sms-for-life-overview), which aims to improve the distribution of malaria drugs in rural areas at the health facility level. Demand for antimalarial drugs is highly unpredictable. Such drugs cost as much as US$10 per course, which is prohibitively expensive for most people in Tanzania (irinnews.org, 2009).

A creative feature of the process is that front-line workers from every clinic send an SMS with their stock count every week. Based on the figures sent by the clinics, senior coordinating staff can determine an appropriate target restocking level at a given clinic to make sure that no stock-out occurs. The WHO reported highly encouraging results. The proportion of clinics with no stock of at least one antimalarial medicine decreased from 78% to 26%. In one of the three districts, stock-outs were completely eliminated by week 8 of the pilot (Newton, 2012). It is worth noting that the data used in SMS for Life is not as big as that of the EWEC initiative. Nonetheless, by aggregating and cross-referencing data sets collected from a number of clinics and other sources, the programme has been able to improve the distribution of malaria drugs. According to Boyd and Crawford's (2012) definition, the data used in SMS for Life can be considered as BD for development.

4.3 Foreign as well as Locally Developed Big Data-Based Health-Care Solutions

4.3.1 Solutions developed in industrialized countries

It was reported in October 2014 that IBM's Watson supercomputer was being deployed in Bumrungrad International Hospital in Thailand, which is the largest private hospital in Southeast Asia. About half of Bumrungrad's 1.1 million patients annually come from 190 countries (Bourne, 2014). Watson will be used to improve the quality of cancer care at Bumrungrad's medical centre in Bangkok, as well as case evaluations at referral offices in 16 countries across four continents. Bumrungrad's plan is to use the IBM Watson for Oncology module (oncology is the study and treatment of tumours), which was developed with New York City-based Memorial Sloan Kettering (MSK) hospital. Using an oncologist-advisor app, Bumrungrad doctors can provide an effective treatment plan for cancer patients. The system uses huge amounts of data and information related to a patient's profile, medical evidence, published research and the clinical expertise of MSK. Watson analyses the information and presents a summary of findings for each patient, which includes treatment options based on National Comprehensive Cancer Network (NCCN) guidelines (ibm.com, 2014). The NCCN is an alliance of 25 US-based cancer centres that have developed a set of recommendations in order to help health-care professionals diagnose, treat and manage cancer patient care. It was reported that Bumrungrad was among the four hospitals worldwide and the first outside North America to implement IBM Watson for Oncology (Pomwasin, 2014).

4.3.2 Locally developed solutions

Kenya's Bespoke Systems has developed a cloud-based application called the Emed Clinic Management System. Its objective is to provide a low-cost health-record management services for small clinics. The system can also be used by pharmacies, X-ray providers and laboratories to collaborate online. In addition, it also provides a unified patient medical record that is accessible to all health-care providers. In this way, it makes it easier to share details of patients' medical histories (ibmsmartcamp.com, 2013).

BD and cloud computing have allowed African biomedical researchers to conduct research and development for diseases such as HIV/AIDS, tuberculosis, malaria and other tropical diseases. Note that these diseases are often ignored by Western pharmaceutical companies (economist.com, 2014a).

4.4 The Role of Big Data in Expanding Access to Health-Care Services

Health-care practitioners and researchers have identified a host of barriers poor people in developing countries face in accessing health-care services. They include limited health insurance and low health literacy. There is a lack of a system that provides consolidated medical records. Most solutions focus on the market's upper end. There is also a lack of a system to exchange information among systems (ibmsmartcamp.com, 2013). The manual systems lead to frequent stock-outs of medicine. There is also the proliferation of counterfeit drugs.

There are many definitions and measures for characterizing access to health services. Most researchers have recognized that access is related to the timely use of services according to the needs of the consumers (Campbell *et al.*, 2000). Some researchers measure access with the actual use of health services (Mooney *et al.*, 1991).

Peters *et al.* (2008) proposed four dimensions of access, each with a supply-and-demand element: (i) geographic accessibility; (ii) availability; (iii) financial accessibility; and (iv) acceptability. Table 4.2 provides some examples regarding the role of BD in expanding access to health-care services.

4.4.1 Geographic accessibility

Regarding obstacles related to geographic accessibility, individuals who live in remote locations are required to spend more time and money to travel to access health care (Peters *et al.*, 2008). BD-based health-care solutions have a potential to address this problem. The Chinese government has established state-owned enterprise zones such as the Chengdu Internet of Things Technology Institute in Sichuan province. The institute is developing a health-care system that allows rural villagers to step into a telephone booth-sized 'health capsule' in order to get a diagnosis and prescription from a doctor in a distant hospital (harborresearch.com, 2014). As of 2013, the institute had installed 11 'health capsules' in a city near Chengdu (Advanced MP Technology, 2013).

The deployment of the Internet of Things (IoT) is also likely to address problems related to geographic access. For instance, sensors can measure and monitor physical activities and multiple physiological variables related to a patient's health status in real time and automatically transmit the data to the health-care provider. Remote patient monitoring of vital signs and health indicators via sensors, which can be embedded in clothing or worn on the arm or wrist, is likely to become the norm (Saunders, 2014).

4.4.2 Availability

The inverse care law states that the availability of health-care services tends to vary inversely with the need (Hart, 1971). Developing countries have higher needs for health care. For instance, sub-Saharan Africa (SSA) accounts for about one-quarter of the world's disease burden but has only 3% of the world's medical workers. According to the World Bank, an additional 90,000 doctors and 500,000 nurses will be needed in SSA economies in the next few years (economist.com, 2013). More people in India and China suffer from cardiovascular diseases than in all the developed economies put together (Wiggins, 2015).

Table 4.2. The role of Big Data in expanding access to health-care services: some examples.

Dimension of access	Explanation	Some examples of BD/ICT deployment
Geographic accessibility	Distance or travel time from the consumer to the health-care service delivery point	Chengdu Internet of Things Technology Institute's 'health capsule' to get a diagnosis and prescription from a doctor in a distant hospital Text messaging and cloud computing to address the shortages and frequent stock-out of essential drugs Remote patient monitoring via sensors
Availability	Right type of care as needed for the patient (e.g. hours of operation and waiting times, appropriate type of service providers and materials)	A health-care worker (not necessarily a cardiac specialist) can use Cardio Pad to perform cardiac tests Improved workflow efficiency and productivity: the Kenyan Ministry of Health's deployment of mobile clouds to reduce the reporting time for HIV test results Reliefwatch reduced expirations of medical supplies by up to 90%
Financial accessibility	Relationship between the price of health-care services and the willingness and ability of users to pay for those services as well as protection from the economic consequences of health costs	Linda Jamii's micro-insurance programme to self-employed Kenyans
Acceptability	Responsiveness of health service providers to consumers' social and cultural expectations	A rural health-care worker rather than a cardiac specialist is likely to use the Cardio Pad: the former is likely to have a lower social distance and hence higher degree of acceptability than the latter

BD, Big Data; ICT, information communication technology.
Source: Peters *et al.* (2008) combined with author's research.

Availability of health care can be measured in terms of the opportunity to access the services when needed. Developing countries suffer from poor performance in terms of availability due to limited hours, long waiting times, unavailability of health-care workers and lack of drug stocks (Chaudhury and Hammer, 2004). A greater proportion of health-care needs are thus unmet. According to the WHO Global Health Observatory data repository, physician density per 1000 people in 2012 varied from 0.031 in Tanzania to 4.281 in Norway and 4.894 in Spain (WHO, 2015b). The demand and supply gap is especially higher in rural areas. For instance, Cameroon is estimated to have less than 50 cardiologists and all of them live in the country's big cities.

These problems are especially acute and prominent in remote areas that are even more underserved (Bhattacharyya *et al.*, 2011). According to the WHO, in many SSA countries a single family doctor oversees the health-care needs of 10,000 to 20,000 individuals. There is also the lack of an adequate supply of life-saving drugs in rural areas.

A key point from our perspective is that the effects of these factors vary across people of different income levels. For instance, poor people in particular are more likely to use informally trained health providers than rich people in Sri Lanka (Akin and Hutchinson, 1999). Poor people are also more likely to buy an incomplete dose of drugs from shopkeepers or inferior quality drugs (Van Der Geest, 1987). Richer people, on the other hand, are more likely to use resources to travel to higher-quality clinics and private health-care providers in order to overcome the barriers related to availability (Peters *et al.*, 2008).

Information communication technology-based solutions may offer promising potential and opportunities to bridge this gap between demand and supply. For instance, an inventor in Cameroon created Cardio Pad, which is arguably Africa's first medical tablet. Using the device, a health-care worker, who is not necessarily a cardiac specialist, can perform cardiac tests and send results to specialists via mobile phones. Cardio Pad has a complete diagnostic kit to examine patients in rural locations. A wireless set of electrodes and a sensor are attached to the patient. Signals are transmitted via Bluetooth to the Cardio Pad, which takes an electrocardiogram reading. The information is sent to a national data centre, where cardiologists diagnose and send back prescriptions and instructions to the health-care worker. The pads are estimated to cost US$1000 to manufacture (Douglas, 2014).

One way to deal with the problem of the shortage of doctors is to improve workflow efficiency and productivity. BD apps have the potential to contribute to this goal. We can illustrate this with Kenya's efforts to fight the HIV/AIDS pandemic. It was reported that it takes up to 3 months to get the results of HIV tests. The consequences of the long delay may prove to be fatal as timely treatment is a key factor for a baby's survival. The Kenyan Ministry of Health has teamed up with several organizations to develop a solution based on mobile clouds in order to reduce the reporting time for HIV test results. A mobile cloud platform enables data gathering on a central server, better structure workflows, delivery of test results and the production of activity reports at short notice. It is expected that implementation of such a platform can reduce the timeline for test result delivery to 2 weeks.

Availability can also be improved by reducing waste and improving the management of health care-related resources. The problems in African health-care clinics include poor record keeping and inadequate databases. Most clinics do not have proper and reliable means to identify patients that have received treatments such as inoculations and vaccines. Due to this, wastage rates are reported to exceed 50% in some clinics. In order to improve this situation, the US-based non-profit organization VaxTrac has created a registry in Kenya, Uganda, Benin and Zambia. Patients returning to clinics in these countries can access their vaccination records by touching a biometric sensor. Their inoculation history is stored on a mobile phone-based vaccination registry (assaabloy.com, 2014).

About 40% of the 1 million clinics treating patients in the developing world experience stock-outs (Levitz, 2014). On the other hand, the shelves of these clinics are often filled with a lot of expired medicines. Expiry of medicines in the supply chain is arguably a serious threat to the access to health care in developing countries (Nakyanzi *et al.*, 2010). For instance, it was reported in 2006 that at least US$550,000 worth of antiretroviral drugs and 10 million antimalarial doses expired in Uganda's National Medical Stores. Likewise, a study found that drugs sold in Afghanistan are often past their expiry date (Harper and Strote, 2011). While medicines used in vertical or stand-alone programmes (which tend to be disease specific, e.g. AIDS, malaria and tuberculosis, and often centrally managed in isolation from general health services), donated medicines and those with a slow turnover are found to be more prone and vulnerable to expiry, research indicates that even essential medicines expire (Nakyanzi *et al.*, 2010).

One organization that has come up with a solution to improve the problem of supply chain performance is Reliefwatch, a for-profit social enterprise. It was a finalist in the 2015 Unilever Sustainable Living Young Entrepreneurs Awards. Reliefwatch is a cloud-based tool, that can be used by health centres in developing economies to track the availability of essential medical supplies and outbreaks of infectious diseases. It uses text messages and voice calls and does not require an Internet connection or costly equipment (theguardian.com, 2015). Reliefwatch automatically makes calls to a health clinic worker's mobile phone at a prescheduled time and schedule (e.g. 5 p.m. every day). Reliefwatch uses an interactive, automated voice-response process that allows the workers to record the quantities of different categories of medicine as 'in supply' or 'in need'. The workers do so by punching in the values on the mobile phone's number pad. The data are then immediately uploaded and stored on the cloud. The support staff can see the updated information on the dashboard and supply the requested medicines on time (theguardian.com, 2015). As of early 2015, Reliefwatch had support for 12 languages.

The founder of Reliefwatch noted that following its launch in 2014, health workers of Global Brigades clinics in three Central American countries (Honduras, Nicaragua and Panama) digitized over 9 million units of medical supplies and reduced their expirations by up to 90% by the end of the year (theguardian.com, 2015).

4.4.3 Financial accessibility

Financial accessibility (or affordability) is arguably among the most important determinants of access to health care. For instance, only 3% of the Kenyan population is reported to have health insurance, which is mainly provided by the employer. This dimension is most closely related to poverty. In addition to the direct cost of treatment, several types of indirect costs act as obstacles to the poor seeking treatment. The indirect costs include the opportunity costs of the patient and accompanying persons, transportation costs, as well as expenses on food and lodging. The economic consequences of paying for health services are no less severe (Peters *et al.*, 2008). These consequences include spending a large proportion of income on health care (catastrophic spending) or those related to borrowing money or selling assets (distress financing). All of these factors contribute to the vicious cycle of poverty (McIntyre et al., 2006).

A positive trend related to financial accessibility concerns the use of BD to increase access to health insurance. BD apps are contributing to the growth of health micro-insurance programmes. Linda Jamii (Swahili for 'protect your family'), is a mobile cloud-based health micro-insurance programme implemented by Safaricom in partnership with Changamka Micro-Health and insurance provider Britam. Linda Jamii's clients are self-employed Kenyans. It provides in-patient and out-patient cover, maternity cover, dental and vision cover, income replacement, funeral expense payout, and other coverage for an annual premium of US$150 per family. While registration for insurance must be done in person, the rest of the processes related to the programme, such as registration and submitting claims, are done through a mobile phone. A cloud-based application manages the entire process (Lemaire, 2013).

4.4.4 Acceptability

Regarding acceptability, little research has been conducted in the context of the developing world to examine consumers' social and cultural expectations and the responsiveness of health service providers to such expectations. We also know very little about how acceptability of health services is related to the poor or vulnerable groups compared to the general population. In particular, village doctors tend to have fewer social and cultural barriers with fellow villagers due to long-standing relationships (Brugha and Zwi, 1998).

Some of the innovations discussed above have the potential to make health-care services more acceptable and desirable. For instance, a rural health-care worker rather than a cardiac specialist is likely to use the Cardio Pad to perform cardiac tests. Since a rural health-care worker is likely to have lower social distance than a cardiac specialist, villagers may find the former more acceptable than the latter.

4.5 Big Data-Based Solutions to Fight Fake Drugs

4.5.1 The prevalence of fake drugs and some Big Data-based solutions to fight the problem

The widespread distribution of fake drugs is a significant problem that has been linked to a large number of deaths in SSA economies. One study published by the *American Journal of Tropical Medicine and Hygiene* found that fake and poorly made malaria drugs contribute to the deaths of more than 100,000 children annually in Africa (Yeebo, 2015). According to the WHO, 700,000 deaths occur due to counterfeit antimalarial and tuberculosis drugs (Rudd, 2012).

Fake drugs often completely lack active ingredients or have just enough to pass quality-control tests. However, there are often no noticeable differences when compared with real drugs in terms of their visual characteristics (Yeebo, 2015). One study conducted in 21 SSA countries found that one-third of malaria drug samples failed chemical testing and one-fifth were confirmed as fake (Nayyar *et al.*, 2012). Likewise, one in three medicines sold in Ghana is estimated to be counterfeit, compared to 1% in the USA and Europe (Yeebo, 2015).

The problem can be attributed to the system's porosity. For instance, most drugs sold in Ghana come from China, India and Malaysia, which are imported by Ghanaian distributors. These drugs are then sold to chemical sellers, pharmacies and hospitals. Some manufacturers lack control over their supply chains. For instance, one drug distributor's warehouse manager was reported to be selling batches of a new malaria treatment drug from a different company (Yeebo, 2015).

In this regard, companies such as Kenya's MPedigree, the US-based companies PharmaSecure and Sproxil, and the Norwegian company Kezzler have introduced scratch-off codes and other forms of technology such as holograms and radio-frequency identification chips to fight counterfeit drugs. As of 2015, PharmaSecure was reported to have its labels on 1.5 billion packs of medicines, mostly in India. Kezzler has also worked with Pfizer in Hong Kong and Royal Dutch Shell in Kenya (Yeebo, 2015).

Sproxil has developed a mobile product authentication (MPA) system. As of 2012, Sproxil operated in Ghana, Kenya, Nigeria and India. Sproxil has attracted venture capital to develop anti-counterfeit technologies (Yeebo, 2015). Drug manufacturers have also utilized Sproxil's MPA system for other purposes. For instance, using the MPA, it is possible to gain insights into locations that are counterfeit hotspots and assess the quantities of counterfeit drugs. Sproxil's cloud database analyses text messages to spot counterfeit drug activity (McBride, 2012). BD- and cloud-based tools such as Sproxil's MPA system can realize economies of scope. Manufacturers of other products have also started using Sproxil's MPA system to eliminate counterfeiters. As of 2012, Nigeria's hair and skin-care product manufacturers and the Swiss company O'tentika had started to collaborate with Sproxil (Bowman, 2012).

The non-profit organization mPedigree has developed an innovative solution, known as GoldKeys (http://goldkeys.org/), to fight this problem. When buying a drug at a pharmacy store, a customer will find a 12-digit code by scratching a sticker on the surface of the package. They will then send a text message to a given number. The code sent by the customer is matched with the ones registered by pharmaceutical companies in the cloud database of Hewlett-Packard (HP). The customer then receives a response back that tells them whether the drug is counterfeit or genuine. In addition, information such as the batch number, expiry date and dosage can also be sent in the same message. In order to maintain the system's integrity, sophisticated enterprise technologies are required to incorporate the secure labelling process with industrial and logistic processes (disrupt-africa.com, 2015). Although this application provides obvious commercial benefits to drug manufacturers and patients, one of the most important benefits is that it helps save lives by enabling the customers to check the authenticity of life-saving drugs.

Among the biggest needs of mPedigree were cloud servers to manage data and partnerships with major mobile phone networks. In December 2010, HP announced it would run the data centres to host mPedigree's codes. mPedigree's founder Bright Simons estimated that it saved the company US$10 million in infrastructure costs. Simons also persuaded Safaricom (a Vodafone subsidiary), MTN Group and other mobile carriers to subsidize the cost of text messages (Yeebo, 2015).

As of September 2015, mPedigree had opened offices in Egypt, Ghana, India, Kenya, Nigeria and Tanzania. However, only four (Egypt, Ghana, India and Nigeria) had a sufficient number of companies that had signed up to make mPedigree's solution profitable (Yeebo, 2015). The company is exploring business opportunities in Bangladesh, Rwanda, Sierra Leone, South Africa, Uganda and Zambia.

mPedigree's labels are printed in China and India, and its data centres are located on three continents. Blackouts can last 24 hours in Ghana. mPedigree tells potential clients it can keep costs within 1% of a product's wholesale value. That limits its own margins (Yeebo, 2015).

4.5.2 Expansion to new market segments

mPedigree has expanded beyond medicine to fight counterfeiting. Its clients include manufacturers of veterinary medicine, electrical products, baby food, cosmetics and high-yield seeds used in agriculture (Douglas, 2015). For instance, Dutch luxury fabric company Vlisco has adopted mPedigree's system since March 2015 to fight the problem of counterfeit and fake products in Ghana. Pirated versions of Vlisco's products are sold for a fraction of the price of the authentic items, and had cut the company's market share from 50% to just 15% over the period 2005–2014. Textile dealers that sell Vlisco products can authenticate the products they buy by sending codes that are on scratch-labels (myjoyonline.com, 2015). Vlisco uses mPedigree's system and uses the data to send text message advertisements to customers (Yeebo, 2015).

4.5.3 Some challenges faced

Innovations like mPedigree become subject to a number of obstacles and constraints in SSA economies. A single authentication code was checked 1500 times in a period of few days. In another case, mPedigree used its data to track down a warehouse that was full of fake malaria medication. In yet another case, a counterfeiter reportedly took a genuine code and used it to make thousands of copycat labels, which were used on counterfeit morning-after pills. mPedigree called everyone who had tested the code to find out where they bought the drug. It then alerted regulators and law enforcement agencies (Yeebo, 2015).

SSA-based firms often face challenges in mobilizing resources. For instance, Simons reported that pharmaceutical companies showed unwillingness to do business with mPedigree. Venture capital firms often do not find local initiatives attractive to fund. Regulators have a tendency to ignore local companies. A further problem noted by Simons was that talented developers do not like to work for local companies.

While the service helped consumers to detect specific fake product packs at retail level, counterfeiters then penetrated the parts of the market with lower consumer education level. Even though a counterfeit product has been detected, there is often a lack of coordinated actions to remove fake products from the shelf. In 2014, mPedigree added another product to the GoldKeys Suite: EarlySensor, which is a data-analytics, mass notifications framework. EarlySensor uses pattern-recognition algorithms to monitor for anomalies and irregularities in the consumer authentication ecosystem on a real-time basis. When certain conditions are breached it promptly sends location-based warnings to diverse stakeholders such as brand owners, regulatory bodies and consumers. In the near future, consumers are expected to receive warnings before purchasing products when suspicious activities are discovered in the supply chain near them (disrupt-africa.com, 2015).

4.6 The Role of Big Data in Promoting Transparency and Accountability in the Health-Care Sector

A huge amount of health-care data exists with hospitals, primary care providers, universities, professional societies, research-driven companies, health insurers, and state and federal government agencies. A major challenge currently facing the health-care system is that each of these organizations acts as a silo (Burg, 2014). This absence of data transparency often encourages actors to pursue their own interests since they have no sense of the motives of other actors (Mantoura *et al.*, 2007). This situation tends to result in a lack of accountability and responsibility among various actors involved in the health-care industry and market. In this regard, a higher degree of data transparency and clearer governance structure can force the relevant stakeholders to be more accountable and responsible. Using BD, these actors can more easily address and resolve most of the major health-care issues (Wyber *et al.*, 2015).

To take an example, in order to reduce its underwriting risk, the South African insurance firm AllLife, which offers affordable life and disability insurance services to people suffering from manageable diseases such as HIV and diabetes, sends its policyholders text messages reminding them to take medications (economist.com, 2014b). Its customers need to agree to adhere to a strict medical protocol. Policyholders are required to get monthly health checks. They also receive personalized advice on managing their conditions. AllLife gets data directly from medical providers with the policyholders' permission. Policyholders not following a treatment protocol or those discontinuing treatment are warned and benefits or coverage can be lowered or even suspended. The company assesses risks every 3 to 6 months. It was reported that the policyholders who participated in the prevention programmes improved their health and lengthened their life expectancies. For instance, 6 months after enrolment, the immune systems of HIV patients improved by 15% on average. AllLife benefits when its customers take voluntary risk-reducing measures and increase the flow of relevant information to the insurer. The company is reported to grow 50% annually and aims to insure 300,000 patients with HIV by 2016. AllLife's model is reported to be highly profitable and the company's risk is not much higher for clients with HIV than it is for other average clients (Brat *et al.*, 2014).

To take another example, the Indian bank ICICI's insurance arm uses web-based applications to develop innovative services such as personalized insurance for patients with diabetes (economist.com, 2008). The premiums are adjusted depending on how well the policyholder sticks to his or her fitness plan.

4.7 The Internet of Things and Health Care

Health care is arguably one of the areas with the biggest applications of IoT supported by BD analytics. One estimate suggested that by 2020, health-care applications will account for 15% of the global IoT market. That amounts to about US$3 billion, 80% of which will be from services rather than products (Saunders, 2014).

By tracking the abrupt onset of heart palpitations and other serious diseases with the IoT, patients, caregivers and health-care workers can be prompted to take appropriate actions in a timely fashion. The IoT thus has the potential to take the current practice of telemedicine to the next level. For instance, sensor-based systems can be used to monitor critical health parameters in health-care facilities such as hospitals, nursing homes, medical centres and clinical laboratories, as well as remotely. In early 2015, the telecommunications operator Etisalat, based in the United Arab Emirates, and Enayati Home Health Care launched a home-monitoring system on a pilot basis in Dubai. The system was developed by the British company Equivital, which focuses on the IoT. The system allows Enayati's health-care staff to monitor huge amounts of physiological data from their patients from sensors in the patient's body. The data can be collected on a real-time basis or retrospectively (ITWeb, 2015).

Using the IoT, patients' flow through an emergency department can be made more efficient and effective. For example, sensors used in an asthma inhaler can help to track when and where asthma patients use their inhalers. The data are analysed and sent back to the asthma patients through a mobile app, which would help understand how triggers like pollen count can affect their symptoms (Hartani, 2015). Using geolocation data, it is possible to build a map of spots in a city where people have problems breathing (Bruzek, 2014). This would help reduce overall health-care costs. Early studies have indicated that it is possible to reduce the number of people with uncontrolled asthma by as much as 50% (Hartani, 2015).

Machine-to-machine applications allow patients with non-life-threatening conditions to be sent home and monitored remotely by medical personnel. They can be issued with sensors to measure blood pressure or blood sugar levels. They can be trained to interpret the data themselves. This will free up hospital beds and physicians' time for more urgent cases (McLellan, 2013).

Finally, the IoT can be employed to prevent rather than cure diseases. For instance, consumer-oriented sensors such as the Fitbit can encourage people to adopt healthier lifestyles (McLellan, 2013).

There are, however, some key issues and challenges surrounding the use of the IoT in health care. For instance, health-care organizations face the challenge of integrating data from consumer-based sensors such as Internet-based blood pressure monitoring system and weight scales into the overall IT architecture. These systems present data exchange challenges. Some home devices may not have the same level of accuracy and need to be recalibrated (Robert, 2014).

4.8 Discussion and Concluding Comments

BD has opened up many exciting opportunities and potentials for developing countries. BD applications are highly beneficial in a number of areas such as research and development involving diseases that are specific to some developing regions, the fight against fake drugs, and efficient drug delivery. The efforts to fight malaria with initiatives such as aWhere's MADIS and mPedigree's solutions to fight fake drugs indicate that health-care problems facing the developing world can be attacked on multiple fronts by employing a variety of BD techniques.

The huge amount of relevant data from the IoT can be used to make informed health-care decisions. Data associated with mobile phones could be invaluable tools in the fight against Ebola and other deadly epidemics and infectious diseases. Such devices can be used to send people public-health information. Citizens can use mobile phones to call helplines if assistance is needed. In addition, the data generated by the mobile phone are likely to be highly valuable and necessary to understand and predict the spatial–temporal pattern of disease spread and the potential impact.

Finally, among the most notable of BD-related developments in SSA is that in some countries such as Nigeria, scratch-off codes have become mandatory on all malaria drugs and antibiotics (Yeebo, 2015). This evidence suggests that successful innovations such as those of mPedigree can bring favourable regulatory changes and help enrich the BD ecosystem by creating a virtuous circle.

References

Advanced MP Technology (2013) Chinese semiconductor outlook part I: IoT in China. Available at: http://www.advancedmp.com/iot-in-china/ (accessed 17 February 2016).

Akin, J.S. and Hutchinson, P. (1999) Health-care facility choice and the phenomenon of bypassing. *Health Policy Planning*, 2, 135–151.

assaabloy.com (2014) Biometric fingerprint sensors help track vaccination patients in developing countries. Available at: http://www.assaabloy.com/en/com/press-news/news/2014/biometric-fingerprint-sensors-help-track-vaccination-patients-in-developing-countries-/ (accessed 17 February 2016).

Bhattacharyya, O., McGahan, A., Singer, P., Daar, A., Khor, S. and Dunne, D. (2011) Innovative health service models for the world's poor. *Rotman Magazine*, 28–35.

Bourne, J. (2014) IBM Watson lands in Thailand, South Africa and Australia. Available at: http://www.cloudcomputing-news.net/news/2014/oct/10/ibm-watson-lands-thailand-south-africa-and-australia/ (accessed 17 February 2016).

Bowman, A. (2012) Scratching out Africa's counterfeit medicines. Available at: http://blogs.ft.com/beyond-brics/2012/08/28/scratching-out-africas-counterfeit-medicines/ (accessed 17 February 2016).

Boyd, D. and Crawford, K. (2012) Critical questions for Big Data: provocations for a cultural, technological, and scholarly phenomenon. *Information, Communication, & Society* 15(5), 662–679.

Brat, E., Clark, P., Mehrotra, P., Stange, A. and Boyer-Chammard, C. (2014) Bringing Big Data to life: four opportunities for insurers. Available at: https://www.bcgperspectives.com/content/articles/insurance_digital_economy_Bringing_big_data_life (accessed 17 February 2016).

Brugha, R. and Zwi, A. (1998) Improving the quality of private health sector services: challenges and strategies. *Health Policy Plan* 2, 107–120.

Bruzek, A. (2014) Medical inhalers to track where you are when you puff. Available at: http://www.popsci.com/every-breath-you-take-theyll-be-tracking-you (accessed 8 April 2016).

Burg, N. (2014) How Big Data will help save healthcare. Available at: http://www.forbes.com/sites/castlight/2014/11/10/how-big-data-will-help-save-healthcare/ (accessed 17 February 2016).

Campbell, S.M., Roland, M.O. and Buetow, S.A. (2000) Defining quality of care. *Social Science & Medicine* 11, 1611–1625.

Chaudhury, N. and Hammer, S.J. (2004) Ghost doctors: absenteeism in rural Bangladeshi health facilities. *World Bank Economic Review* 3, 423–441

Clapp, J. (2011) St. Tammany will use satellite surveillance to find, destroy mosquitoes. Available at: http://www.nola.com/politics/index.ssf/2011/03/st_tammany_will_use_satellite.html (accessed 17 February 2016)

connectaschool.org (2013) Ericsson launches 3G and connect to learn in the millennium village in Ethiopia. Available at: http://connectaschool.org/fr/node/4448/ (accessed 8 April 2016).

disrupt-africa.com (2015) mPedigree EarlySensor: ahead of its time. Available at: http://disrupt-africa.com/2015/08/mpedigree-earlysensor-ahead-of-its-time (accessed 17 February 2016).

Douglas, K. (2014) How Cameroon's Rolex award winner created Africa's first medical tablet. Available at: http://www.howwemadeitinafrica.com/how-cameroons-rolex-award-winner-created-africas-first-medical-tablet/41552/ (accessed 17 February 2016).

Douglas, K. (2015) How mPedigree built a business by combating counterfeit products. Available at: http://www.howwemadeitinafrica.com/how-mpedigree-built-a-business-by-combating-counterfeit-products/51384/ (accessed 16 February 2016).

Dutton, S. (2011) What Justin Bieber proves about the human face of big data. Available at: http://www.business2community.com/big-data/what-justin-bieber-proves-about-the-human-face-of-big-data-01321898 (accessed 8 April 2016).

economist.com (2008) The long nimbus, *The Economist* 389 (8603), 15–17. Available at: http://www.economist.com/node/12411864 (accessed 2 August 2016).

economist.com (2013) A middle way? Insurers have spotted an opening for no-frills but life-saving health care. Available at: http://www.economist.com/news/middle-east-and-africa/21589925-insurers-have-spotted-opening-no-frills-life-saving-health-care (accessed 17 February 2016).

economist.com (2014a) Scientific research in Africa is gathering momentum. Available at: http://www.economist.com/news/middle-east-and-africa/21611112-scientific-research-africa-gathering-momentum-rise (accessed 8 April 2016).

economist.com (2014b) A phoneful of dollars: the world's poor need the stability and security that banks have traditionally offered, but increasingly they do not need banks to provide it. Available at: http://www.economist.com/news/briefing/21632441-worlds-poor-need-stability-and-security-banks-have-traditionally-offered (accessed 17 February 2016).

harborresearch.com (2014) IoT in the news: China invests heavily in the Internet of Things. Available at: http://harborresearch.com/iot-in-the-news-china-invests-heavily-in-the-iot/ (accessed 17 February 2016).

Harper, J. and Strote, G. (2011) Afghanistan pharmaceutical sector development: problems and prospects. *Southern Med Review* 4(1), 29–39.

Hart, J.T. (1971) The inverse care law. *Lancet* 1, 405–412.

Hartani, R. (2015) Into the Internet of Things era: the African context. *Africa Telecom & IT*, February, 47–48.

ibm.com (2014) IBM Watson accelerates global expansion. Available at: https://www-03.ibm.com/press/us/en/pressrelease/45022.wss (accessed 17 February 2016).

ibm.com (2015) Medicine on demand. Available at: http://www-03.ibm.com/ibm/history/ibm100/us/en/icons/medicineon-demand/ (accessed 17 February 2016).

ibmsmartcamp.com (2013) Entrepreneurs changing healthcare in Kenya. Available at: http://ibmsmartcamp.com/2013/08/29/entrepreneurs-changing-healthcare-in-kenya/ (accessed 17 February 2016).

irinnews.org (2009) Tanzania: anti-malarial drugs too expensive – minister. Available at: http://www.irinnews.org/report/82984/tanzania-anti-malarial-drugs-too-expensive-minister (accessed 17 February 2016).

ITWeb (2015) Internet of Things to boost healthcare. Available at: http://www.itweb.co.za/index.php?option=com_content&view=article&id=143841 (accessed 17 February 2016).

Kirkpatrick, R. (2013) Use big data wisely and it can provide big insights. Available at: http://www.scidev.net/global/data/opinion/use-big-data-wisely-and-it-can-provide-big-insights.html (accessed 18 August 2014).

Lemaire, J. (2013) Scaling up mobile health: developing mhealth partnerships for scale. Commissioned by advanced development for Africa. Available at: https://www.k4health.org/toolkits/mhealth-planning-guide/scaling-mobile-health-developing-mhealth-partnerships-scale (accessed 8 April 2016).

Levitz, D. (2014) Winner spotlight: preventing 'stock outs' in developing countries' clinics. Available at: http://challengecup.1776dc.com/news/winner-spotlight-preventing-stock-outs-in-developing-countries-clinics/ (accessed 17 February 2016).

Lomborg, B. (2015) This child doesn't need a solar panel. Available at: http://www.wsj.com/articles/this-child-doesnt-need-a-solar-panel-1445466967 (accessed 17 February 2016).

Mantoura, P., Gendron, S. and Potvin, L. (2007) Participatory research in public health: Creating innovative alliances for health. *Health & Place* 13(2), 440–451.

McBride, R. (2012) Software provider to Merck taps IBM cloud to fight fake drugs. Available at: http://www.fiercebiotechit.com/story/software-provider-merck-taps-ibm-cloud-fight-fake-drugs/2012-05-03 (accessed 17 February 2016).

McIntyre, D., Thiede, M., Dahlgren, G. and Whitehead, M. (2006) What are the economic consequences for households of illness and of paying for health care in low- and middle-income country contexts? *Social Science & Medicine* 4, 858–865.

McLellan, C. (2013) M2M and the Internet of Things: a guide. Available at: http://www.zdnet.com/article/m2m-and-the-internet-of-things-a-guide/ (accessed 17 February 2016).

Mooney, G., Hall, J., Donaldson, C. and Gerard, K. (1991) Utilization as a measure of equity: weighing heat? *Journal of Health Economics* 4, 475–480.

myjoyonline.com (2015) mPedigree launches Goldkeys technology to fight textile piracy in Ghana. Available at: http://www.myjoyonline.com/business/2015/March-3rd/mpedigree-goldkeys-technology-to-fight-textile-piracy-in-ghana.php (accessed 28 April 2016).

Nakyanzi, J.K., Kitutu, F.E., Oria, H. and Kamba, P.F. (2010) Expiry of medicines in supply outlets in Uganda. *Bulletin of the World Health Organization* 88(2), 154–158.

Nayyar G.M.L., Breman J.G., Newton, P.N. and Herrington J. (2012) Poor-quality antimalarial drugs in southeast Asia and sub-Saharan Africa. *The Lancet Infectious Diseases* 12(6), 488–496. Available at: http://www.thelancet.com/journals/laninf/article/PIIS1473-3099%2812%2970064-6/fulltext (accessed 8 April 2016).

Newton, A. (2012) Big Data for development: beyond transparency. Available at: https://blogs.worldbank.org/psd/big-data-for-development-beyond-transparency (accessed 18 August 2014).

Peters, H.D., Garg, A., Bloom, G., Walker, G.D., Brieger, R.W. and Rahman, R.H. (2008) Poverty and access to health care in developing countries. *Annals of the New York Academy of Sciences* 1136, 161–171.

Pomwasin, A. (2014) Bumrungrad aims to grow more than 10%. Available at: http://www.nationmultimedia.com/business/Bumrungrad-aims-to-grow-more-than-10-30246441.html (accessed 17 February 2016).

Robert, L.M. (2014) Internet of Things (cover story). *Computerworld* 48(7), 12–16.

Rosemary, W., Vaillancourt, S., Perry, W., Mannava, P., Folaranmi, T. and Celi, L.A. (2015) Big data in global health: improving health in low- and middle-income countries. *Bulletin of the World Health Organization* 93(3), 203–208.

Rudd, M. (2012) Fake anti-malarial drugs could cost 'millions of lives'. Available at: http://www.africanbusinessreview.co.za/financeinafrica/1034/Fake-anti-malarial-drugs-could-cost-millions-of-lives (accessed 17 February 2016).

Saunders, A. (2014) The internet of everything. *Management Today* 5, 40–43.

Schmidt, E. and Cohen, J. (2015/2016) Technology: inventive artificial intelligence will make all of us better. Available at: http://time.com/4154126/technology-essay-eric-schmidt-jared-cohen/ (accessed 8 April 2016).

Surdak, W.C. and Agarwal, S. (2014) The benevolent side of Big Data. *Finance & Development*, 51(4). Available at: http://www.imf.org/external/pubs/ft/fandd/2014/12/surdak.htm (accessed 17 February 2016).

theguardian.com (2015) The cloud-based tool improving healthcare across the developing world. Available at: http://www.theguardian.com/sustainable-business/2015/jan/07/the-cloud-based-tool-improving-healthcare-across-the-developing-world (accessed 16 February 2016).

unglobalpulse.org (2015) Data visualisation and interactive mapping to support response to disease outbreak. Available at: http://www.unglobalpulse.org/mapping-infectious-diseases (accessed 17 February 2016).

UN Global Pulse (2014) Advocacy Monitoring through Social Data: Womens and Children's Health. Available at: http://www.unglobalpulse.org/EWEC-social-data-analysis (accessed 18 August 2014).

UNICEF (2013) Tracking anti-vaccination sentiment in Eastern European social media networks. UNICEF. Available at: http://www.unicef.org/ceecis/Tracking_anti-vaccine_sentiment_in_Eastern_European_social_media_networks.pdf (accessed 8 April 2016).

Van Der Geest, S. (1987) Self-care and the informal sale of drugs in south Cameroon. *Social Science & Medicine* 3, 293–305.

WHO [World Health Organization] (2014) Fact sheet on the World Malaria Report 2014. Available at: http://www.who.int/malaria/media/world_malaria_report_2014/en/ (accessed 8 April 2016).

WHO (2015a) Typhoid fever – Uganda. Available at: http://www.who.int/csr/don/17-march-2015-uganda/en/ (accessed 17 February 2016).

WHO (2015b) Global Health Observatory data repository: density per 1000 data by country. Available at: http://apps.who.int/gho/data/node.main.A1444?lang=en (accessed 21 April 2016).

WHO (no date) SMS for Life: An RBM initiative. Available at: http://www.rollbackmalaria.org/commodity-access/sms-for-life/sms-for-life-overview (accessed 2 August 2016).

Wiggins, D. (2015) Connected healthcare: extending the benefits of growth. Available at: http://reports.weforum.org/global-information-technology-report-2015/1-9-connected-healthcare-extending-the-benefits-of-growth/ (accessed 17 February 2016).

Wyber, R., Vaillancourt, S., Perry, W., Mannava, P., Folaranmi, T. and Celi, L.A. (2015) Big data in global health: improving health in low- and middle-income countries. *Bulletin of the World Health Organization* 93(3), 203–208, DOI: 10.2471/BLT.14.139022.

Yeebo, Y. (2015) Taking on fake drugs in Africa. Available at: http://www.businessweekme.com/Bloomberg/newsmid/190/newsid/1187/Taking-On-Fake-Drugs-in-Africa#cnttop (accessed 17 February 2016).

5 Big Data in Agriculture

Abstract

The visible impacts of BD are already underway in primary industries such as agriculture. Farmers based in the developing world can benefit tremendously if data from diverse sources are employed in important farming decisions such as planting date, varietal choice and applications of fertilizer. This chapter highlights the various data sources and technological trends affecting farming activities in the developing world. The role of smallholder farmers in the production and consumption of data and information is explored. This chapter presents a range of opportunities offered by BD to smallholder farmers based in the developing world. It describes agricultural BD projects with diverse impacts using a comparison of Vietnam's TH Milk and Kenya's Agrilife. It also probes the influence of various types of pressures in the adoption of BD technologies in farming activities. This chapter also offers an analysis of various challenges and obstacles faced by smallholder farmers in making BD-based decisions.

5.1 Introduction

Agriculture is entering into what Lance Donny, founder of the agricultural technology (Ag Tech) start-up OnFarm Systems, refers to as the third stage or Ag 3.0 (Lohr, 2015). Ag 3.0 involves exploiting data from diverse sources such as sensors embedded on farm equipment and plants, satellite images and weather tracking. The idea is that by deploying techniques such as micro-drip irrigation systems, using drought-resistant seeds and expanding microloan schemes, it may be possible to improve the livelihood of smallholder farmers and increase their income.

Donny points out that the first stage (i.e. preindustrial agriculture), which lasted until about the 1920s, involved labour-intensive activities and was subsistence farming on small farms. It took two acres to feed one person. The second stage (Ag 2.0) is industrial agriculture (1920 to about 2010), which entailed the use of tractors, combine harvesters, chemical fertilizers and seed science. It led the development of large commercial farms. In the Ag 2.0, there were big gains in productivity. One acre of land could feed as many as five people.

Now the era of Ag 3.0 has begun. Over the past few years there has been a rapid increase in investment activity in Ag Tech. The investment in the Ag Tech sector was estimated at US$500 million in 2010, which increased to US$4.2 billion in 2015 (Daneshkhu, 2016). In the first half of 2015, Ag Tech raised US$2.06 billion in venture capital investment in 228 deals. Precision agriculture technologies, such as drones and satellite imagery attracted US$400 million (Burwood-Taylor, 2015).

It is argued that in the not too distant future, the use of water, fertilizer and other input is likely to involve detailed measurement and monitoring. Sometimes such measurements are made on a plant-by-plant basis (dimsums.blogspot.ca, 2014). Moreover, BD is likely to help provide smallholder farmers with a highly personalized and customized set of solutions. It is, for instance, anticipated that not far into the future a rural African farmer working in his farm can be geo-located with the help of an app installed in his mobile phone. The soil type and needs of the field can be identified and advice regarding appropriate seeds can be offered. Then the farmer will be told where they can be purchased, and how they can be planted and harvested (Patel, 2013). The availability of sensors to accurately and cost-effectively monitor and measure various needs of the field is likely to make this happen.

Overall, the most positive effects of BD are likely to occur in improving agricultural productivity. Wolfgang von Loeper, a former farmer and the founder of MySmartFarm app, estimates that the average African smallholder farmer produces only one-quarter to one-half of the productive potential. BD can help them make full use of their productive potential. BD can also help farmers reduce costs by providing access to detailed information about irrigation and reduce wastage in resources (Jacobs, 2014).

This effect is likely to have tremendous developmental benefits as the agricultural sector employs over 60% of the active labour force in sub-Saharan Africa (SSA) economies (Oluoch-Kosura, 2010). According to the UNCTAD's 2009 World Investment Report, over 900 million people in the world were undernourished and 65 countries faced 'serious' or 'alarming' danger of food shortages and famine (UNCTAD, 2009). Studies have suggested that ineffective farm operations such as late planting/weeding, the lack of proper land preparation and harvesting techniques, and poor housing and feeding of livestock can reduce smallholder farmers' productivity by up to 40% (Oluoch-Kosura, 2010). BD has a potential to improve this condition. According to Monsanto, the world's biggest seed company, tailoring information and advice to farmers could increase annual worldwide crop production by about US$20 billion (Bunge, 2014).

There are additional forces present that increase the importance of BD and stimulate investments in Ag Tech. Environmental advocacy groups such as Greenpeace are vigorously opposing genetic modification and other enhancements. They are lobbying for more research involving various types of biotechnology application. BD facilitates marker-assisted selection (MAS), an indirect selection process in which a trait of interest (e.g. productivity, disease resistance) is selected based on a marker associated with it. Genomics and MAS enable researchers to find gene combinations that occur naturally instead of making new genetically modified organisms (Daneshkhu, 2016).

In summary, if BD solutions can be designed to help small-scale farmers make better decisions in order to increase efficiency and profitability, this may provide the greatest improvements in economic and social welfare. BD apps can help farmers know the best period to plant and harvest a crop by linking market demands with weather patterns and other relevant indicators. Such tools can also help farmers understand factors affecting crops such as precipitation and soil conditions. The apps can also alert farmers if crop diseases spread and provide them with information to prevent infections (Sudrak and Agarwal, 2014).

5.2 Various Data Sources and Technological Trends

Multiple data sources and technology applications are used in agricultural activities. Below we discuss key data sources and technological trends in the agricultural sector.

5.2.1 The Internet of Things and agriculture

The Internet of Things (IoT) is emerging as a key source of data for monitoring agricultural activities. In particular, China has been undertaking various IoT projects to increase farm productivity and enhance standards for quality and safety of agricultural and food commodities. A project involving an intelligent engineering system, which is designed for artificial control of greenhouse temperature and air, is underway in the port city of Tianjin in northern China. It collects data and sends out warnings when the temperature falls below a certain critical level during the winter season. A second project involves monitoring microorganisms in milk at each stage 'from cow to table'. The monitoring is expected to enhance transparency and strengthen the reputation and competitiveness of dairy companies.

Another example of an agricultural project that uses the IoT is Ez-Farm, a water management solution for agriculture. It was designed by Water Research Scientists at IBM Research-Africa and targets 'telephone farmers' who live in cities and can visit farms only at the weekends. These farmers need better reports on water usage and other aspects of operations. Farms have water tank sensors, soil moisture sensors and infrared light sensors that monitor the health of plants. As of July 2015, IBM had set up pilot projects with farms around Nairobi where sensors send data to IBM's cloud-based Data Centers every minute. Using BD and apps on smartphones and tablets, the system delivers information to farmers and water service providers on a real-time basis about current and predicted water and soil moisture levels (allafrica.com, 2015). The future plan is to incorporate data from the Kenya meteorological department and other sources. For instance, information about rainfall patterns and predictions will be delivered to farmers' mobile phones. Additional data about farms such as real-time operating status of farm equipment (e.g. pump failure) will also be provided in the future, which will help save costs (Kariuki, 2015).

5.2.2 Drip irrigation systems

Drip irrigation systems are being increasingly deployed in developing countries. Trung Nguyen Corporation, which is Vietnam's biggest domestically owned roasting and instant coffee business, has installed Israeli-sourced drip irrigation systems. The system provides irrigation directly to the root of coffee plants and fertilizes based on need. The system helps save water during the dry season (gcrmag.com, 2013).

Drip irrigation systems are reported to have a visible impact on productivity. Following the deployment of drip irrigation systems, yields of Arabica coffee in Tanzania were reported to increase from 400 kg per hectare to 2.5 tons per hectare. Yields per hectare of the Robusta variety were reported to increase from 1.2 to 3 tons in India and from 2.4 to 5.5 tons in Brazil. Likewise, cocoa bean production in Bahia Brazil was reported to increase from 400–500 kg per hectare to 3 tons per hectare by applying drip irrigation (Netafim, 2014).

The future shows a potential for further development in this technology. In 2015, the Israeli drip irrigation provider Netafim, which is the world's largest drip irrigation service provider, raised over US$500 million to fund an effort to further develop drip irrigation technology. This technology is likely to benefit farmers in the developing world such as those in China, India, Brazil and Africa (Street, 2015).

5.2.3 Soil infrared spectroscopy

Data about soil characteristics such as texture, organic matter and fertility help determine fertilizer needs and can be used as a basis for precise prescriptions. One way to get information about soil characteristics is to use orbiting satellites, which can collect data in a cost-effective manner by measuring electromagnetic radiation reflected from farmlands (economist.com, 2009). Industrialized countries already have soil data with a high level of granularity. As early as 2009, the data from RapidEye, which covered Europe and the Americas, was precise to the level of just 5 m^2 (economist.com, 2009). The level of granularity for such data is not yet fine enough for developing countries.

Nonetheless, efforts have been made to develop national and regional databases for soil properties. In 2009, the Kenyan-based World Agroforestry Centre started cataloguing the radiation signature of about 100,000 samples of African soils. It also announced a plan to give the information to the Colombia-based International Centre for Tropical Agriculture in order to build the Digital Soil Map database. The goal of the project was to combine the information with regularly updated satellite imagery of farmland in 42 African countries in order to provide farmers with free forecasts (economist.com, 2009). The Africa Soil Information Service (AfSIS) has developed a soil infrared spectroscopy technique to predict the characteristics of a soil sample based on the light reflected by the sample. A test costs only US$1 to the farmer. AfSIS has also launched a soil properties map of Africa at a 250 m × 250 m resolution. AfSIS was reported to be helping SSA economies such as Ethiopia, Ghana, Nigeria and Tanzania to establish national soil information systems and services, which are based on soil spectroscopy and digital soil-mapping technology (Mumero, 2015).

5.2.4 Data and information created via agriculture and farming platforms

Data and information are created via various agriculture and farming platforms. Smallholder farmers have various roles and functions in the production and consumption of data and information via such platforms. Table 5.1 describes some such platforms in terms of BD's roles in facilitating input availability, providing access to resources (e.g. loans, seeds and insurance), enhancing farming processes and productivity, and improving market access, marketability of products and bargaining power for smallholders.

In some tools, farmers play active roles in the production and consumption of information. As an example, Farmforce, a US$2 million cloud-based mobile platform developed by Syngenta Foundation and backed by the Swiss government, operates on a subscription-based software as a service model, which tracks pesticide residues in produce. It was developed in 2011 by a team based in Switzerland with inputs from a team based in Kenya. Smallholders in Kenya access it for free online via mobile phones to store and manage data on pesticide content in crops (Sambira, 2013). The Nigerian farm services company Babban Gona (http://

Table 5.1. Smallholder farmers' roles in the production and consumption of data and information via farming platforms.

	Individual farmers' active roles in the production and consumption of data and information	Individual farmers' minor or no roles in the production and/or consumption of data and information
Access to inputs and resources	iCow's help in finding nearest vets	Kilimo Salama's weather-based index: information for banks/MFIs to provide loans Agrilife: service providers tailor offerings to farmers
Enhancing farming process and productivity	Farmforce's digitization of farm activities and operations. iCow's positive impact on milk production	FACE: Agrilife lowered data-collection costs
Increasing access to market, marketability of products and bargaining power	Esoko: information on current market prices, bids and offers. Farmforce: identify/document requirements related to quality standards and pesticide traceability	Agrilife connects farmers with buyers CKWs help to find markets for products

CKW, community key worker; MFI, microfinance institutions.

www.babbangona.com/) (which means 'great farm' in Hausa) has been using Farmforce since 2013. A total of 692 farmers were enrolled in the first year, which covered 583 ha (farmforce.com, ND). The number of farmers enrolled increased to more than 2000 in 2014 (Syngenta Foundation for Sustainable Agriculture, 2015a). Farmforce records information about farmers' personal profiles, growing activity, yields and other indicators.

Guatemala's Adisagua, which is a smallholder agricultural initiative, adopted Farmforce in 2013. Syngenta Foundation for Sustainable Agriculture claimed that the traceability and precision of smallholder groups increased by a factor of ten due to Farmforce. Adoption of the platform increased from 16% of the farmers in 2013 to 100% in 2014 (Syngenta Foundation For Sustainable Agriculture, 2015b). It was reported that a number of developing countries such as Ghana, Indonesia and Zimbabwe had also expressed interest in Farmforce (Syngenta Foundation for Sustainable Agriculture, 2015b; The AgTechXChange, 2015).

As another example, the Apps4Africa award-winning mobile app iCow, developed by Kenya's Green Dreams, helps small-scale dairy farmers track and manage cows' fertility cycles. The app educates farmers about important stages of a cow's gestation period, collects and stores milk and breeding records, and sends best practice information. It also helps find the nearest vets and other service providers. Green Dreams has formed a system involving Google Docs. If Green Dreams and a vet contacted by a farmer are unable to answer the farmer's question, it is uploaded onto the system. The vets send messages among themselves and come up with the best answer, which is forwarded to the farmer. As of 2012, iCow was used by 42,000 farmers in 42 countries.

In some BD tools, most individual farmers have minor or no roles in the production and consumption of information. BD tools are used to obtain information on farmers, their farms and practices, as well as external conditions affecting farming productivity. For instance, Uganda's so-called 'community knowledge workers' (CKWs) use phones loaded with open-source data-collection applications. The concept was developed by the Grameen Foundation. It offers selected farmers, who act as CKWs, loans to buy Android phones. The phone is loaded with information about the time and methods of planting crops, caring for farm animals and finding markets for products. Data are automatically fed into Salesforce.com clouds. As of 2011, about 400 CKWs interacted with farmers and gathered information (Gohring, 2011). They use solar power, bicycles and other means to recharge phone batteries.

The project created a cloud-hosted database for Ugandan farmers. Farmers contribute questions and answers about agricultural practices to the database. It also contains answers to frequently asked questions, which can be accessed via a free text message service. The project generated US$1 million when government agencies and commercial organizations paid for farming data, for example, a brewery requested information on barley crop supply chains (Hall, 2012).

As a further example, the social enterprise Kilimo Salama ('safe agriculture' in Swahili) has developed a weather-based index insurance that uses weather stations across Kenya to serve small-scale farmers. Kilimo Salama is a partnership between the Syngenta Foundation, UAP Insurance and Safaricom. Farmers buy the insurance at the beginning of the season for 10–20% of the amount invested in seeds and inputs (Kalan, 2013). The insurance is completely automated and distributed through dealers who use an advanced phone application with a camera to scan and capture policy information. The information is uploaded to Safaricom's mobile cloud-based server, which administers policies. Farmers receive information about the policy and payouts via text messages (Schneider, 2013). Weather stations are equipped with wireless SIM cards that transmit data every 5 minutes to clouds. At the season's end, the data are aggregated and coupled with satellite data, and are used to map out rain patterns. Kilimo Salama works with agronomists to calculate the index to identify locations with too much rain, too little rain, or rain at the wrong time. Farmer payouts are based on crops, location and the amount of seeds purchased (Kalan, 2013).

5.3 The Origin of Big Data-Related Innovations in the Agricultural Sector

5.3.1 Big Data technologies developed in industrialized countries

BD technologies developed in industrialized countries have been a key driving force for the adoption of BD in developing countries. As of 2015, AfiMilk technologies have been implemented in 50 countries, including China, Belarus and Vietnam (investinisrael.gov, 2014). Vingroup, which is Vietnam's biggest privately owned company, uses BD and other agricultural technologies from Israel, Japan and the Netherlands in its agricultural projects. Vingroup formed a new wholly owned subsidiary, VinEco, in March 2015 for this purpose. According to Vingroup's founder and chairman, Pham Nhat Vuong, the aim of the newly established unit is to supply fresh produce throughout the year at low costs to its supermarket chain in Vietnam and to export to other countries.

Vuong noted that Israel produces 300–700 tons of tomatoes per hectare compared to 30–60 tons in Vietnam (Coren, 2015). In August 2015, VinEco started the construction of a VND1,000 billion (US$45 million) greenhouse in the Vinh Phuc province, which is the first of its kind in Vietnam. It will produce organic vegetables and sprouts that comply with VIETGAP and GLOBALGAP (GAP: good agriculture practices) standards. VinEco's greenhouse is expected to produce 3500 metric tonnes (about 3857 tons) of organic vegetables annually, which will be sold through Vinmart supermarkets and stores in the country (VOV, 2015). Two Israeli companies, Teshuva Agricultural Projects and Netafim, provide technology for greenhouses. KUBOTA will assist in the mechanization and automation of operations (talkvietnam.com, 2015).

In August 2015, Vingroup signed a US$17 million agreement with Netafim, which provides turnkey greenhouse projects and drip and smart-irrigation solutions (Netafim, 2015). Netafim's drip irrigation system can precisely control nutrient and water flows. It does so by wirelessly monitoring the flows with atmospheric sensors. It also utilizes self-cleaning pipes that are installed under the surface, which can reduce water loss through evaporation and lessen the severity of contamination due to surface water runoff (Levitt, 2013). According to the agreement, Netafim will supply VinEco with greenhouse structures, drip products, automated systems for climate control, crop growing platforms, know-how, and agronomic and other support services (Netafim, 2015).

Vietnam's FPT Telecom and Japan's Fujitsu have reached an agreement to deploy Fujitsu's Akisai cloud technology to support agricultural management (Goldberg, 2015). The two companies agreed to sell systems that remotely manage the cultivation of high-quality agricultural products. The target markets for the systems are agricultural groups and retailers. As a component of its smart agriculture model for Vietnam, Fujitsu announced a plan to build a greenhouse in Hanoi and launch a pilot project involving the Akisai cloud (vietnam.vnanet.vn, 2015b). FPT handles sales, and Fujitsu monitors and controls conditions from its Japanese data centres. The system remotely opens and closes cold frame lids, greenhouse windows and skylights and adjusts temperatures as needed. The plan is to first control the conditions from Japan. After gathering more data on climate and soil, the plan is to then transfer to local data centres in Vietnam (Asian Review, 2014). Fujitsu is also working closely with another Japanese provider of farming technology, Aeon Agri Create. In October 2015, authorities from Vietnam's Ha Nam province held a working session with executives from Aeon Agri Create and Fujitsu to discuss the deployment of BD in agricultural development. The farming information technology (IT) solutions introduced by Aeon Agri Create include smartphone appliances that record data on indicators related to plant growth and insects, which are then transmitted to farmers (baodanang.vn, 2015).

5.3.2 Undertaking Big Data-related innovations locally

As noted above, China is one of the developing countries that are actively pursuing innovations in IoT applicable in the agricultural sector. There are reports that a significant proportion of milk, meat, rice, vegetables and other food items sold in the country are heavily tainted and contaminated. The government has thus made food safety a top priority. In 2011, Fudan University's Auto-ID Lab collaborated with 17 other research teams at universities, research institutes and enterprises on a project called Agriculture Internet of Things and Food Safety and Quality. The project was supported by the Ministry of Science and Technology, which uses the IoT to track agricultural products from the field through the supply chain and food-processing environments (Wang and Min, 2013). Businesses are also responding by developing products that monitor food safety. For instance, Baidu announced a plan to launch a pair of smart chopsticks that can detect contaminants in food (Higginbotham, 2014).

In 2014, the International Rice Research Institute, the Shenzhen-based Beijing Genomics Institute and the Chinese Academy of Agricultural Sciences completed sequencing the genomes (i.e. a complete set of an organism's DNA) of 3024 rice varieties originating from 89 countries (flar.org, 2014). The project accumulated over 120 TBs of data consisting of over 30 million genetic variations (Wheatly, 2015). The significance of the 3K RGP (3000 Rice Genomes Project) stems from the fact that about half of the world's population depends on rice as a dietary staple and main source of energy (Anderson, 2015). Estimates suggest that rice accounts for more than 20% of human calorie intake (Wheatly, 2015).

5.4 The Appropriateness and Impacts of Big Data Tools on Smallholder Farmers in Developing Economies

A number of strategic implications may be noted when viewing the land constraints facing farmers and the increased demand for food due to population growth. Boserup's (1965) framework proposes two strategies:

1. A labour-intensive strategy in which farmers just add more labour to the production process, which allows them to crop more densely and engage in more intensive weeding and harvesting.
2. A capital-intensive strategy in which farmers improve their agricultural productivity by increasing investments in fertilizer, organic matter, machinery, equipment and other capital goods.

Boserup noted that a capital-intensive strategy is likely to lead to a higher productivity than a labour-intensive strategy. Similarly, Matlon and Spencer (1984) argued that a capital-intensive path is more sustainable and productive, especially in fragile and resource-poor areas. The fertility-enhancing inputs can help repair the progressive exhaustion of the soil and investments in land improvements can help avoid erosion.

In tropical highlands and other areas characterized by demographic pressure, which are facing severe degradation, farmers who follow a labour-intensive strategy are more prone to long-run ecological disaster and further economic impoverishment (Matlon and Adesina, 1992; Cleaver and Schreiber, 1994). Farmers in SSA economies have exhibited a tendency to engage in a labour-intensive strategy, which is unsustainable and may result in land degradation and stagnation of land productivity (Reardon and Vosti, 1995). BD can act as a force that will shift farming activities towards capital intensiveness and reduce the land-degradation problem.

In order to better analyse and evaluate the poverty-environment nexus, Reardon and Vosti (1995) proposed the use of a measure of 'investment poverty'. They define the cut-off point for investment poverty as 'the ability to make minimum investments in resource improvements to maintain or enhance the quantity and quality of the resource base – to forestall or reverse resource degradation' (p. 1498). The commonly used measures of poverty, or what Reardon and Vosti refer to as 'welfare poverty', on the other hand, are based on criteria such as income, consumption and nutrition. Farmers who are welfare-poor also tend to be investment-poor but the converse is not necessarily true. The cut-off point for investment poverty is a function of local factors such as labour and non-labour input costs, and the nature of investment needed for the particular environmental problems and risks faced by the farmer. Farmers that are investment-poor have shown a tendency to convert forest to farmland in order to offset land degradation with more land under cultivation (Reardon and Vosti, 1995).

Investment-poor farmers that face fragile and degrading environments and land constraints are not in a position to make investments in resources in order to improve economic conditions. They may consequently engage in activities that may further increase the degradation and their vulnerability. There is thus a vicious circle between poverty and environmental degradation (Pearce and Warford, 1993; Mink, 1993).

One way to break the vicious circle is to make use of BD in smallholders' farming decisions and activities. Some argue that BD is the source of the next revolution in farming (Bunge, 2014). An overview of the deployment of BD in industrialized countries would be helpful for assessing how conditions can be improved in developing countries. On this front, precision agriculture or precision farming has been a key trend in industrialized countries. Data collected on soil conditions, seeding rates, crop yields and other variables from farmers' tractors, combines and drones are combined with detailed records on historical weather patterns, topography and crop performance collected by the providers of prescriptive-planting technology (foxnews.com, 2014; Bunge, 2014). Human experts may need to perform tasks involving decision problems and processes for which no algorithm exists or the algorithm has not yet been developed. In some cases, due to unknowns no algorithm can solve all instances of the problem. In agriculture, some examples of situations include tasks involving unknown soil types and extreme weather conditions, which often need to be performed by humans rather than algorithms.

The data are thus crunched by algorithms and human experts and turned into customized useful advice which is sent directly to farmers and their machines instructing the optimum amount of pesticides, herbicides, fertilizer and other applications.

Many tractors and combines are guided by global positioning system satellites. An article published in Usatoday.com explained that a maize and soybean farmer in Iowa used a US$30,000 drone to study how the yield in his 900 acre farm is affected by changes in topography and other factors (Doering, 2014). This example is illustrative of a widespread adoption and diffusion of BD in the agricultural sector in industrialized countries. Many farmers who have implement data-driven prescriptive planting based on the analysis of nutrients in soil and other factors have reported a significant increase in productivity (Bunge, 2014). The point is that even small alterations in planting depth or the distance between rows of crops can lead to a significant increase in agricultural productivity.

The diffusion of BD is associated with and facilitated by measures taken by the providers of prescriptive-planting technology to strengthen their resources and capabilities. In 2013, Monsanto acquired the weather data mining firm Climate Corp. Likewise, the agricultural cooperative Land O'Lakes bought satellite-imaging specialist Geosys. In the same vein, in order to provide real-time climate and market information to its data services users, DuPont announced a collaboration with the weather and market analysis firm DTN/The Progressive Farmer. In 2013, Deere agreed to send data from its tractors, combines and other machinery to the computer servers of DuPont and Dow (Bunge, 2014).

While BD does not have the same level of effects in developing countries, the impacts can be clearly seen to occur in some key areas. Some impact areas are discussed below.

5.4.1 Access to inputs and resources

An area in which BD might have potential to facilitate agricultural and farming activities in developing countries relates to the availability of near real-time data and information regarding farmers' needs and capabilities, which can be used by value-chain partners to effectively serve the farmers. One example is the cloud-based platform Agrilife.

BD tools have enhanced farmers' access to inputs and resources. For example, iCow helps farmers find the nearest vet and other service providers. Likewise, thanks to Kilimo Salama's insurance scheme, banks and microfinance institutions are more comfortable in giving loans to farmers. As of 2013, Kilimo Salama insured over 100,000 farmers in Kenya and Rwanda (Kalan, 2013).

5.4.2 Access to insurance and other risk-spreading mechanisms

Insurance could affect farm household utility through various channels. For instance, income is stabilized if the farm income is not affected because of adverse weather or other natural disasters. A farmer with agricultural insurance can also take decisions that can maximize his profits (e.g. investing in high-return cash crops) because he does not need to worry about potential damage due to adverse weather conditions (Binswanger-Mkhize, 2012).

Due to problems such as high costs and moral hazard, individual crop insurance is almost non-existent in developing countries as a tool to insure farmers or farm credits. Since the 1990s, the focus of the agricultural insurance industry has gravitated towards index-based insurance. Index-based insurance utilizes an index (e.g. area-wide yields or a weather index) that is correlated with the farmers' yields and thus incomes. Index-based insurance thus does not pay the policy holder on the basis of their individually assessed loss. If insurance companies are able to come up with an index that has a sufficiently high degree of correlation with the farmers' yields, index-based insurance can resolve the key problems associated with individual insurance: (i) since payments to the policyholders are based on a sub-regional measurable index, there is no moral hazard; (ii) there is no requirement to make field-level assessments, which reduces costs; and (iii) the fact that the insurance is based on a reliable and independently verifiable index makes it possible to reinsure, which allows local insurance companies to efficiently transfer part of the risk to the global market (un.org, 2007).

Binswanger-Mkhize (2012) described two conditions in index-based insurance:

1. **The supply-side condition:** It is commercially viable for the insurance company if:
insurance premium > expected loss + risk margin + administrative costs.
2. **The demand-side condition:** A farmer will invest in insurance if:
expected utility without formal insurance < expected utility with formal insurance.

BD, especially IoT, is likely to change the conditions in both the demand and supply sides. Additional data provided by sensors and devices can be supplemented with human input on safety and prevention, which is likely to provide a better and more accurate understanding of exposure, hazards and risk (resulting in lower expected loss and risk margin in point 1). It is thus possible to offer loss control on an individualized scale. Insurers can reward behaviours such as locking doors when leaving homes, or turning off stoves and ovens when not in use. In the non-IoT environment, there is no measurable or reliable way for home insurers to know this information. The IoT and Smart Homes allow this data to be collected, managed and shared. This will decrease the left-hand side and increase the right-hand side in point 2.

The Indian insurance system has been criticized on the grounds of political interference and the perception that it lacks scientific basis and transparency (Gulati, 2015). India's limited weather station infrastructure has been a challenge. Historical weather data is only available from about 550 weather stations of the Indian Meteorological Department (IMD). These are insufficient to cover India's arable land, which according to the World Bank was more than 157 million ha in 2011 (tradingeconomics.com, 2016). Moreover, IMD weather stations are rarely available in rural areas. At a workshop held in 2013, senior government officials, researchers and industry representatives discussed possible ways to improve insurance to serve Indian farmers in a better way. Some of the recommendations made by the participants of the workshop included:

1. Identifying and applying appropriate technologies such as remote sensing, simulation modelling (creation and analysis of a digital prototype in order to predict the impact of different weather conditions on crops) and information communication technology (ICT) tools to improve the assessment of adverse weather's impact on crop yield loss.
2. Creating a repository where all insurance-related data on weather and crop yield can be accessed.
3. Building historical time series data on crop yields at the village, panchayat and block levels (Parthasarathy, 2014).

Crop insurance is not available in Bangladesh. In 2014, the Asian Development Bank announced a grant of US$2 million to develop weather index-based crop insurance in the country, which uses historical weather and crop production data. This approach reduces farm-level monitoring and transaction costs and thus is considered to be cost effective and efficient compared to traditional agricultural insurance. The project involves collaboration with a number of partners, such as agricultural banks, multilateral financial institutions and farmer cooperatives to develop and pilot new models of distribution. In order to improve the accuracy of weather data, space technology through remote sensing will be used in collaboration with the Japan Aerospace Agency. Initially, a pilot programme will generate a new weather index based on data for the past 25 to 30 years in collaboration with agriculture research institutions and weather and meteorological departments (adb.org, 2013).

The project entails upgrading at least 20 weather stations. Training and education on weather-indexed insurance will be provided to at least 400 staff from government and meteorological agencies, insurance companies, agricultural institutions and civil society groups. Among the key benefits of the proposed scheme are reduced premiums and improved distribution, farmers' access to credit and a lower rate of loan defaults. There are plans to provide insurance literacy and climate risk awareness seminars to at least 6000 smallholder farmers. The project also supports the development of a regulatory and legal framework to accommodate weather index-based crop insurance (southasia.oneworld.net, 2014).

5.4.3 Impacts on farming process and productivity

Many examples of the impact of BD on farming process and productivity can be cited. iCow has reportedly helped increase milk production by 2–3 litres per cow per day. Likewise, Farmforce eliminated the need to use manual record keeping of farm activities/operations. Similarly, FACE's use of Agrilife to collect information about their farmer clients has led to lower data-collection costs compared to paper-based questionnaires.

Nutrient management is another area where BD may be relevant. In Africa, outdated knowledge in recommendations for nutrient management is pervasive and ubiquitous. This often leads to too much fertilizer in relation to potential crop demand on a uniform basis irrespective of the type of land (Giller *et al.*, 2011). A model-based and data-driven approach is thus likely to reduce the costs of fertilizer and increase productivity.

5.4.4 Increase in small-scale farmer's access to market, marketability of products and bargaining power

Small-scale farmers in the developing world face several key challenges. Studies conducted in Sri Lanka and other countries have indicated that farmers are not able to sell their harvests because of oversupply or not getting the planned harvest, and the lack of necessary information (Walisadeer *et al.*, 2013). These obstacles can be partly overcome by using BD.

BD tools have increased small-scale farmers' access to market, marketability of products and bargaining power. For instance, despite the rising demands in industrialized countries for fruit and vegetables, small-scale farmers based in the developing world face barriers related to quality standards and pesticide traceability (Dinham, 2003). The use of Farmforce would help small-scale farmers identify and document important requirements related to quality standards and pesticide traceability in order to improve marketability of their crops. The platforms thus enable smallholder farmers' access to formal markets. Likewise, in Mauritius and Ghana, a mobile-enabled cloud service (Esoko) collects and provides information to farmers on topics such as current market prices, bids/offers, weather and tips. Advice is sent by voice messages, and call centres run by agricultural experts are available (Brock, 2015). Similarly, Agrilife and CKWs help find markets for products.

Researchers have recognized that farmers based in the developing world face difficulties in meeting the quality and safety standards set by the developed world (Oluoch-Kosura, 2010). In this regard, the availability of easily accessible data, which includes digital records of farming activities (e.g. the amount of seeds and pesticides), will obviously play a major role in documenting the quality standards of agricultural products.

5.4.5 Improving efficiency of the downstream activities in the supply chain

BD can also help to better manage logistics and transportation after harvesting. A large proportion of food waste occurs throughout the supply chain. It is thus important to transport the food under the right weather conditions. At the same time, it may not be appropriate to hold the produce for a long time. For instance, in some countries such as Brazil, a large proportion of roads are of low quality. During the rainy season, trucks can get stuck in mud. If farmers know in advance which locations are likely to experience rain and the routes that are likely to be affected, then they can make better logistical decisions to transport food (IBM, 2015).

According to the Food and Agriculture Organization, food losses and waste amounts to roughly US$680 billion in industrialized countries and US$310 billion in developing countries. In medium- and high-income countries, supply chains account for a large proportion of food waste. Some possible measures to decrease the volume of loss and waste of food include increasing coordination between actors in the supply chain (e.g. through farmer–buyer agreements), raising awareness among industries, retailers and consumers, and finding a beneficial use for food that is otherwise thrown away (fao.org, 2016). BD can help improve the efficiency of activities downstream in the supply chain of agricultural products. For instance, in industrialized countries retailers are using BD to minimize food wastage by using customer data collected from the loyalty cards used by shoppers. For instance, the US retailer Walmart's analysis of the shopping patterns of customers and weather data found useful correlations. The retailer found that people eat more steak during warm and windy weather but not when it is raining. The retailer also found that the most ideal weather condition for eating berries is when the temperature is under 27°C with low winds. This information can help the retailer to tailor their procurement from producers in order to meet customer demands with the lowest possible wastage (Daneshkhu, 2016).

Alibaba's logistic affiliate, China Smart Logistics (also known as Cainiao), has developed a logistics network in the country. In 2015, a huge distribution centre was established to support Alibaba's supermarket sales in eastern China. The centre makes next-day delivery possible in 25 cities if the groceries are purchased online via Tmall Supermarket in Jiangsu Province, Zhejiang province and Shanghai. In June 2015, Cainiao set up three fresh food distribution centres in Beijing, Shanghai and Guangzhou, which makes it possible to deliver fresh food purchased on Taobao and Tmall.com to Chinese consumers within 24 hours (Knowler, 2015).

5.4.6 Improving crop quality

A further mechanism by which productivity can be increased is through the development of better crop quality. In order to improve crop quality characteristics, it is important to identify the genetic basis of the traits that are of interest. In this regard, 3K RGP is among the most impressive and most closely watched BD projects where organizations from the developing world have a lead role. 3K RGP has been supported by grants from the Bill and Melinda Gates Foundation and the Chinese Ministry of Science and Technology. The goal of this multi-agency project is to acquire genomic information, which can be used to accelerate rice breeding programmes by enabling the rapid development of 'higher-yielding, drought-tolerant, pest- or disease-resistant strains of rice with high nutritional value' (Anderson, 2015).

To take another example, Suzhou-based Anwood Logistics Systems provides radiofrequency identification (RFID)-based returnable packaging solutions and intelligent logistic services for agricultural products. Anwood's solutions are used by Fruitday, which grows, imports and sells its fruits online. Fruitday organizes cold chain storage and transports 2700 tons of citrus from its farms in Kunming to major Chinese cities. Fruitday uses an automatic system to clean and sort freshly harvested citrus fruits. The fruits are loaded into protective crates and provided with unique RFID codes, which are scanned. When the fruits arrive at the warehouse, the RFID codes are scanned again. During the entire process, the temperatures and truck footprints are monitored and measured. This process substantially reduced losses and improved product quality. It was reported that Anwood's solutions helped Fruitday reduce logistic costs by more than 50% and improve transparency. Anwood's other major customers include Yihaodian, which is a subsidiary of Walmart, and the state-owned agriculture and fresh produce company COFCO Womai (freshplaza.com, 2015).

5.5 Some Challenges and Obstacles

From the standpoint of BD deployment, the agricultural sector in the developing world faces specific challenges and obstacles that are unique to this sector. Against the backdrop of rapid diffusion of BD among big farmers in industrialized countries, a comparison of their BD ecosystems with those of developing countries would be helpful to understand critical challenges and problems in the effective utilization of BD for developmental issues. Firstly, and perhaps most importantly, agricultural firms in the industrialized world have a long history of data production and consumption. For instance, DuPont has been making use of farm-level data since the early 2000s (Bunge, 2014). Likewise, it is increasingly common for farmers to monitor the progress of their agricultural activities on iPads and tablets. In industrialized countries, firms in diverse industries such as satellite imaging, weather data mining, and weather and market analysis have enabled a rich ecosystem of BD.

Small farmers do not have enough financial resources to afford specialized machineries. The conditions that stimulated the growth of BD in the US farming industry (e.g. the widespread adoption of mechanized tractors, genetically modified seeds, and computers and tablets for farming activities) are less prevalent in developing countries. Smallholder farmers often have no means to access the data and lack the ability to interpret it. Therefore a major concern is that BD collection efforts will only benefit big and well-educated farmers (Palmer, 2012).

There is a lack of appropriate database systems for agribusiness development, agriculture management and produce distribution. A BD attempt is greatly hampered by the lack of a reliable infrastructure to collect information. Consider, for instance, climate-related historical data. African countries have limited capacity to develop, generate, disseminate and effectively use climate data and information (Twomlow *et al.*, 2008). National institutions, leadership and the civil society are inherently weak and cannot determine the types of climate data and information needed for agriculture and other economic activities. An extremely low number of meteorological stations for climate data collection and the lack of digitization of the data exacerbates the problems faced by policy makers and practitioners in the provision of effective responses to climate change and other climate-related effects (UNFCC, 2007).

There is also the risk that agricultural insurance becomes a cover-up for not tackling other more fundamental problems that farmers face, which have nothing to do with the weather. These include the use of traditional low-productivity techniques and the lack of health care, which increase livelihood risks. Moreover, the aggregators often do not insure farm revenues but only credit or input costs. Without addressing these challenges, government policies will not have large welfare impacts on the smallholder farmers. A higher priority thus needs to be placed on BD projects that lead to an increase in the productivity of smallholder farmers and their access to health care.

Measures such as, inter alia, development of broader indices, reduction in risks and transactions costs, facilitation in farmers' understanding of insurance, and improvement in weather data are likely to accelerate farmers' adoption of index-based insurance. However, these conditions are helpful but not sufficient. That is, there is often very little that can be done to overcome farmers' inability to buy insurance (Binswanger-Mkhize, 2012).

Transnational corporations (TNCs) are likely to be a driving force behind the diffusion of BD in the agricultural sector of developing countries. Large food and biotechnology TNCs such as Monsanto and Syngenta already have a notable presence in developing countries, which is a positive factor from the standpoint of BD-led productivity growth in these countries. During 2005–2007, the share of agriculture in foreign direct investment inflows was 15.1% in Cambodia and 12% in Laos (UNCTAD, 2009). Monsanto reportedly has control of over 95% of the Indian cotton seed market (Vidal, 2011). TNCs, which are often producers, processors or traders of agricultural products or sellers of inputs or machinery, engage in a contracting system in which they assume a variety of responsibilities including providing technical assistance and marketing to small-scale farmers based in the developing world (Glover, 1984). TNCs such as Monsanto and Syngenta, which have become a driving force behind the utilization of BD in the industrialized world, are thus likely to act as a key channel in the international technology transfer of BD.

A related point is that international technology transfer in BD is likely to have differential effects across different categories of crops. For instance, foreign companies are more active in newly emerging export crops that are integrated into the international supply chain. Traditional cash crops such as coffee, cotton, tea and tobacco are thus more likely to realize the need to adopt various aspects of BD (Hoeffler, 2006).

Other potential mechanisms and determinants of BD diffusion among farmers also exist. For instance, Oluoch-Kosura (2010) reported that non-governmental organizations, farmers' organizations and the private sector in Africa are playing important roles in facilitating farmers' education, access to agricultural information and training. International supply chain structures often tend to exclude smallholder farmers. In Mozambique, farmers who are engaged in contract farming pool their resources to get technical advice and other services. More than 400,000 smallholders with less than 1 ha of land each are reported to benefit from such arrangements (Hoeffler, 2006).

5.6 Adapting to Various Types of Pressures

One's power arguably 'resides implicitly in the other's dependency' (Emerson 1962, p. 32). This view suggests that inter-organizational pressures from trading partners based in the industrialized world are of paramount importance for firms in the developing world to adopt ICT. In the case of a low bargaining power, on the other hand, less powerful firms may resist ICT adoption pressures. Schware and Kimberley (1995) found that some organizations from developed countries accepted new suppliers only if they could demonstrate an electronic data interchange capability. US multinational corporations such as Walmart and JC Penney require their foreign suppliers to transact on the Internet, which led the suppliers from developing Asian countries to adopt the Internet sooner because of such pressure (Woodall, 2000). It is reported that supermarkets in Southeast Asian nations are becoming increasingly concerned with safety and quality and are asking suppliers to comply with standards similar to those of EUREPGAP. Unbelievable as it may sound, small-scale farmers are now being asked to provide traceability to guarantee a safe water supply and other key issues (Berdegue *et al.*, 2003). One chain in El Salvador is reported to be asking for barcodes to be applied to pre-packaged produce (Shepherd, 2005).

The agriculture and farming industry in the developing world also needs to respond to various types of pressures. Vietnam's biggest firms such as the steelmaker Hoa Phat Group, the largest listed property company, Vingroup, and the real estate firm Hoang Anh Gia Lai (HAGL) have diversified their businesses and ventured into the agricultural sector, which is estimated at US$37 billion. Overseas market opportunities created by free trade agreements (FTAs) are among the key motivating factors behind these firms' entry into the agricultural sector (Nguyen, 2015). As of 2015, Vietnam had 15 FTAs (adb.org, 2015). The Vietnamese agricultural sector has come under ongoing pressure to be internationally competitive due to increased competition brought about by trade liberalization. Such opportunities also require increasing BD expertise among Vietnamese agricultural firms.

Consumers have become more health conscious and are placing greater emphasis on environmental sustainability. In response, governments all over the world are tightening standards for food production. The demand is rising for healthier foods and for traceable and certified foods that meet a certain level of safety and environmental or corporate social responsibility. Producers and food companies are adopting stringent environmental and social standards, organic-certification requirements, and traceability standards. In 2010, Unilever announced plans to source 100% of its agricultural raw materials sustainably by 2020. By the end of 2014, the company had reached 55% (Goedde *et al.*, 2015).

There is a concern that a large proportion of seafood products sold in the USA may be mislabelled. Concerns have also been expressed that illegally caught fish from other countries are entering the US market. In June 2014, the White House asked federal agencies to team up with the fisheries industry and foreign partners to develop and implement measures, including traceability programmes, in order to fight seafood fraud (Plumer, 2014).

Many farmers are adopting IoT devices such as sensors not by choice, but as a result of pressures from supermarkets. In many cases, installing sensors in the farm would in no way affect farmers' BD capability. The farmers are, however, feeding the BD ecosystem of big supermarkets in order to make the latter more efficient. In this way, smallholder farmers in the developing world are thus forced to be a part of big firms' BD capability.

5.7 Agricultural Big Data Projects with Diverse Impacts: A Comparison of TH Milk and Agrilife

In this section, we discuss two BD projects (Vietnam's TH Milk facility and Kenya's Agrilife) in the agricultural sector of developing countries and compare them in terms of various parameters.

5.7.1 The TH Milk facility

Some developing countries have been able to attract foreign investment in mega BD projects in the agricultural sector. One such example is the TH Milk facility based in Vietnam. A group of Israeli companies, led by the milking technology developer AfiMilk based in Kibbutz Afikim near the Sea of Galilee, teamed up with TH Milk to construct an 8100 ha milk facility in central Vietnam. The initial agreement was signed in 2009 and construction began in October of that year.

It is the world's largest dairy farming project undertaken by an Israeli company. It was reported that the original cows for the dairy were from New Zealand. They were inseminated with sperm sourced from Israeli and European cows to maximize the milk's quality and the yield (Bland, 2011).

As of March 2011, 12,000 cows had arrived from New Zealand of which 2000 were milked daily. About 300 workers had been hired. As of March 2015, the TH Group had invested US$450 million on importing and raising cattle. It had 45,000 cattle. The plan is to increase the total pastured area to 37,000 ha (Tung, 2015).

Some impressive accomplishments have been achieved in increasing milk production. A cow in the TH Milk facility was reported to be capable of generating 9300 litres of milk annually despite tropical conditions (Udasin, 2015). This means that cows at the TH Milk facility have about the same level of milk productivity as those in the USA. Note too that an average cow in Vietnam is estimated to produce about 3500 litres of milk a year (Leichman, 2011).

Big Data tools

Each cow is tagged with a chip. A warning is sounded if breast inflammation is detected and the milking machine is then automatically shut down. This process ensures that the milk is of high quality (vietnam.vnanet.vn, 2015a). One of AfiMilk's flagship products is the milk meter, which is customized for goat milking. The meter has been approved for goat milking by the International Committee for Animal Recording. AfiMilk's system uses electrodes to measure the quality and quantity of the milk. AfiMilk also produces tags to attach to each animal's leg that collects movement data. For instance, the leg tag records if the goat is moving, standing or lying down. The farmer will be alerted when an animal is lying down for longer than normal or at unusual times, which can indicate an illness (Chan, 2013). The data can be used to choose the next generation of goats. If a farm has a capacity for 100 goats, the farmer can decide which of the baby goats to grow based on the mother goat's health records.

BD and the cloud has also helped to improve the efficiency of the distribution channel. In 2013, TH Milk switched to the Cloud enterprise resource planning (ERP) platform provided by the software firm Acumatica. A single database is hosted on TH Milk's private cloud, which provides real-time information to staff, distributors and salespersons. By June 2014, all of TH Milk's 180 distributors were connected to the Cloud ERP platform. The company's 1000 salespersons gather at the distributors' offices each morning to get sales plans. TH Milk salespersons synchronize their sales data with TH Milk's server via an app. It allows them to get new pricing or sales promotions (Acumatica, 2015).

Impact

Atkinson (1999) has proposed the resultant system (the product) and the benefits to diverse stakeholders such as the users, customers or the organization's employees as possible criteria to measure a project's success. The venture started selling milk in December 2010. The goal is to increase the number of cows to 137,000 by 2017 and about 203,000 by 2020, and increase the total investment to more than US$1.2billion (Tung, 2015). TH Group's 2014 revenue from milk was over US$200 million, which accounted for one-third of the fresh-milk market in Vietnam (Tung, 2015). After the completion of the project, TH Milk's goal is to capture a 50% share in the Vietnamese fresh-milk market. TH Milk will then become the biggest milk producer in Vietnam, overtaking Vinamilk (Rabinovitch, 2015).

5.7.2 The Agrilife platform: expanding access to credits for African farmers

The Agrilife platform, launched in 2012, was developed by the Kenyan-based IT company MobiPay. Mercy Corps supported the expansion of Agrilife to Uganda and helped build relationships with other service providers and integrate them into the platform so they can reach rural clients more effectively. The platform is also being used in Zimbabwe, Zambia and Senegal. Its targeted beneficiaries are farmers who are excluded from formal agricultural finance.

AgriLife is a cloud-based mobile platform used for collecting and analysing distant, rural farmers' needs, production capability and history. Agrilife is accessible via mobile phones. In order to ensure fast, easy and efficient availability of resources and services to distant, rural farmers, the platform also acts as an integration point for financial institutions, mobile network operators, and produce buyers and their agents (Yeoman, 2013). The data analysis provides a better understanding of small-scale farmers' needs and production capability. Service providers can tailor their offerings (e.g. crop insurance, input payment, and savings accounts) based on the data (Yeoman, 2013). It provides financial institutions and suppliers with near-real-time information on farmers' ability to pay for services (capacity.org, 2013). In this way, Agrilife is a 'one-stop-virtual-agri-info-shop' (CTA, 2014). Agrilife reduces transaction costs by linking various value-chain actors.

Service providers tailor offerings such as insurance, input payments and savings accounts. Uganda's Farmers Centre (FACE) was an early adopter of Agrilife. FACE started uploading information on its 10,000 farmer clients, who travel long distances to purchase inputs and aggregate their produce at FACE warehouses for processing/sale. Before using Agrilife, FACE collected information by paper-based questionnaires. The data had been stored on a computer, which had crashed. Transaction data from small-scale farmers help them build a credit history, which is used by value-chain actors to provide credit and other resources such as seeds, fertilizers and pest control chemical agents. The transaction data are used to create and maintain their financial identities, at both the individual or group level, which helps them build a credit history (Yeoman, 2013). In the past, a farmer's needs may have been known by a field officer or a programme manager of a development organization only if the farmer was part of a household survey. Survey data also take a relatively long time to analyse.

By analysing data related to mobile money and other types of transactions of a large number of farmers, a credit appraiser assesses a farmer's creditworthiness. Based on the milk sold to a dairy processor, a farmer receives a short code text message that can be used to access credit to purchase inputs. In this way, the farmer can use the future production of milk as collateral. When a farmer sells milk, a Bluetooth-enabled digital scale is used. The transaction's 'weight details' are also transferred to the platform, which minimizes data discrepancies (CTA, 2014). In this way, digitization minimizes the governing or transaction costs that are associated with opportunistic behaviours and uncertainty (Williamson, 1979, 1985; Rindfleisch and Heide, 1997).

Agrilife also offers a social networking application, which links smallholder farmers with traders and other players in the value chain. The social networking application, known as USSD, facilitates the identification of new opportunities for users. It also helps to generate new sources of revenue for mobile operators and local partners.

Impact

By September 2013, AgriLife had facilitated over US$2 million in revolving credit lines to about 120,000 small-scale farmers in Kenya and Uganda (AKCP, 2013). As of mid-2014, AgriLife's business turnover had exceeded US$18 million (fin4ag.org, 2014).

5.7.3 A comparison of Agrilife platform and TH Milk facility

Both Agrilife and the TH Milk facility contribute to the growth of the local dairy industries, but in quite different ways. Agrilife's main use of BD is in expanding smallholder farmers' access to market, finance and inputs. The TH Milk facility, on the other hand, is a massive capital-intensive mega project that uses BD to modernize the milk production process. Table 5.2 compares these two projects in terms of a number of indicators.

Not all firms are created equal. To highlight the contrasts between BD deployments in Agrilife and TH Milk facility, we might detour briefly to point out that their entrepreneurial impacts are of a different nature.

Entrepreneurial impacts reflect the value created by entrepreneurs and entrepreneurship and are the ultimate objectives that policy makers want to accomplish. Various objectives such as job creation, economic growth, poverty reduction and the formalization of the informal sector have been identified (Ahmad and Hoffman, 2008). The nature of impacts may vary across BD projects. While some developing economies have experienced significant economic growth, the lack of mechanisms to trickle down the benefits to the poor represents a fundamental

Table 5.2. A comparison of Big Data deployment in Agrilife and TH Milk facility.

	Agrilife	TH Milk facility
Local input in the design of the BD system	High	Low
Mechanisms associated with entrepreneurial impacts	Economic growth via higher productivity, reducing poverty, formalizing informal businesses	Economic growth via higher productivity
Capital intensiveness	Low	High
Main sources of data	Transaction data from the farmers	IoT
Targeted beneficiaries	Smallholder farmers	Vietnamese consumers
Key concerns and challenges faced in the implementation	A significant proportion of farmers in the targeted countries still lack access to mobile phones. Privacy concerns of farmers' data	Vietnam's lack of a professional knowledge related to dairy farming Lack of physical infrastructures Negative environmental impacts

BD, Big Data; IoT, Internet of Things.

challenge facing them. The benefits of economic growth in most developing economies are highly concentrated and disproportionately distributed to the well-connected and wealthiest individuals. In this regard, mega BD projects such as those implemented by TH Milk, notwithstanding overall positive impacts on economic growth, may have limited effects on poverty reduction.

BD projects such as Agrilife could be more effective in reducing poverty than mega-projects such as TH Milk. Informal businesses often tend to avoid attention and like to keep their activities secret. Digitization of their economic activities, however, forces them to be more transparent. In this way, BD can also provide incentives and pressures for small informal businesses to formalize.

In general, the proportion of informal economy tends to be higher if a country is economically less developed. A large informal sector significantly reduces a country's development potential and acts as a constraining factor in fighting against poverty. Various potential advantages to formal sector participation include police and judicial protection (and less vulnerability to corruption and the demand for bribes), access to formal credit institutions, and the ability to use formal labour contracts (economist.com, 2009). Formal sector participation also leads to greater access to a wider marketplace, including foreign markets that would allow these businesses to specialize and make them more productive and competitive. Most informal businesses pay lower wages and have lower growth rates than formal businesses. They also have poorer safety records, are less likely to pay taxes and are targets of corrupt government officials (Schneider and Enste, 2000).

BD projects face a range of concerns, challenges and problems. In the case of Agrilife, a significant proportion of farmers in the targeted countries still lack access to mobile phones. According to International Telecommunications Union's statistics page (ITU, ND), Kenya's and Uganda's mobile phone penetration rates in 2014 were 73.8% and 52.4%. Privacy concerns in the TH Milk facility are low because the data are mainly collected from animals, but privacy concerns are evident for farmers' data in Agrilife.

For a mega BD project such as TH Milk, environmental concerns also deserve attention. According to the US Environmental Protection Agency, a dairy operation with 2500 cows creates as much waste as a city of 400,000 people (MacDonald, 2014). This means that TH Milk could be producing as much waste as 22 million people.

TH Milk's case indicates that Vietnam severely lacked the key ingredients needed to successfully deploy mega BD projects. For instance, the lack of professionals such as veterinarians as well as animal health products and other critical resources such as medicines and vaccines significantly increased the costs of the project. This fundamental reality needs to be kept in mind in the launch of big BD projects.

BD projects do not exist in a vacuum. It was reported that all the infrastructure needed for TH Milk in Vietnam, including veterinarians, medicines and vaccines, were built around this project. This included unloading the cows at the port (Udasin, 2015). In order to reduce costs, Vietnamese dairy farmers are being trained and given as much responsibility as possible (Bland, 2011).

Another challenge that TH Milk faced was the shortage of professional knowledge of dairy farming in Vietnam. This means that the Israelis needed to develop systems, manage the farms and train the Vietnamese farmers in different procedures. In order to teach the most basic jobs to the Vietnamese team, AfiMilk uses relevant examples. For more skilled jobs, manuals describe the process with step-by-step protocols. Specially created courses in Israel and Vietnam are used for upper-level management jobs (Leichman, 2011).

5.8 Relevance of Big Data Dimensions

It would be interesting to assess the above examples related to the use of data in farming activities in developing countries in terms of BD dimensions. Table 5.3 presents how various BD dimensions are relevant in agricultural decision making.

Many BD solutions utilize huge amounts of data from multiple sources. For instance, aWhere collects and analyses billions of pieces of data every day. Obviously higher volumes of data on farming activities are available now than in the past. For instance, data such as farmers' credit history and the amounts of seeds and pesticides used were not available in the pre-BD environment.

As to the data speed, real-time (e.g. TH Milk) or near real-time (e.g. Agrilife) data and information on agricultural and farming activities and farmers' needs and capabilities are available. This means that financial institutions, produce buyers and other relevant actors can fulfil farmers' needs more quickly than in the past. Regarding the variety, most data currently used in farming-related activities are structured data. Such data can be combined with unstructured data. For instance, farmers can upload pictures and videos related to a problem they are facing, which can then be analysed by experts to offer customized advice.

Data flow may vary depending on the phases of crop growth and stages of animal reproduction. For instance, a user of iCow may experience high rates of data flow during the gestation period of his cow. For some farmers with low-end phones, their limited storage capacities have presented barriers to fully utilize

Table 5.3. BD dimensions in agriculture: some examples and explanations.

Characteristic	Some examples in the context of environmental monitoring and protection
Volume	More data are available and analysed than in the pre-BD environment (e.g. aWhere collects and analyses billions of pieces of data daily).
Velocity	Real-time (e.g. TH Milk) or near-real time (e.g. Agrilife) data and information on agricultural and farming activities and farmers' needs and capabilities are available.
Variety	Structured data can be combined with unstructured data (e.g. farmers can upload pictures and videos related to a problem they are facing).
Variability	Data flow may vary depending on the phases of crop growth and stages of animal reproduction (iCow users may experience high rates of data flow during cows' gestation periods).
Complexity	Data from multiple sources are needed to make more accurate agricultural decisions (aWhere's weather app pulls data from the National Doppler Weather Sites, regional satellite radar and other sources).

iCow's potential. For example, it was reported that a Kenyan dairy farmer received 310 text messages from iCow and his phone ran out of storage (Mbuvi, 2013).

Agricultural data are derived from multiple sources that require linking, matching, cleansing and transforming across systems. For instance, in order to help smallholders, aWhere is teaming up with Apigee, an application program interface (API) software platform company to offer a platform for apps. Its weather app pulls data from multiple sources such as the National Doppler Weather Sites and regional satellite radar and provides weather forecasts at the field level. Another product is an open-source Community Development Platform, which can be used by software developers to create their own apps using aWhere's APIs and Apigee's platform.

5.9 Discussion and Concluding Comments

BD applications have the potential to transform farming systems and practices in developing countries. Thanks to the low cost of sensors and other related technologies, monitoring of various parameters related to agricultural decision making could be accomplished in a cost-efficient manner. The cases of TH Milk and other business cases indicate that BD-driven businesses may disrupt existing business models, practices and operations.

It is important to develop and gather more detailed and appropriate data related to agriculture and farming. More granular data (e.g. for every 10 m × 10 m square of a field) and analytical capability to integrate various sources of information (e.g. weather, soil and market prices) can help increase crop yield and optimize resource usage. Inexpensive data on land is valuable to governments as well. The availability of such data can help environmental and land-use agencies to introduce and enforce regulation to minimize the excessive use of fertilizers and toxic pesticides.

When formulating policies and designing BD systems aimed at smallholder farmers in developing countries it is helpful to consider whether the end users are technologically challenged or less savvy. Due to ease of use, affordability and convenience, iCow has high retention and satisfaction rates. For instance, iCow's surveys indicated that 82% of farmers who started using the platform in June 2011 were still using it in January 2012 (Kshetri, 2013).

Among the most intriguing aspects of the data and information is the functioning of markets by matching smallholders with providers of inputs and facilitating the exchange of information, goods, services and payments. This function has a critical role in the overall well-being of smallholders because developing economies are characterized by the lack, or poor performance, of credit rating agencies providing information about the creditworthiness of small and medium-sized enterprises.

Researchers and practitioners have advocated the development and use of index insurance contracts to manage the risks faced by farmers and agricultural producers (Barnett and Mahul, 2007). Whereas conventional insurance schemes compensate an insurer based on verifiable losses, under an index insurance scheme, such as that of Kilimo Salama, payment to an insured farmer depends on the observed value of a specified index (Miranda and Gonzalez-Vega, 2011). The benefits of index insurance are greater to lending institutions such as agricultural/industrial development banks and microfinance institutions (MFIs) than to borrowers (Skees and Barnett, 2006). The loan portfolios of most MFIs are typically concentrated in urban areas. Systemic risks associated with droughts, floods, cyclones and other extreme weather-related events make agricultural loans less attractive and hinder the ability and enthusiasm of MFIs to expand to rural areas. An index would provide an accurate measurement of systemic agricultural production shocks in a lending institution's geographic boundaries to help effectively track cash flows. By diversifying a large proportion of the borrower-specific idiosyncratic risks, a lending institution faces lower basis risk than its borrowers individually.

In the developing world's context, an even bigger question than whether agricultural productivity can be improved using BD is: who is likely to benefit from the BD-led growth in productivity? One possibility is that agricultural productivity associated with BD utilization in developing countries may provide benefits primarily to foreign companies. This is because while a number of positive outcomes of agricultural TNCs' operation in developing countries have been recorded, there are also possible negative effects such as the potential abuse of their market power and dominant position. One estimate suggested that foreign investors acquired (or sought) about 15–20 million ha of farmland in developing countries during 2006–2009 (UNCTAD, 2009). The increasing globalization of agriculture and the food chain means that agricultural giants based in the industrialized world may expand such activities globally.

Political as well as economic factors are of crucial importance in determining the distribution of benefits resulting from the system (Glover, 1987). Farmers who are able to mobilize and organize themselves (e.g. in cooperatives or other forms of groups) may increase their bargaining power vis-a-vis TNCs based in industrialized countries.

The conditions in developing countries provide limited incentives to encourage the public and private sectors to invest in the creation of relevant databases. It is important to develop means to make usable and relevant knowledge available to smallholder farmers in a timely manner. Data accessibility is more challenging in developing countries. For example, in light of the usefulness of climate-related data as noted above, more investment into climate observation networks is needed to enhance climate forecasting capacity. Historical and projected data on climatic conditions would be of great help to farmers. While the creation of a database that is completely customized to meet the need of every field and every farm may not be feasible in the short run, making information available regarding a basis for even a broad categorization (e.g. soil type) can be of great help. For instance, in Kenya and Zimbabwe, while a wide heterogeneity exists among farms, they can be arguably reduced into three categories in relation to a response to fertilizers: (i) fertile fields unresponsive to fertilizers, which require only maintenance fertilization; (ii) intermediate fields highly responsive to fertilizers, which require the efficient management of fertilizers; and (iii) infertile fields unresponsive to fertilizers, which may require complete restoration and rehabilitation (Giller *et al.*, 2011). Providing advice and guidance to farmers based on the responsiveness to fertilizers of their farms is likely to lead to a more appropriate management of fertilizer use.

References

Acumatica (2015) Vietnam's leading fresh milk producer transforms distribution management system with Acumatica, 15 January, Available at: www.acumatica.com, CS-01-36-1-20150116 (accessed 4 May 2016).

adb.org (2013) Bangladesh crop insurance: helping farmers weather the storm. Available at: http://www.adb.org/features/pilot-crop-insurance-help-bangladesh-farmers-after-bad-weather (accessed 18 February 2016).

adb.org (2015) Free trade agreements. Available at: https://aric.adb.org/fta-country (accessed 18 February 2016).

Ahmad, N. and Hoffmann, A.N. (2008) A Framework for Addressing and Measuring Entrepreneurship. OECD Statistics Working Paper. Available at: http://www.olis.oecd.org/olis/2008doc.nsf/LinkTo/NT000009FA/$FILE/JT03239191.PDF (accessed 18 February 2016).

AKCP (2013) Credit information sharing: Unlocking access to affordable credit: alternative data to drive financial inclusion. The 2nd Regional Credit Information Sharing Conference, 24–25 September 2013, Nairobi: Kenya. Available at: http://www.ciskenya.co.ke/sites/default/files/2nd%20Regional%20CIS%20Conference%20Report%202013.pdf (accessed 9 April 2015).

allafrica.com (2015) East Africa: IBM Research – Africa targets telephone farmers with their Ez-Farm solution. Available at: http://allafrica.com/stories/201507021201.html (accessed 17 February 2016).

Anderson, A. (2015) Big data rice research helps to feed the world. Available at: http://blog.dnanexus.com/2015-06-08-big-data-rice-research-helps-to-feed-the-world/ (accessed 9 April 2015).

Asian Review (2014) Fujitsu to sell agricultural IT systems in Vietnam. Available at: http://asia.nikkei.com/Business/Deals/Fujitsu-to-sell-agricultural-IT-systems-in-Vietnam (accessed 18 February 2016).

Atkinson, R. (1999) Project management: cost, time and quality, two best guesses and a phenomenon, it's time to accept other success criteria. *International Journal of Project Management* 17(6), 337–342.

baodanang.vn (2015) Japanese firms seek to adopt IT in agriculture in Ha Nam. Available at: http://www.baodanang.vn/english/education-science/201510/japanese-firms-seek-to-adopt-it-in-agriculture-in-ha-nam-2450169/ (accessed 18 February 2016).

Barnett, B.J. and Mahul, O. (2007) Weather index insurance for agriculture and rural areas in lower-income countries. *American Journal of Agricultural Economics* 89, 1241–1247.

Berdegue, J.A., Balsevich, F., Flores, L., Mainville, D. and Reardon, T. (2003) Case study – supermarkets and quality and safety standards for produce in Latin America: food safety in food security and food trade, Washington, D.C. International Food Policy Research Institute (IFPRI), Available at: http://www.ifpri.org/2020/focus/focus10/focus10_12.pdf (accessed 16 February 2016).

Binswanger-Mkhize, H.P. (2012) Is there too much hype about index-based agricultural insurance? *Journal of Development Studies* 48(2), 187–200.

Bland, B. (2011) Israelis teach Vietnam how to milk it. Available at: http://www.ft.com/cms/s/0/7ee50218-50c7-11e0-9227-00144feab49a.html (accessed 18 February 2016).

Boserup, E. (1965) *The Conditions of Agricultural Growth: The Economics of Agricultural Change Under Population Pressure.* Aldine, Chicago, USA.

Brock, J. (2015) Africa Business-With iCow and M-Farm, smartphones reboot African agriculture. 16 March. Available at: http://www.reuters.com/article/africa-farming-idUSL5N0WB34920150316 (accessed 18 February 2016).

Bunge, J. (2014) Big Data comes to the farm, sowing mistrust; seed makers barrel into technology business. *Wall Street Journal* (Online). Available at: http://www.wsj.com/articles/SB10001424052702304450904579369283869192124 (accessed 8 April 2016).

Burwood-Taylor, L. (2015) Moving to mainstream: AgTech gathers $2.06bn in the first half of 2015. Available at: https://agfundernews.com/moving-to-mainstream-agtech-gathers-2-06bn-in-the-first-half-of-2015.html (accessed 17 February 2016).

capacity.org (2013) Agrilife platform. Available at: http://www.capacity.org/capacity/opencms/en/topics/gender-and-social-inclusion/agrilife-web-platform-kenya.html (accessed 8 April 2016).

Chan, L.Y. (2013) How Israel Became The World Leader In Milking Technologies. Available at: http://nocamels.com/2013/03/how-israel-became-the-world-leader-in-milking-technologies/ (accessed 8 April 2016).

Cleaver, K.M. and Schreiber, G.A. (1994) Reversing the spiral: the population, agriculture, and environment nexus in Sub-Saharan Africa. The World Bank, Washington, DC, USA.

Coren, O. (2015) Vietnamese Conglomerate to Tap Israeli Farm Technology. Available at: http://www.haaretz.com/israel-news/business/.premium-1.651805 (accessed 18 February 2016).

CTA (2014) Agrilife: Bringing the agriculture value chain finance ecosystem to life. Available at: http://blogs.cta.int/2014/07/14/agrilife-bringing-agriculture-value-chain-finance-ecosystem-life/ (accessed 18 February 2016).

Daneshkhu, S. (2016) Future farming relies on new technology. Available at: http://www.ft.com/cms/s/2/53960dd4-981e-11e5-9228-87e603d47bdc.html (accessed 17 February 2016).

dimsums.blogspot.ca (2014) "Internet of Things" for China's agriculture. Available at: http://dimsums.blogspot.ca/2014/01/internet-of-things-for-chinas.html (accessed 17 February 2016).

Dinham, B. (2003) Growing vegetables in developing countries for local urban populations and export markets: problems confronting small-scale producers. *Pest Management Science* 59, 575–582.

Doering, C. (2014) Growing use of drones poised to transform agriculture. Available at: http://www.usatoday.com/story/money/business/2014/03/23/drones-agriculture-growth/6665561/ (accessed 18 August 2014).

economist.com (2009) Harvest moon: artificial satellites are helping farmers boost crop yields. Available at: http://www.economist.com/node/14793411 (accessed 17 February 2016).

Emerson, R.M. (1962) Power-dependence relations. *American Sociological Review* 27,31–40.

farmforce.com (ND) Doreo Partners, an impact investment firm in Nigeria, signed up to Farmforce in 2013 on behalf of one of its investee companies, Babban Gona. Available at: http://www.farmforce.com/case-studies/doreo (accessed 26 April 2016).

fao.org (2016) Save food: global initiative on food loss and waste reduction. Available at: http://www.fao.org/save-food/resources/keyfindings/en/ (accessed 18 February 2016).

fin4ag.org (2014) Revolutionising finance for agri-value chains. Available at: http://fin4ag.org/en/session/agrilife-platform.html (accessed 11 April 2016).

flar.org (2014) Dawn of a new era in rice improvement. Available at: http://flar.org/en/dawn-new-era-rice-improvement/ (accessed 18 February 2016).

foxnews.com (2014) American farmers confront big data revolution Available at: http://www.foxnews.com/us/2014/03/29/american-farmers-confront-big-data-revolution/ (accessed 18 August 2014).

freshplaza.com (2015) CEO Anwood: "tracebility and transparency key drivers innovation China" Hop-on, hop-of logistics solutions for online retailers. Available at: http://www.freshplaza.com/article/151008/Hop-on,-hop-of-logistics-solutions-for-online-retailers (accessed 11 April 2016).

gcrmag.com (2013) Vietnam, Buon Ma Thuot – a coffee success story. Available at: http://gcrmag.com/market-reports/view/vietnam-buon-ma-thuot-a-coffee-success-story (accessed 11 April 2016).

Giller, K.E., Tittonell, P.A., Rufino, M.C., van Wijk, M., Zingore, S. and Mapfumo, P. (2011) Communicating complexity: integrated assessment of trade-offs concerning soil fertility management within African farming systems to support innovation and development. *Agricultural Systems* 104, 191–203.

Glover, D.J. (1984) Contract farming and smallholder outgrower schemes in less-developed countries. *World Development* 12(11/12), 1143–1157.
Glover, D.J. (1987) Increasing the benefits to smallholders from contract farming: problems for farmers' organizations and policy makers. *World Development* 15(4), 441–448.
Goedde, L., Horii, M. and Sanghvi, S. (2015) Pursuing the global opportunity in food and agribusiness. Available at: http://www.mckinsey.com/insights/food_agriculture/pursuing_the_global_opportunity_in_food_and_agribusiness (accessed 18 February 2016).
Gohring, N. (2011) Android phones help poor farmers in Uganda. Available at: http://www.pcworld.com/article/236194/article.html (accessed 18 February 2016).
Goldberg, S. (2015) Good morning Vietnam agriculture opportunities. Available at: http://www.trefis.com/stock/vnm/articles/279564/good-morning-vietnam-agriculture-opportunities/2015-02-10 (accessed 18 February 2016).
Gulati, A. (2015) Drones and doves. Available at: http://indianexpress.com/article/opinion/columns/drones-and-doves/ (accessed 18 February 2016).
Hall, M. (2012) Cloud and mobiles fighting corruption in developing nations. Available at: http://www.theage.com.au/it-pro/cloud/cloud-and-mobiles-fighting-corruption-in-developing-nations-20120514-1ylsf.html?page=1 (accessed 25 February 2013).
Higginbotham, S. (2014) In China, the internet of things is a social phenomenon. Available at: https://gigaom.com/2014/09/30/in-china-the-internet-of-things-is-a-social-phenomenon/ (accessed 17 February 2016).
Hoeffler, H. (2006) Promoting the Kenyan potato value chain: can contract farming help build trust and reduce transaction risks? *Proceedings of the 99th EAAE (European Association of Agricultural Economists) Seminar, Trust and Risks in Business Networks, 8–10 February, Bonn, Germany*. Available at: http://ageconsearch.umn.edu/bitstream/7726/1/sp06ho02.pdf (accessed 18 August 2014).
IBM (2015) Precision agriculture. Using predictive weather analytics to feed future generations. Available at: http://www.research.ibm.com/articles/precision_agriculture.shtml (accessed 18 February 2016).
ITU [International Telecommunications Union] (ND) Statistics. Available at: https://www.itu.int/en/ITU-D/Statistics/Pages/stat/default.aspx (accessed 14 May 2016).
investinisrael.gov (2014) How to milk technological innovation. Available at: http://www.investinisrael.gov.il/NR/exeres/37FB305D-7A59-4096-B3BE-920D3DE1BD6F.htm (accessed 8 February 2015).
Jacobs, S. (2014) Big Data comes to Africa. Available at: http://www.thisisafricaonline.com/News/Big-Data-comes-to-Africa (accessed 17 February 2016).
Kalan, J. (2013) Tech fix for Africa's big farming challenge. Available at: http://www.bbc.com/future/story/20130408-tech-taps-africas-farm-potential (accessed 18 February 2016).
Kariuki, D. (2016) The Internet of Things: making smart farms in Africa. Available at: http://cleanleap.com/internet-things-making-smart-farms-africa (accessed 17 February 2016).
Knowler, G. (2015) Chinese farmers go Internet shopping — for tractors. Available at: http://www.joc.com/international-logistics/chinese-farmers-go-internet-shopping-%E2%80%93-tractors_20150715.html (accessed 11 April 2016).
Kshetri, N. (2013) Cloud computing in Sub-Saharan Africa. *IEEE IT Professional* 15(6), 64–67.
Leichman, K.A. (2011) Milking Israel's dairy expertise in Vietnam. Available at: http://www.israel21c.org/milking-israels-dairy-expertise-in-vietnam/ (accessed 18 February 2016).
Levitt, J. (2013) Start-up nation: TaKaDu and Netafim apply Israeli ingenuity to improve global water use. Available at: http://www.algemeiner.com/2013/07/30/start-up-nation-takadu-and-netafim-bring-israeli-ingenuity-to-improve-global-water-use/# (accessed 18 February 2016).
Lohr, S. (2015) The Internet of Things and the future of farming. Available at: http://bits.blogs.nytimes.com/2015/08/03/the-internet-of-things-and-the-future-of-farming/ (accessed 17 February 2016).

MacDonald, M. (2014) Will 'Milk Life' go global? Big dairy sets its sights on Asia. Available at: http://www.huffingtonpost.com/mia-macdonald/will-milk-life-go-global-_b_5249166.html (accessed 18 February 2016).

Matlon, P.J. and Adesina, A.A. (1992) Agricultural growth and sustainability – prospects for semi-arid West Africa. In: Vosti, S., Reardon, T. and von Urff W. (eds), *Agricultural Sustainability, Growth and Poverty Alleviation: Issues and Policies*. DSE, Feldafing, Germany.

Matlon, P. and Spencer, D.S. (1984) Increasing food production in Sub-Saharan Africa: Environmental problems and inadequate technological solutions. *American Journal of Agricultural Economics* 66(5), 671–676.

Mbuvi, D. (2013) Kenyan dairy farmers to benefit from Safaricom's partnership with iCow. CIO East Aftica (online). Available at: http://www.cio.co.ke/news/main-stories/kenyan-dairy-farmers-to-benefit-from-safaricom%27s-partnership-with-icow (accessed 11 April 2016).

Mink, S.D. (1993) Poverty, Population, and the Environment. World Bank Discussion Paper, No. 189. The World Bank, Washington, DC, USA.

Miranda, M.J. and Gonzalez-Vega, C. (2011) Systemic risk, index insurance, and optimal management of agricultural loan portfolios in developing countries. *American Journal of Agricultural Economics* 93(2), 399–406.

Mumero, M. (2015) Spectroscopy analysis of soil to help farmers. Available at: http://www.africanfarming.net/technology/machinery-equipment/spectroscopy-analysis-of-soil-to-help-farmers (accessed 17 February 2016).

Netafim (2014) Drippers and the cup of joe – A love story. Available at: http://blog.netafim.com/?p=1405 (accessed 11 April 2016).

Netafim (2015) Netafim signs $17 million greenhouse deal with Vietnam's Vingroup. Available at: https://www.netafim.com/news-item/206177 (accessed 11 April 2016).

Nguyen, M. (2015) With farms, fruit and feed, Vietnam's tycoons explore agribusiness ventures. Available at: http://www.reuters.com/article/2015/07/27/vietnam-agriculture-idUSL3N0Z53GS20150727 (accessed 18 February 2016).

Oluoch-Kosura, W. (2010) Institutional innovations for smallholder farmers' competitiveness in Africa. *African Journal of Agricultural and Resource Economics* 5(1), 227–242

Palmer, N. (2012) ICT for data collection and monitoring and evaluation. E-agriculture. Available at: http://www.fao.org/docrep/017/aq003e/aq003e.pdf (accessed 11 April 2016).

Parthasarathy, D. (2014) Strategising a new approach to crop insurance in India. Available at: https://ccafs.cgiar.org/fr/blog/strategising-new-approach-crop-insurance-india#.VkKwaL_i_m4 (accessed 11 April 2016).

Patel, P. (2013) Feeding the world with Big Data. Available at: http://spectrum.ieee.org/computing/networks/feeding-the-world-with-big-data (accessed 18 August 2014).

Pearce, D.W. and Warford, J.J. (1993) *World Without End: Economics, Environment, and Sustainable Development*. Oxford University Press, New York, USA.

Plumer, B. (2014) Obama calls for a crackdown on "seafood fraud" and illegal fishing. Available at: http://www.vox.com/2014/6/17/5818388/the-obama-administration-wants-to-crack-down-on-seafood-fraud (accessed 18 February 2016).

Rabinovitch, A. (2015) RPT-Milking it: Israel leads the way in dairy tech. Available at: http://www.reuters.com/article/2015/05/19/israel-dairy-idUSL5N0Y44V820150519 (accessed 11 April 2016).

Reardon, T and Vosti, A, S. (1995) Links between rural poverty and the environment in developing countries: asset categories and investment poverty. *World Development* 23(9), 1495–1506.

Rindfleisch, A. and Heide, B.J. (1997) Transaction cost analysis: past, present, and future applications. *Journal of Marketing* 61(4), 30–54.

Sambira, J. (2013) Simple invention brokers peace between humans and wildlife. Available at: www.un.org/africarenewal/magazine/august-2013/africa-wired (accessed 25 February 2013).

Schneider, S. (2013) Five ways cell phones are changing agriculture in Africa. Available at: http://foodtank.com/news/2013/04/five-ways-cell-phones-are-changing-agriculture-in-africa (accessed 6 May 2016).

Schneider, F. and Enste, D. (2000) Shadow economies: size, causes and consequences. *Journal of Economic Literature* 38 (1), 77–114.

Schware, R. and Kimberley, P. (1995) Information technology and national trade facilitation. World Bank, Technical Paper No.317. World Bank, Washington, DC, USA.

Shepherd, W.A. (2005) The implications of supermarket development for horticultural farmers and traditional marketing systems in Asia, Agricultural Management, Marketing and Finance Service. *Revised version of paper first presented to the FAO/AFMA/FAMA, Regional Workshop on the Growth of Supermarkets as Retailers of Fresh Produce, Kuala Lumpur.*

Skees, J.R. and Barnett, B.J. (2006) Enhancing microfinance using index-based risk-transfer products. *Agricultural Finance Review* 66, 235–250.

southasia.oneworld.net (2014) ADB, Japan to develop crop insurance for Bangla farmers. Available at: http://southasia.oneworld.net/news/adb-japan-to-develop-crop-insurance-for-bangla-farmers-1#.VkMn8L_i_m4 (accessed 11 April 2016).

Street, C. (2015) Silicon valley Agtech deals double in first half of 2015. Available at: http://www.breitbart.com/california/2015/10/18/silicon-valley-agtech-deals-double-first-half-2015/ (accessed 17 February 2016).

Sudrak, W.C. and Agarwal, S. (2014) The benevolent side of Big Data. *International Monetary Fund,* 51(4). Available at: http://www.imf.org/external/pubs/ft/fandd/2014/12/surdak.htm (accessed 11 April 2016).

Syngenta Foundation for Sustainable Agriculture (2015a) Doreo Partners: creating companies, creating wealth, creating jobs, case study. Available at: http://www.farmforce.com/case-studies/doreo (accessed 17 February 2016).

Syngenta Foundation for Sustainable Agriculture (2015b) FairFruit, case study. Available at: http://www.farmforce.com/case-studies/adisagua (accessed 17 February 2016).

talkvietnam.com (2015) Vingroup spends VND1 trillion on foreign technology. Available at: http://www.talkvietnam.com/2015/07/vingroup-spends-vnd1-trillion-on-foreign-technology/ (accessed 18 February 2016).

The AgTechXChange (2015) Farmforce: a force for good for the world's smallholder farmers. Available at: http://agtech.partneringforinnovation.org/community/commercialization/blog/2015/10/05/farmforce-a-force-for-good-for-the-world-s-smallholder-farmers (accessed 17 February 2016).

tradingeconomics.com (2016) Arable land in India. Available at: http://www.tradingeconomics.com/india/arable-land-hectares-wb-data.html (accessed 18 February 2016).

Tung, T. (2015) Vietnam's dairy queen courts fame. Available at: http://english.vietnamnet.vn/fms/business/125135/vietnam-s-dairy-queen-courts-fame.html (accessed 18 February 2016).

Twomlow, S., Mugabe, F.T., Mwale, M., Delve, R., Nanja, D., *et al.* (2008) Building adaptive capacity to cope with increasing vulnerability due to climatic change in Africa – A new approach. *Physics and Chemistry of Earth* 33, 780–787.

Udasin, S. (2015) Israeli-Vietnamese commercial milking venture nears completion. Available at: http://www.jpost.com/Business/Israeli-Vietnamese-commercial-milking-venture-nears-completion-390874 (accessed 18 February 2016).

un.org (2007) Developing index-based insurance for agriculture in developing countries. Available at: https://sustainabledevelopment.un.org/content/documents/no2.pdf (accessed 11 April 2016).

UNCTAD (2009) World Investment Report 2009: transnational corporations, agricultural production and development. Available at: http://unctad.org/en/docs/wir2009_en.pdf (accessed 11 April 2016).

UNFCC (2007) Climate change: impacts, vulnerabilities and adaptation in developing countries. Available at: unfccc.int/resource/docs/publications/impacts.pdf (accessed 18 August 2014).

Vidal, J. (2011) GM crops promote superweeds, food insecurity and pesticides, say NGOs. Available at: guardian.co.uk (accessed 18 August 2014).

vietnam.vnanet.vn (2015a) TH true Milk – a leading brand in Vietnam's fresh milk market. Available at: http://vietnam.vnanet.vn/english/th-true-milk-a-leading-brand-in-vietnams-fresh-milk-market/190058.html (accessed 18 February 2016).

vietnam.vnanet.vn (2015b) Japan seeks to promote agricultural projects in Vietnam. Available at: http://vietnam.vnanet.vn/english/japan-seeks-to-promote-agricultural-projects-in-vietnam/113728.html (accessed 11 April 2016).

VOV (2015) With Israeli tech, Vingroup goes green. Available at: http://english.vov.vn/Economy/Trade/With-Israeli-tech-Vingroup-goes-green/299748.vov (accessed 18 February 2016).

Walisadeer, A.I., Wikramanayake, G.N. and Ginige, A. (2013) An ontological approach to meet information needs of farmers in Sri Lanka. In: Murgante, B. *et al.* (eds), Computational Science and Its Applications – ICCSA 2013. 13th International Conference, Ho Chi Minh City, Vietnam, June 24–27, 2013, *Proceedings, Part I, Lecture Notes in Computer Science* 7971, 228–240. Springer, Berlin and Heidelberg.

Wang, J. and Min, H. (2013) Improving food safety and quality in China. Available at: http://www.rfidjournal.com/articles/view?11034 (accessed 11 April 2016).

Wheatly, M. (2015) Feeding the world with Big Data: the 3000 Rice Genome Project. Available at: http://siliconangle.com/blog/2015/09/23/the-3000-rice-genome-project-bids-to-feed-the-world-with-big-data/ (accessed 11 April 2016).

Williamson, O.E. (1979) Transaction-cost economics: the governance of contractual relations. *Journal of Law and Economics* 22(2), 233–261.

Williamson, O.E. (1985) *The Economic Institutions of Capitalism*. The Free Press, New York, USA.

Woodall, P. (2000) Survey: the new economy: falling through the net? *The Economist* 21 September, 34-S39. Available at: http://www.economist.com/node/375645 (accessed 28 April 2016).

Yeoman, K. (2013) Mobile phones unleash farmers in Uganda. Available at: http://www.csmonitor.com/World/Making-a-difference/Change-Agent/2013/0509/Mobile-phones-unleash-farmers-in-Uganda (accessed 11 April 2016).

6 Big Data's Roles in Increasing Smallholder Farmers' Access to Finance

Abstract
General consumer and business finance companies and microcredit organizations have had limited success in serving the needs of farmers and other economically active low-income families. BD has dramatically transformed this landscape by changing the way the financial industry operates. A key mechanism underlying this transformation concerns the use of BD in assessing, evaluating and refining the creditworthiness of potential borrowers. Case studies of developing world-based BD companies involved in this business are discussed. This chapter looks at various categories of personal financial and non-financial information that are being used as proxy measures for a potential borrower's identity, ability to repay and willingness to repay. It also provides a glimpse at the role of BD in enabling and incentivizing smallholder farmers to participate in the market. Also discussed are various risks and challenges.

6.1 Introduction

Disadvantaged groups in developing countries (e.g. smallholder farmers) often lack access to financial services. For instance, whereas 65% of Africa's labour force is in agriculture, less than 1% of commercial bank loans are estimated to go to this sector. Information asymmetry has been recognized as a major problem facing consumers and small businesses in the developing world. Only a few participants in Africa are reported to have the kind of data needed to take advantage of trading relationships between the producer and the market (Mohammad, 2015).

A related point is that poor people are often forced to pay a premium for credit or savings. A complete lack of access to financial products such as insurance for their crops, livestock or lives is of even bigger concern. We noted in Chapter 1 that 15-month-old Latifa Ramadani of Palembang, Indonesia, died due to respiratory infection. Latifa did not have health insurance. It was reported that Latifa was moved from intensive care in one of the city's modern hospitals to a lower-quality facility because her parents could not pay her medical bills (mongabay.com, 2015).

In many cases, the problem is not the lack of cash with banks and other financial institutions, but the lack of sufficient information to assess the creditworthiness of disadvantaged groups. For instance, it is reported that big banks in China such as China Construction Bank (CCB) have a lot of money to lend and are looking for attractive borrowers (Rabinovitch, 2013). These banks, however, lack information to assess the creditworthiness of potential borrowers. In general, most developing economies are characterized by the lack or poor performance of credit-rating agencies to provide information about the creditworthiness of disadvantaged groups such as farmers and small to medium-sized enterprises (SMEs). A national credit bureau would collect and distribute reliable credit information and hence increase transparency and minimize banks' lending risks. This situation puts smallholder farmers in a disadvantaged position in the credit market. This is because SMEs tend to be more informationally opaque than large corporations because the former often lack certified audited financial statements and thus it is difficult for banks to assess or monitor the financial conditions (Kshetri, 2014). Thus, an important reason why smallholder farmers face barriers to access financial products concerns informational opacity (Stiglitz and Weiss, 1981).

In that connection, it is relevant to note that of the estimated 570 million farms in the world, more than 500 million are family farms. A key characteristic of family farms is that they are tiny in size. It is estimated that 400 million farmers own less than 1 ha, and 475 million own less than 2 ha of land. A study of a sample of 30 countries indicated that family farms produce more than 80% of the food in these countries (fao.org, 2014). Studies have indicated that the average farm size tends to be smaller in developing countries than in developed countries (Eastwood *et al.*, 2010). This means that most farmers in the developing world have an extremely limited choice of financial services due primarily to their size.

The lack of insurance to cover the cost of damage caused by adverse weather is often a bigger roadblock than the lack of credit in farmers' decisions to expand their businesses. A field study conducted with different groups of farmers in Ghana gave the participants cash grants, which could be used in funding investments in farm inputs, crop insurance, or both. The participants with crop insurance invested more in agricultural inputs such as chemicals, land preparation and labour. On average, they spent US$266 more on cultivation compared to the farmers without insurance (Jake and Rodger, 2014). The results of this experiment and other studies and anecdotal evidence indicate that agricultural insurance is likely to play a key role in unleashing entrepreneurial spirit among farmers by promoting risk-taking behaviours and allowing farmers to cope with unexpected shocks and stresses.

Most farmers are not in a position to hedge risks and uncertainties due to the lack of such insurance products. In Tanzania, for instance, uninsured small-scale farmers tend to plant only crops that they can eat such as maize, rice, wheat and cassava. Such crops offer smaller returns than cash crops such as coffee, tea, cotton, cashews, sisal, cloves and pyrethrum. Likewise, in Uganda, uninsured poor farmers are unable to lock in future prices for their crops. Such farmers are less likely to invest in high-return crops such as coffee due to uncertainties as to how much they will get paid (economist.com, 2014a). It is worth noting that in Vietnam, an average family earns just US$100 a month from cultivating rice in An Giang province, which is at the heart of the Mekong delta. This amount is about one-fifth of what coffee-growers earn in Vietnam's Central Highlands (economist.com, 2014a).

BD is evolving as a key force that has the potential to promote access to finance in disadvantaged economic groups. Kshetri (2016) reported that BD is playing a key role in expanding access to financial services in China. In August 2015, the Agricultural Bank of China announced a plan to expand its farming finance policy to all of its county branches in order to serve rural businesses in a better way. The bank will establish a specialized department with trained staff to serve agro-related business at the bank's major levels (Xueqing, 2015). It is worth noting that the bank's activities are becoming increasingly data-driven, and it has generated extensive amounts of information on its customers. The bank was estimated to generate 100 TB of structured data and 1 PB of unstructured data in 2014 (ABC, 2014).

Some foundations for BD-based credit expansion have already been laid down. As of mid-2014, there were 242 mobile-enabled e-money providers that operated in 89 countries and served 203 million customers. In nine African countries (Cameroon, the Democratic Republic of Congo, Gabon, Kenya, Madagascar, Tanzania, Uganda, Zambia and Zimbabwe), there were more mobile money accounts than bank accounts (Mirani, 2014).

6.2 Diverse Models and Multiple Approaches to Assess Creditworthiness

BD companies operating in the developing world utilize business models and algorithms of various degrees of complexity, sophistication and capability. The credit product offered for prepaid mobile phone users who run out of airtime is a widely used form of credit. Most airtime advances are less than US$1. Using prepaid mobile phone data, companies such as Tiaxa and MODE provide immediate nano-credits if customers run out of airtime (Ehrbeck, 2015). It was reported that Tiaxa makes 50 million small airtime credits every month for various mobile operators. Tiaxa was reported to be building a team in order to expand its analytics services to support lenders' decisions for larger loans (Herrera, 2014).

The procedures and mechanisms for rating creditworthiness of farmers have been based on various models of consumer behaviour and environmental quality. The Kenyan-based Gro Ventures group is working on a data platform that integrates information on crops and environmental factors to improve credit models, which would increase a bank's confidence to lend to farmers. An offering based on the platform allows multiple farmers to pool their data to apply for collective loans so that they can buy tractors and other equipment (Korte, 2014). Gro Ventures is creating a network of farmers whose data are collected to create credit models. Gro Ventures describes its model as the social relationship aspect of micro-lending. The company aims to focus on larger-sized loans, which will lower the cost of capital (Byme, 2013).

As noted in Chapter 1, some BD companies based in the developing world (e.g. Alibaba) are constantly sharpening and renewing their ability to stay at the cutting edge of new developments. BD technologies of Alibaba have a broad market potential. Other BD providers have targeted a narrower market segment. For instance, business management software provider Kopo has started offering a credit advance to small businesses, known as Grow, which is based on their sales records (kopokopo.com, 2015). The size of a loan is determined by a merchant's transaction history and over 150 other factors (Kaffenberger and Lyon, 2015). Likewise, the Zambia-based Zoona creates profiles for all new agents on the Kiva website so that they can receive start-up funding. Before this partnership, Zoona relied on agents who already had an income or savings to cover their initial costs. Now, Zoona calculates the exact amount of funding that an agent needs based on the cost of a kiosk, and an affordable minimum monthly payment based on the agent's expected commission (Gray, 2015). This means that people all over the world can crowdfund Zoona agents. As of September 2015, Zoona had a presence in South Africa, Zambia and Malawi and was focusing on Ghana and Mozambique (Tredger, 2015). It had 1000 operating outlets in Zambia.

6.3 Big Data Companies Operating in the Developing World

In this section, we discuss a number of big data companies operating in the developing world that have used various models in order to evaluate the creditworthiness of individuals and businesses.

6.2.1 Cignifi

US-based Cignifi (Cambridge, MA) provides credit scores for people that lack traditional credit histories, which helps them to get access to financial services. The company mainly relies on mobile phone behavioural data. A technology developed by the company can recognize patterns in consumers' phone-calls, text messages and data usage, which are used to predict lifestyle and credit-risk profiles (bigdata-startups.com, 2013). As of 2014, the company was working with mobile carriers and financial institutions in emerging markets such as Brazil, Ghana, Mexico and Chile. The company had offices in Sao Paulo (Brazil), Mexico City (Mexico) and Accra (Ghana) (Kokalitcheva, 2014).

6.2.2 Kreditech

Kreditech is a German technology company that uses an online platform to assess loan applicants' creditworthiness. Kreditech was reported to process over 8000 data points in real time (such as location, social media activity and e-commerce behaviour) to generate a credit score for a consumer. It then sells the score to retailers. The company's risk model does not require an external credit bureau to make identification, fraud detection and scoring decisions (Wicem, 2014). As of September 2015, Kreditech was focusing on customers in Poland, Spain, the Czech Republic, Mexico and Russia, who lacked the credit history to borrow money through other means (Lunden, 2015).

6.2.3 Lenddo

Lenddo was founded in the Philippines in 2011. As of mid-2014, Lenddo operated in the Philippines, Colombia and Mexico (Lapowsky, 2014). Lenddo allows its members to use their online social connections in order to build creditworthiness and get access to financial services (Saloom, 2015). As of mid-2014, Lenddo's network had about 1 million members, who gave Lenddo access to all of their social media activities from Twitter, Facebook, LinkedIn, Google, Yahoo and Hotmail. It was reported that a typical Lenndo credit application had over 12,000 data points that can be used to assess creditworthiness (aws.amazon.com, 2016). Lenddo mines the data to see who an individual talks to and how often, as well as the contents of their communication. Lenddo also asks its members to provide a list of 'trusted friends' who are used as references. If a member's friends have not paid back their loans, it will affect the member's LenddoScore negatively. In April 2014, Lenddo teamed up with Scotiabank to give 100,000 Colombians access to credit cards based on LenddoScores.

Lenddo's typical loans are reported to be in the range of US$300 to US$400. Lenddo, however, does not lend money itself. It charges other institutional lenders for assessing the borrowers' creditworthiness. A consumer's LenddoScores and the local rates in that country determine the interest rates for a loan. The company claimed that compared to other resources, its loans are typically cheaper by about one-third (Beltran, 2011). Lenddo loans are reported to be used for education, medical and other purposes. Lenddo users are required to fill out an application form, which takes about 15 minutes. Lenddo claimed that it responds in as little as 24 hours (Beltran, 2011).

6.2.4 Alibaba

Alibaba has developed its own credit ratings and risk control models based on information on payment and e-commerce transactions. It mainly utilizes its huge online ecosystem, which, as of early 2015, consisted of over 300 million registered users and 37 million small businesses on Alibaba Group marketplaces including Taobao and Tmall.com (alibabagroup.com, 2015).

In 2007, Alibaba launched AliLoan, which was backed by the CCB. The CCB had a lot of money to lend and was looking for attractive borrowers but was cautious of lending to small businesses that lacked credit histories (Rabinovitch, 2013). AliLoan focused on small companies. Alibaba provided transaction data from its e-commerce site to the CCB so that the latter could make better-informed lending decisions.

The relationship terminated in 2011 when Alibaba reportedly asked the CCB to pay more for its credit information. Alibaba then used its own funds to lend via its AliFinance website. By mid-2012 AliFinance extended Rmb 28 billion in loans to more than 130,000 small businesses (Rabinovitch, 2013). During the three-year period following its creation, AliFinance issued over Rmb 100 billion (US$16 billion) of credit (Li *et al.*, 2014). Every loan is estimated to cost 0.3 yuan or roughly one-thousandth of what a traditional loan by a bank would cost (Li, 2014). Its non-performing loan ratio was reported to be less than 1% (Li *et al.*, 2014).

In June 2013 Alibaba launched a new fund management service called Yu'E Bao ('extra treasure' in Chinese) to compete with the deposit business of commercial banks. Yu'E Bao allows e-commerce customers to deposit leftover cash into a high-interest fund. A few months after it was launched, the service attracted over US$1 billion in investments (economist.com, 2013). Yu'E Bao is an attractive alternative to traditional bank accounts. The annual interest rate for Yu'E Bao is about 4.5%, which is significantly higher than the 0.35% rate on current account deposits in traditional bank accounts. They also have the same liquidity as traditional bank accounts, that is, funds can be withdrawn at any time (Rabinovitch, 2013). Yu'E Bao had attracted 574 billion yuan (about US$90 billion) of funds by June 2014 (Chen, 2014).

In April 2014, Alibaba started the platform Zhao Cai Bao, which allows small businesses and individuals to borrow from investors directly. It had created a 14 billion yuan (US$2.3 billion) marketplace as of September 2014. A borrower can get loans from up to 200 investors after a financial institution guarantees the loan and makes sure the money will be paid back. Zhao Cai Bao worked with over 40 financial institutions to help guarantee the credit (Chen, 2014).

A vendor's willingness and ability to repay loans are assessed based on information such as the borrower's credit rating and customer reviews. As of 2014, more than 70 people worked on developing models for open data processing service (ODPS) in the small-loan business. All decisions related to granting a loan are made by the system without human intervention (Li, 2014).

Sesame Credit, which provides credit ratings of consumers and small businesses, was launched in January 2015. Sesame mainly utilizes data from Alibaba's huge online ecosystem. It also makes use of BD collected from Alibaba's various partners, as well as the online and offline history of transactions. Sesame provides credit providers with more accurate and data-driven insights, which can help assess potential borrowers' creditworthiness and offer loans and microfinance and other credit-related services.

In June 2015, Ant Financial Services Group, the financial affiliate of Alibaba Group Holding, launched MYbank, which is an Internet bank run entirely on the cloud. Rural users are one of the key target groups of MYbank (Asia Unhedged, 2015). The company aspires to provide credit to farmers to allow them to buy agricultural machines and tools (Alois, 2015). Ant Financial plans to issue loans of up to US$800,000 to small businesses and consumers (Kshetri, 2016).

MYbank's goal is to extend loans to 10 million SMEs in 5 years (Bloomberg.com, 2015). MYbank's data come from Ant Financial as well as from credit evaluation companies such as Zhima Credit, which is Alibaba's personal credit-scoring service launched in January 2015. In determining a user's credit score, Zhima uses information such as court reports default on debts, late returns of rented cars and transactions on the Alipay online payment service (wantchinatimes.com, 2015).

Alibaba is exploiting its massive amount of data related to online consumption in the offline setting by accessing the relevant data through Alipay (china.org, 2015). Alipay credits can be used to buy consumer goods with offline retailers. In June 2015, Ant Financial announced a partnership with Walmart stores in which the latter would accept the Alipay mobile payments service. The partnership started with 25 stores in Shenzen and aimed to cover all 410 Walmart stores in China by the end of 2015 (Wahba, 2015). Alibaba's BD research on customer preferences, behavioural habits and credit ratings is expected to help Walmart to better utilize consumer profile information. This is expected to help the company launch more effective marketing promotions and reduce operational costs (china.org, 2015).

6.2.5 Tencent

Tencent's huge online ecosystem consists of the users of WeChat, which offers a number of features such as celebrity marketing, free calls and texts, and QQ, the online messaging software. In mid-2015, WeChat was reported to have about 550 million active users, which was about twice that of Twitter (Davidson, 2015). As of early 2015, QQ had over 800 million users (Zhou, 2015).

In early 2015, Tencent-backed private lender, WeBank, was launched. WeBank carries out all services online and it has no plan to have bricks-and-mortar outlets. A key aspect of WeBank's financial innovations involves BD. To apply for a loan, an applicant takes her/his picture using the mobile phone camera and submits it online. WeBank's system matches the picture with data provided by the Ministry of Public Security in order to verify the person's identity.

The system gives the applicant a credit rating based on data collected from a number of sources such as online shopping, activities on social network sites, games and other online activities. The credit rating is used to decide the amount of credit that the applicant can obtain (Zhou, 2015).

Tencent's key strategy has been to make credits available to regular WeChat users in order to encourage them to shop at selected retailers. By the end of 2014, over 100 million users' bank cards had been linked with Tencent's payment system through WeChat and QQ (Yining, 2015). The firm is planning to launch a point scheme and membership plan, which will give WeChat users a better deal if they use the WeChat payment system (china.org, 2015).

6.2.6 Kueski (Mexico)

Banks in Mexico are extremely risk-averse. Only 15% of Mexicans have a credit card and 5% have access to an overdraft (economist.com, 2015). Most Mexicans also lack a meaningful credit score, which has hindered the traditional banks' ability to provide consumer loans. Based in Guadalajara, Mexico, Kueski provides loan services to Mexicans without any collateral or a personal meeting with the borrower. Kueski uses alternative information such as the number of social media friends to provide faster and easier credit. Individuals can apply for a loan with Kueski via a computer or a smartphone.

Unlike some other BD companies such as Cignifi, which work with mobile carriers and financial institutions, Kueski itself is a loan service provider. The company's BD team uses machine-learning methods for risk assessment using an algorithm. It analyses credit history, information collected using a credit questionnaire, online activity, sociodemographic information and other relevant data. The cloud-computing firm Mambu provides to Kueski technology and computing power such as a customer relationship management platform, and accounting and systems integration. Mambu also helps Kueski connect its payment gateways with banks (Holley, 2014). Customers receive loans averaging US$150, which average 22 days (economist.com, 2015).

6.2.7 JD.com (Jingdong Mall)

JD.com is a Chinese online retailer. As of mid-2015, it had 100 million active customers and is reported to generate an annual revenue of US$20 billion (Lohr, 2015). In June 2015, ZestFinance and JD.com announced a joint venture, JD-ZestFinance Gaia, to provide a consumer credit-scoring service in China. In the early stages, JD-ZestFinance will focus on assessing credit risk and offer instalment loans for purchases on JD.com. In the future, the venture aims to offer a credit-analysis service to corporate customers in China (Lohr, 2015).

ZestFinance reportedly uses 'tens of thousands of data points' to assess a potential borrower's ability to pay back loans. Consumers who want to buy items on JD.com can apply for a line of credit. ZestFinance and JD.com utilize data from the applicants' past and present online shopping habits to predict the risk of default. ZestFinance's algorithms also take into account factors such as the time of day the person is shopping online (which is used as an indication of whether the applicant has a job), the type of items being purchased, and the history of buying expensive items (Kshetri, 2016).

6.3 The Role of Big Data in Facilitating Access to Finance for Smallholder Farmers

BD companies use information from a variety of sources to assess potential borrowers' creditworthiness. In China, some companies use e-commerce data, others use public record data, and still others use traditional consumer financial data to determine consumers' creditworthiness (scmp.com, 2015). Shanghai-based China Rapid Finance utilizes data from the Internet company Tencent Holdings and the country's largest search engine, Baidu, to find potential borrowers. The company pre-approved 50 million potential borrowers in early 2015. The pre-approval decision was based on information such as frequency of instant messages, number of online friends, length of phone registration and use of mobile shopping and games. According to the founder of China Rapid Finance, individuals who search for photography or hiking on Baidu are more likely to be looking for unsecured small loans compared to those looking for information on cars or scuba diving. Individuals searching for lottery tickets may be risky borrowers (Bloomberg.com, 2015).

6.3.1 Utilizing different categories of financial and non-financial information

Potential sources of data and information about a potential borrower include telecommunications providers, utility companies, wholesale suppliers, retailers and government agencies. In addition, financial institutions might have data that were previously overlooked (Baer *et al.*, 2013). In attempting to explain the potential uses of BD in assessing the creditworthiness of poor people and micro-enterprises, analysts have suggested the importance of paying greater attention to three categories of data that can be potentially used as reliable proxies for creditworthiness: identity, ability to repay, and willingness to repay (Baer *et al.*, 2013). Table 6.1 presents the functions of different categories of financial and non-financial information used by lending organizations.

Table 6.1. Functions of different categories of financial and non-financial information.

	Financial information	Non-financial information
Identity (to reduce fraud)	Third party information: high degree of trustworthiness	From government agencies (WeBank from the Ministry of Public Security) A South African mobile payments company: mobile phone's nightly location patterns. FIRM developed by PERC and EMA: farmers can opt-in to provide biometrics such as fingerprints. Information about job status from social media sites (e.g. LendUp and Moven)
Ability to repay	Income/current debt Prepaid-minute purchase patterns: steady/uneven cash flow (e.g. topping up mobile phones on the same day every week) Estimates of future production (collateral)	The number of social media friends of a borrower (e.g. LendUp and Moven) Reputation of social media friends Frequency of interaction on social media Hobbies (e.g. time spent playing video games) Mobility: passing by more than two mobile phone masts during the week
Willingness to repay	Past credit experience Utility bill payment history	Items bought (e.g. buying diapers = responsibility) Customer reviews (in the case of an organization) Books read RevolutionCredit: participation in enhanced education

EMA, Experian MicroAnalytics; FIRM, Financial Identity Risk Management.

Identity

Identity-related information helps to ensure that the state or fact about a potential borrower is the same as that which is provided or described by the borrower. Such information helps reduce potential frauds. The San Francisco, California-based online-only direct lender of small-dollar amounts, LendUp, and the New York-based mobile banking service provider Moven check if a potential borrower has posted about losing a job on social media sites such as Facebook (Jeffries, 2014).

Sometimes the source of the information is more important than the content. Information coming from a third party often has a higher degree of source credibility and trustworthiness than information that is self-reported by the potential borrower.

Some encouraging technological developments are likely to further improve this landscape. A South African mobile payments provider was reported to be piloting the use of location data as a low-cost mechanism to validate self-reported addresses. To do so, it looks at the nightly location pattern of a potential borrower's mobile phone (Ehrbeck, 2015). Biometrics such as eye scanning and fingerprinting can also be used to address the problem of producing identification for illiterate clients who are unable to provide a signature.

Some BD companies are taking measures to create a unique 'financial identity' for a farmer, which can be used by financial institutions in the process of assessing and quantifying the credit risk. PERC and Experian MicroAnalytics (EMA) have developed a tool called Financial Identity Risk Management (FIRM). Farmers can opt-in to provide biometric data (e.g. fingerprints) and authorize access to their mobile transactions and other data such as utility bills and phone records. PERC and EMA use the data to create a credit score using an algorithm. The credit score is passed to partner financial institutions (Babcock and Satham, 2014).

Ability to repay

In order to determine the ability to repay a loan, possession of the means need to be assessed. Factors such as income and current debt load are some examples of proxies. Various measures of stability are being employed to predict the ability to repay. For instance, LendUp uses the frequency of social media interactions of a borrower as an indicator of stability (sjnewsonline.com, 2013). Accion is reported to be working with companies whose data suggest that individuals living in a rural area who top up their mobile phones on the same day every week and who pass by more than two mobile phone masts during the week are likely to have more reliable financial habits than those who top up irregularly and do not travel (economist.com, 2014b).

Various proxies of social capital are also being used as a measure of a user's ability to repay. Some researchers have measured a person's social capital by counting the number of contacts to specific groups or individuals (Glaeser *et al.*, 2001). The idea here is that creating and maintaining contacts with people or groups entail investment of time and other resources (Becker, 1964). LendUp and Moven take into account the number of social media friends a borrower has as a proxy for the ability to pay (Jeffries, 2014).

This simple counting, however, can be considered to be only a crude measure of social capital. In order to refine this measure, BD lending companies are relying on the quality of the contacts. Some BD companies use the reputation of social media friends to predict a user's ability to repay. The principle is that a borrower's likelihood can be predicted by her/his friends' credit reputation (Cullerton, 2013).

Willingness to repay

Possession of the means, however, may not be a sufficient condition to repay a loan. It is also important to assess whether the borrower has a strong disposition or inclination towards paying down debt. Past credit history and payment behaviour of a borrower are used to assess the willingness to repay.

Financial and technology companies are launching services that are likely to help consumers address challenging behaviours and learn new behaviours so that they will be assessed favourably in terms of the willingness to repay. One such example is RevolutionCredit, whose long-term vision is to promote financial inclusion in the developed as well as emerging markets. RevolutionCredit describes its programme to be like 'traffic school' for credit. Customers can participate in enhanced education to compensate for a minor mistake. The company offers bite-sized, 'gamified' financial education videos at the point of transaction in order to improve individuals' use of credit cards. Customers can improve their credit by watching a series of 1-minute videos and passing corresponding tests (Faz and Noor, 2014). Accion, which as of 2015 helped create 63 microfinance institutions in 32 countries, invested US$10 million in RevolutionCredit (prnewswire.com, 2014).

6.3.2 The role of BD in reducing information opacity and transaction costs

Table 6.2 presents the role of BD in reducing information opacity and transaction costs and compares the approaches of some of the BD firms. As is clear, various sources of data are being used to reduce information opacity. For instance, CreditEase utilizes data obtained from spot investigations and other sources. It uses BD to assess farmers' credit capabilities. The company's research in Gansu province indicated that about 70% of the people in rural areas used smartphones, which is considered to be the foundation for Internet finance. CreditEase started its focus on China's rural areas from 2009. As of early 2015, the CreditEase platform had disbursed a cumulative loan of more than 900 million yuan through its service outlets in Gansu, Shaanxi, Yunnan and Sichuan provinces, and the Inner Mongolia autonomous region (Xiao, 2015).

Transaction costs are reduced by digitizing the activities and/or minimizing or completely eliminating physical interactions between the lender and the borrower. For instance, the lack of an instantaneous credit-scoring tool means that lenders need to go to people's homes and places of business and evaluate net worth and ability to repay. The Canadian firm First Access has developed a cloud-based platform for the Tanzanian market that analyses how often a potential borrower replenishes airtime, buys data and interacts with social networks. The

Table 6.2. The role of BD in reducing information opacity and transaction costs.

	Reducing information opacity	Reducing transaction costs
Kilimo Salama	Modernized solar power and computerized gauges/farmers linked to nearest weather station Data from satellite	All transactions via mobile phones No requirement to file a claim No farm visits
Kueski	Partnership with Mambu BD team: machine-learning methods using an algorithm. Alternative information	Applying for a loan: computer/smartphone No personal meeting with the borrower
Alibaba	Proprietary data: online purchasing habits/creditworthiness ODPS Data from various platforms/partners, online/offline history of transactions Scoring system–online/offline data	No human intervention My bank: Internet-only bank

BD, Big Data; ODPS, open data processing service.

company charges about US$1.25 per transaction to lenders. Using the information provided by First Access, lenders, on average, are reported to save between US$12 and US$16 per evaluation (Browdie, 2013).

The costs associated with collecting small cash payments act as a barrier for financial institutions to offer services to poor or rural consumers. According to the Consultative Group to Assist the Poor, digitizing these transactions with mobile money accounts can reduce the cost of these payments to US$0.10 per transaction (Faz and Noor, 2014). The rapid diffusion of mobile phones and advances in cloud-computing and data-crunching technologies have lowered the cost of lending money, as well as moving and storing money, to poor people. Thanks to these innovations and advances, a number of financial services such as mobile wallets, crop insurance and new types of microloans are available to poor people. For instance, time saving is a major benefit of the M-PESA system. It is estimated that each M-PESA transaction requires 2 to 3 hours of time and costs US$3 if it is processed through the traditional financial channels (Schwartz, 2014). Likewise, M-Shwari allows customers to use mobile phones to deposit savings into 'locked' accounts. The savings can be unlocked on a specific date, such as the day when school fees for their children need to be paid (economist.com, 2014b).

6.4 Enabling and Incentivizing Smallholder Farmers to Participate in the Market

One strategy for the rural poor to diversify incomes and assets is to participate in economic activities in the non-agricultural sector, which helps them to manage risks. Rural populations in developing countries with a fragile resource base have a lower availability of off-farm activities. Workers that are released from primary industries such as agriculture tend to have a limited labour market-relevant education to get new employment in other industries (Gylfason, 2001). If non-agricultural activities are available to absorb farmers, the jobs often tend to be labour intensive that require little capital to enter, such as small commerce or unskilled labour for construction (Reardon and Vosti, 1995).

Information communication technologies have also helped farmers find off-farm activities. Integrating poorly organized and isolated people in rural communities into the global marketplace is probably the most important mechanism (Brock, 2015). For instance, Vietnamese farmers regularly get text messages that provide updates on the global coffee market. A farmer can text 'CA' to the number 8288, which belongs to a data supply firm, from any Vietnamese mobile phone. The farmer instantly receives a message that provides the London price for Robusta coffee beans and the New York price for Arabica beans. Farmers are reported to check the coffee price regularly and take their coffee to market when there is a possibility of getting a high price (tuoitrenews.vn, 2013). Likewise, Cameroon's Mewanko Farm has established an e-marketplace for farmers to sell fresh produce. It is expected to increase the income of 13 million people. Esoko charges farmers US$1 per month to use the service. Businesses pay US$3000 to US$20,000 annually (Brock, 2015).

In China many farmers have transformed themselves into Internet entrepreneurs thanks to Alibaba's BD services and other Internet-based tools. As of 2013, over 22% of the 7 million stores on Alibaba's Taobao Marketplace and Tmall.com originated from IP addresses in villages and towns. In 2013, 16 Chinese villages generated 5 billion yuan (about US$750 million) or more in online sales and created 40,000 jobs. It has also helped to slow down rural–urban migration. A success story of a farmer from rural Qinghe County has been reported on Bloomberg.com. The farmer made more than 10 million yuan (US$1.6 million) from selling woollen yarns (Chen, 2013).

Politicians are encouraging farmers to use online retail to improve their lives. In 2014, Alibaba signed contracts to help farmers to do e-commerce in the western regions of Xinjiang and Gansu (xinhuanet.com, 2015).

In 2015, Taobao Marketplace launched a shopping channel dedicated to farm products. This means that China's 700 million farmers can buy tractors and other farm machinery as well as pesticides, fertilizers and seedlings online through Taobao. As of July 2015, about 100,000 Taobao merchants were offering farming products on the platform (Knowler, 2015).

Taobao has partnered with the government of Shuyang County in Jiangsu Province to establish a US$1.6 million fund to refine and regulate local seedling e-commerce. The fund is used to provide refunds to farmers if they receive inferior seedlings from Taobao shops that are operated by merchants in Shuyang. As of mid-2015, there were over 10,000 Shuyang-area seedling e-retailers on Taobao. Taobao and the local government inspected about 3000 merchants and offered them training on regulations and Chinese laws related to the sale of live plants (Knowler, 2015).

The role of information communication technology in promoting transparency discussed in earlier chapters deserves a mention. Jeremy Rifkin, the author of *The Zero Marginal Cost Society* noted: 'For the first time in history, everyone is going to have a transparent picture of the economic life in society. We are leveling the playing field. If this network stays open, everyone is going to know what everyone knows. Everyone is going to know what is going on across the value chain' (McKendrick, 2015). The Internet of Things is likely to disrupt key developments of the industrial era such as those in communications, energy and transportation.

A popular version of the theory of transparency is that, thanks to their purchasing power, consumers play a key role in controlling the economy by choosing the businesses that are likely to succeed or fail (Sirgy and Su, 2002). In order to exercise their power, consumers like to have information about the attributes of the products they purchase. Manufacturers thus provide information such as calorie values and the types and levels of vitamins and nutrients on food labels. According to the transparency theory, this disclosure enables consumers to make informed choices and reward the businesses that provide the preferred products. This practice puts businesses that disregard consumers' preferences at a disadvantage (Sirgy and Su, 2002). In this book's context, firms based in developed countries are in a strong position to exercise their power over farmers from developing countries. The use of BD is likely to force farmers to use less pesticide, which is likely to help them enhance the quality of their products and stay competitive. As noted earlier, the availability of digital records of farming activities plays a major role in documenting quality standards of agricultural products.

Prior research indicates that transparency is likely to be more useful when the level of information costs is lower (Etzioni, 2010). In this regard, the rapidly falling costs of collecting, processing, storing and transmitting data and information are likely to play major roles in promoting transparency and accountability in the public and the private sectors. This benefit is especially stronger for SMEs engaged in exporting products.

6.5 Risks and Challenges

It is important to look at the potential risks, challenges and caveats associated with the deployment of BD in expanding farmers' access to finance and the market. Firstly, there has been a proliferation of illegitimate lenders in some developing countries. In China, over 700 online lenders were shut down in the first 10 months of 2015 alone. According to Henry Yin, managing director of CreditEase, two main categories of such businesses that were closed included: (i) 'run away platforms' in which purported lenders start questionable and suspicious platforms, take deposits and then disappear; and (ii) a 'self-funding' model in which owners start lending platforms with deceitful intents and use deposits to fund their personal projects (Williams-Grut, 2015). Unsuspecting farmers are likely to be deceived by illegal or illegitimate lenders.

Due primarily to the newness, reliability and validity issues have not been adequately addressed in the processes used in assessing consumers' and businesses' creditworthiness. For instance, the use of factors such as reputation of friends, hobbies, time of the day an individual shops online, and types of items purchased in assessing individuals' creditworthiness may be of questionable validity and subject to a number of limitations.

Finally, there are various privacy, confidentiality and security risks associated with the collection, use or disclosure of personal information of disadvantaged groups such as farmers. Some online lenders engage in practices that are questionable. For instance, it is reported that Lenddo broadcasts messages about repayment status to a borrower's social network (Jeffries, 2014). These risks are discussed in more detail in Chapter 7.

6.6 Discussion and Concluding Comments

Recent innovations have brought an array of financial services to poor people. This chapter has outlined the economic, ethical and public policy issues associated with this new development.

Despite some limitations, caveats and potential inaccuracies, BD tools have helped increase the access of finances to poor people who were previously deprived of such services. This capacity is powerfully illustrated in China and many other countries noted above. Rural farmers in China are not likely to have access to a bank branch in close geographic proximity. However, they can benefit from Internet-only banks. Indeed, smallholder rural farmers constitute a major target market for China's Internet-only banks. Having a mobile phone allows rural farmers to access Internet banking services such as savings, payment transactions, e-commerce and fund transfers (Seth, 2015). For instance, both Alibaba and Tencent have mobile payment services which allow rural farmers to store funds in their accounts.

Nonetheless, in some countries (e.g. China) there is the proliferation of fraudulent BD firms that, in most cases, focus on illicit economic gain by victimizing innocent and naïve consumers. In particular, many farmers are more susceptible to such frauds because they lack the capabilities to determine which online lenders are genuine and which are bogus. The previous discussion indicates that there is a need for measures and interventions that target farmers and other early adopters of the Internet in order to reduce their vulnerability to such threats. It is particularly important to initiate programmes that increase the public's awareness of such frauds through education and training.

One estimate suggested that the number of tractors per 100 km^2 of arable land is 13 in Africa and 129 in Asia compared to the world average of 200 (Byme, 2013). According to the Mo Ibrahim Foundation, Africa needs 3.5 million more tractors in order to reach the average level of other regions (Ibrahim Forum, 2011). Increased access to financial products is likely to enable farmers to buy tractors and other agricultural equipment and products in order to improve agricultural yields.

The above discussions have important public policy implications. A study by the World Bank found that countries with similar levels of economic development are often characterized by significantly different levels of financial inclusion, which can be mainly attributed to government policy (Demirguc-Kunt and Klapper, 2012). For instance, regulations introduced in 2008 in India allow only banks to operate mobile money schemes. It is thus difficult for an M-PESA-type player to enter into the market (CGAP, 2010).

Public policy experts argue that there is too much enthusiasm in new lending models without sufficient consideration regarding their appropriateness. Aaron Rieke, a former lawyer for the Federal Trade Commission and director of technology projects for Upturn, a policy-consulting firm, was quoted as saying that the 'accuracy and fairness of big data credit technology is unproven' (Lohr, 2015). The questionable reliability and validity of social media data as an indicator of consumers' creditworthiness has not prevented many BD firms from selling customer data to financial institutions. While there are many BD firms to provide creditworthiness of individuals and businesses, most are still at an early stage of development and not technically mature. However, it can be expected that the models and data used in assessing the creditworthiness of individuals and organizations are likely to be further developed, improved and refined in the future.

References

ABC [Agricultural Bank of China] (2014) Annual Report of ABC 2013. Beijing. Available at: www.abchina.com/en/investor-relations/performance-reports/annual-reports (accessed 16 February 2016).

alibabagroup.com (2015) Ant Financial unveils China's first credit-scoring system using online data. Available at: http://www.alibabagroup.com/en/news/article?news=p150128 (accessed 18 February 2016).

Alois, J.D. (2015) MYBank, a privately owned internet bank in China, is set to challenge traditional banks. Available at: http://www.crowdfundinsider.com/2015/07/70665-mybank-a-privately-owned-internet-bank-in-china-is-set-to-challenge-traditional-banks/ (accessed 18 February 2016).

Asia Unhedged (2015) Jack Ma's online bank lifts off. Available at: http://atimes.com/2015/06/jack-mas-online-bank-lifts-off/ (accessed 18 February 2016).

aws.amazon.com (2016) AWS case study: Lenddo. Available at: https://aws.amazon.com/solutions/case-studies/lenddo/ (accessed 18 February 2016).

Babcock, H.L. and Statham, C. (2014) The agricultural mobile finance revolution, 76. Available at: http://ictupdate.cta.int/Feature-Articles/The-agricultural-mobile-finance-revolution/%2876%29/1392201374 (accessed 18 February 2016).

Baer, T., Goland, T. and Schiff, R. (2013) New credit-risk models for the unbanked. Available at: http://www.mckinsey.com/insights/risk_management/new_credit-risk_models_for_the_unbanked (accessed 18 February 2016).

Becker, G.S. (1964) *Human Capital: A Theoretical and Empirical Analysis with Special Reference to Education*. Columbia University Press, New York, USA.

Beltran, L. (2011) Lenddo provides loans for consumers in emerging markets. Available at: https://www.pehub.com/2011/07/lenddo-provides-loans-for-consumers-in-emerging-markets/ (accessed 18 February 2016).

bigdata-startups.com (2013) How Big Data can help the developing world beat poverty. Available at: http://www.bigdata-startups.com/big-data-developing-world-beat-poverty/ (accessed 18 August 2014).

Bloomberg.com (2015) Big Data pumps money at 500 million Chinese lacking credit. Available at: http://www.bloomberg.com/news/articles/2015-11-30/big-data-pumps-money-at-500-million-chinese-with-no-bank-credit (accessed 18 February 2016).

Brock, J. (2015) Africa business: with iCow and M-Farm, smartphones reboot African agriculture. Available at: http://www.reuters.com/article/2015/03/16/africa-farming-idUSL5N0WB34920150316 (accessed 18 February 2016).
Browdie, B. (2013) First Access, Cignifi use Big Data to bring economic security to the unbanked. Available at: http://www.americanbanker.com/issues/178_246/first-access-cignifi-use-big-data-to-bring-economic-security-to-unbanked-1064537-1.html (accessed 18 February 2016).
Byme, C. (2013) Data-driven lending could help African farmers feed the world. Available at: http://www.fastcolabs.com/3019953/data-driven-lending-could-help-african-farmers-feed-the-world (accessed 18 February 2016).
CGAP (Consultative Group to Assist the Poor) (2010) Technology program focus country: India. Available at: http://www.cgap.org/ (accessed 18 February 2016).
Chen, L.Y. (2013) China farmer turns yarn baron as villages embrace Alibaba. Available at: http://www.bloomberg.com/news/articles/2013-11-06/china-farmer-turns-yarn-baron-as-villages-embrace-alibaba (accessed 18 February 2016).
Chen, L.Y. (2014) Alibaba arm to create $163 billion loans marketplace. Available at: http://www.bloomberg.com/news/articles/2014-09-23/alibaba-arm-aims-to-create-163-billion-loans-marketplace (accessed 11 April 2016).
china.org (2015) China establishes credit score website. Available at: http://www.china.org.cn/china/2015-06/02/content_35716132.htm (accessed 10 May 2016).
Cullerton, N. (2013) Behavioral credit scoring. *Georgetown Law Journal* 101, 807–838.
Davidson, L. (2015) Is Colonel Sanders helping the Chinese censor the Internet? Available at: http://www.newsweek.com/colonel-sanders-helping-chinese-censor-internet-344988 (accessed 18 February 2016).
Demirguc-Kunt, A. and Klapper, L. (2012) *Measuring Financial Inclusion: The Global Findex Database*. The World Bank Development Research Group, Finance and Private Sector Development Team, Policy Research Working Paper, 6025.
Eastwood, R., Lipton, M. and Newell, A. (2010) Farm size. In: P. Pingali and R. Evenson (eds) *Handbook of Agricultural Economics* 4 (65), 3323–3394. North Holland, Amsterdam, The Netherlands.
economist.com (2013) Giant reality-check: four of the world's biggest lenders must face some nasty truths. Available at: http://www.economist.com/news/finance-and-economics/21584331-four-worlds-biggest-lenders-must-face-some-nasty-truths-giant-reality-check (accessed 18 February 2016).
economist.com (2014a) Rice farming in Vietnam: against the grain. Available at: http://www.economist.com/news/asia/21594338-vietnams-farmers-are-growing-crop-no-longer-pays-its-way-against-grain (accessed 18 February 2016).
economist.com (2014b) A phoneful of dollars: the world's poor need the stability and security that banks have traditionally offered, but increasingly they do not need banks to provide it. Available at: http://www.economist.com/news/briefing/21632441-worlds-poor-need-stability-and-security-banks-have-traditionally-offered (accessed 18 February 2016).
economist.com (2015) A nascent tech hub may succeed by solving local problems. Available at: http://www.economist.com/news/business/21647624-nascent-tech-hub-may-succeed-solving-local-problems-techs-mex (accessed 18 February 2016).
Ehrbeck, T. (2015) Driving financial inclusion at 4G speed. Available at: http://www.huffingtonpost.com/tilman-ehrbeck/smartphones-driving-finan_b_7011282.html (accessed 18 February 2016).
Etzioni, A. (2010) Is transparency the best disinfectant? *Journal of Political Philosophy* 18(4), 389–404.
fao.org (2014) The State of Food and Agriculture (SOFA). Available at: http://www.fao.org/publications/sofa/2014/en/ (accessed 18 February 2016).

Faz, X. and Noor, W. (2014) New CGAP research points to the potential game-changing power of "second generation" digital payments products. Available at: http://paymentweek.com/2014-10-22-new-cgap-research-second-generation-digital-payments-products-5923/ (accessed 18 February 2016).

Glaeser, E.L., Laibson, D. and Sacerdote, B. (2001) *The Economic Approach to Social Capital*. Discussion paper no. 1916. Harvard Institute of Economic Research, Cambridge, MA, USA.

Gray, K. (2015) How to get a loan and start a business: when Zoona met Kiva. Available at: http://accionambassadorsblog.com/2015/07/20/how-to-get-a-loan-and-start-a-business-when-zoona-met-kiva/ (accessed 18 February 2016).

Gylfason, T. (2001) Natural resources, education, and economic development. *European Economic Review* 45(4), 847–859.

Herrera, M. (2014) Leveraging mobile phone data: Tiaxa's balance advance. CGAP Blog. Available at: http://www.cgap.org/blog/leveraging-mobile-phone-data-tiaxa%E2%80%99s-balance-advance (accessed 11 April 2016).

Holley, E. (2014) Financial services looking up, down Mexico way. Available at: http://www.bankingtech.com/206102/financial-services-looking-up-down-mexico-way/ (accessed 18 February 2016).

Ibrahim Forum (2011) African agriculture: from meeting needs to creating wealth. Tunis, Mo Ibrahim Foundation. Available at: http://static.moibrahimfoundation.org/downloads/publications/2011/2011-facts-&-figures-african-agriculture-from-meeting-needs-to-creating-wealth.pdf (accessed 11 April 2016).

Jeffries, A. (2014) FICO may start including your Facebook presence in your credit score. Available at:http://www.theverge.com/2014/1/9/5292568/fico-may-start-including-your-facebook-presence-in-your-credit-score (accessed 11 April 2016).

Kaffenberger, M. and Lyon, B. (2015) Responsible digital finance for Kenyan merchants: five priorities. Available at: http://www.ruralfinancenetwork.org/responsible-digital-finance-for-kenyan-merchants-five-priorities/ (accessed 18 February 2016).

Kendall, J. and Voorhies, R. (2014) The mobile-finance revolution. *Foreign Affairs* 93(2), 9–13.

Knowler, G. (2015) Chinese farmers go Internet shopping — for tractors. Available at: http://www.joc.com/international-logistics/chinese-farmers-go-internet-shopping-%E2%80%93-tractors_20150715.html (accessed 11 April 2016).

Kokalitcheva, K. (2014) Cignifi raises funding to model credit scores for emerging market consumers. Available at: http://venturebeat.com/2014/09/05/cignifi-raises-funding-from-to-model-credit-scores-for-emerging-market-consumers/ (accessed 11 April 2016).

kopokopo.com (2015) We're hiring! Business development and partnership manager. Available at: http://kopokopo.com/blog/ (accessed 18 February 2016).

Korte, T. (2014) How data and analytics can help the developing world. Available at: http://www.datainnovation.org/2014/07/how-data-and-analytics-can-help-the-developing-world/ (accessed 18 February 2016).

Kshetri, N. (2014) China's data privacy regulations: a tricky trade-off between ICT's productive utilization and cyber-control. *IEEE Security & Privacy* 12(4), 38–45.

Kshetri, N. (2016) Big Data's role in expanding access to financial services in China. *International Journal of Information Management* 36 (3), 297–308.

Lapowsky, I. (2014) How to get a loan without leaving Facebook. Available at: http://www.wired.com/2014/05/lenddo-facebook/ (accessed 18 February 2016).

Li, J.P., Zhang, Y.J., Wu, D.S. and Zhang, W. (2014) Impacts of Big Data in the Chinese financial industry. *The Bridge* 44(4). Available at: https://www.nae.edu/Publications/Bridge/128772/129193.aspx (accessed 18 February 2016).

Li, X.X. (2014) Alibaba has big hopes for new Big Data processing service. Caixin Online. Available at: http://english.caixin.com/2014-07-17/100705224.html (accessed 18 February 2016).

Lohr, S. (2015) ZestFinance takes its Big Data credit scoring to China. Available at: http://bits.blogs.nytimes.com/2015/06/26/zestfinance-takes-its-big-data-credit-scoring-to-china/ (accessed 18 February 2016).
Lunden, I. (2015) Kreditech Nabs $92M to build financial services for the 'underbanked'. Available at: http://techcrunch.com/2015/09/28/kreditech-series-c/ (accessed 18 February 2016).
McKendrick, J. (2015) Why the Internet of Things heralds the next great economic disruption. Available at: http://www.forbes.com/sites/joemckendrick/2015/03/25/is-the-internet-of-things-heralding-the-next-great-economic-shift/ (accessed 16 February 2016).
Mirani, L. (2014) How to manage all your financial affairs from a $20 mobile phone. Available at: http://qz.com/218988/how-to-manage-all-your-financial-affairs-from-a-20-mobile-phone/ (accessed 18 February 2016).
Mohammad, O. (2015) Reliable data is the answer to Africa's $1 trillion agriculture opportunity. Available at: http://qz.com/501379/reliable-data-is-the-answer-to-africas-1-trillion-agriculture-opportunity/ (accessed 18 February 2016).
mongabay.com (2015) Indonesian healthcare in focus as haze worsens; NASA data show Papua ablaze. Available at: http://news.mongabay.com/2015/10/indonesian-healthcare-in-focus-as-haze-worsens-nasa-data-show-papua-ablaze/ (accessed 18 February 2016).
prnewswire.com (2014) Accion Venture Lab invests in RevolutionCredit. Available at: http://www.prnewswire.com/news-releases/accion-venture-lab-invests-in-revolutioncredit-258287631.html (accessed 18 February 2016).
Rabinovitch, S. (2013) Alibaba digs deep for Chinese banking treasure. Available at: http://www.ft.com/cms/s/0/f956b004-ffee-11e2-9c40-00144feab7de.html (accessed 18 February 2016).
Reardon, T. and Vosti, A.S. (1995) Links between rural poverty and the environment in developing countries. Asset categories and investment poverty. *World Development* 23(9), 1495–1506.
Saloom, K. (2015) Lenddo continues to grow as a social-network based lending platform for emerging markets, raises an additional US$6 million for global expansion. Available at: http://www.prweb.com/releases/lenddo/1017/prweb11236476.htm (accessed 18 February 2016).
Schwartz, P. (2014) Peripheral vision: Climate change and global development in the 21st century (Pt. IV: Long-Tail Liberation). Available at: http://www.huffingtonpost.com/peter-schwartz/peripheral-vision-climate_1_b_5591640.html (accessed 11 April 2016).
scmp.com (2015) The big score: making or breaking China's consumer credit market. Available at: http://www.scmp.com/business/banking-finance/article/1878528/big-score-making-or-breaking-chinas-consumer-credit-market (accessed 11 April 2016).
Seth, S. (2015) Will "Internet-only" banks change Chinese banking? Available at: http://www.investopedia.com/articles/investing/042015/will-internetonly-banks-change-chinese-banking.asp (accessed 18 February 2016).
Sirgy, M.J. and Su, C. (2002) The ethics of consumer sovereignty in an age of high tech. *Journal of Business Ethics* 28, 1–14.
sjnewsonline.com (2013) Are your deadbeat Facebook friends costing you money? Available at: http://www.sjnewsonline.com/article/20130919/NEWS/130919066 (accessed 18 February 2016).
Stiglitz, J.E. and Weiss, A. (1981) Credit rationing in markets with imperfect information. *American Economic Review* 71(3), 393–410.
Tredger, C. (2015) Zambia's Zoona isn't flustered by competition. Available at: http://www.itwebafrica.com/mobile/339-africa/235153-zambias-zoona-isnt-flustered-by-competition (accessed 18 February 2016).
tuoitrenews.vn (2013) Tech-savvy Vietnam coffee farmers brew global takeover. Available at: http://tuoitrenews.vn/business/8868/techsavvy-vietnam-coffee-farmers-brew-global-takeover (accessed 18 February 2016).
Wahba, P. (2015) Wal-Mart to accept Alipay in a bid for growth in China. Available at: http://fortune.com/2015/05/13/walmart-alibaba-china/ (accessed 18 February 2016).

wantchinatimes.com (2015) Alibaba unveils 'smart living' strategy. Available at: http://www.wantchinatimes.com/news-subclass-cnt.aspx?id=20150427000109&cid=1102 (accessed 18 February 2016).

Wicem, S. (2014) Big Data-driven credits and loans startup Kreditech raises $15M in debt to expand. Available at: http://technlogienews.blogspot.com/2014/01/big-data-driven-credit-and-loans.html (accessed 18 February 2016).

Williams-Grut, O. (2015) Chinese investors lost $1.2 billion in the country's wild west online lending industry. Available at: http://www.businessinsider.com/crediteases-henry-yin-chinese-investors-lost-12-billion-from-online-lending-2015-10 (accessed 18 February 2016).

Xiao, C. (2015) P2P lending covers rural areas. Available at: http://usa.chinadaily.com.cn/epaper/2015-02/17/content_19613336.htm?from=timeline (accessed 18 February 2016).

xinhuanet.com (2015) Xinhua insight: undeveloped west China joins Singles' Day shopping spree. Available at: http://news.xinhuanet.com/english/2015-11/11/c_134806559.htm (accessed 11 April 2016).

Xueqing, J. (2015) Agricultural Bank of China expands farming finance service. Available at: http://europe.chinadaily.com.cn/business/2015-08/14/content_21602503.htm (accessed 18 February 2016).

Yining, D. (2015) Over 100m users pay through Tencent's WeChat and QQ. Available at: http://www.shanghaidaily.com/business/it/Over-100m-users-pay-through-Tencents-WeChat-and-QQ/shdaily.shtml (accessed 18 February 2016).

Zhou, X.Y. (2015) A small bank makes a big difference. Available at: http://www.bjreview.com.cn/quotes/txt/2015-04/01/content_663611.htm (accessed 18 February 2016).

7 Data Privacy and Security Issues Facing Smallholder Farmers and Poor Communities in Developing Countries

Abstract

Among the key issues that BD projects will have to address are privacy and security. This chapter analyses the privacy, data protection and security issues associated with BD and discusses some key challenges associated with such issues in developing countries. A key focus is also on agriculture- and health care-related data. This chapter also promotes an understanding of the institutionalization of data privacy and security issues in developing countries. It gives special consideration to institutions at various levels that can influence cybersecurity and privacy issues in developing countries. This chapter also delves into the variation in institutionalization of cybersecurity and privacy issues across developing countries and different groups of people.

7.1 Introduction

Data and information do not exist in a vacuum or stand complete on their own. Data-related issues thus cannot be addressed in isolation. Among the key issues that BD projects will have to address are privacy and security. Serious concerns have been raised about privacy and security issues associated with BD and cloud computing in developing countries. For instance, 32% of South African businesses and 33% in Egypt have expressed concerns about cloud security. The proportion for the Middle East and Africa was 26% (Mzekandaba, 2014).

Privacy, data protection and security are also among the issues of key concern to farmers. For instance, there is a fear and danger that a farmer's data could be sold to a neighbour, a seed retailer, a fertilizer company or an agricultural corporation, who can then use the data against the farmer (Gilpin, 2014).

Many developing countries are strengthening cybersecurity (CS)-related regulatory and enforcement capacity. Privacy is also becoming an increasingly important issue. Legal institutions in developing countries have also recently recognized that citizens have a fundamental right to protect their privacy. In

September 2013, India's Supreme Court issued an interim order which ruled that people cannot be required to have the Aadhaar identification (ID) in order to collect state subsidies (Ribeiro, 2014). Note that the government of India led by the Bharatiya Janata Party indicated that it would require residents to have biometric identification in order to collect government benefits. The project had set a target of 1 billion enrolments by 2015 (cio.de, 2014). The biometric ID assigns a person a 12-digit number, which is called the Aadhaar number. It requires the collection of ten fingerprints, iris scans and other information such as a name, date of birth and address and will be hosted in the e-governance cloud platform.

Institutionalization of cybersecurity is also greatly increased at the supranational level. For instance, the African Union Convention on Cyber Security and Personal Data Protection requires member states to establish a legal framework for 'protection of physical data' and 'national Data Protection Authorities' (allafrica.com, 2015).

It is important to discuss the importance of CS *vis-á-vis* privacy. It is reported that in some developing economies, while there has been an increasing awareness, understanding and knowledge about CS and they have exhibited a higher degree of preparedness to address CS problems, there is the lack of regulatory and enforcement capacity for privacy protection. For instance, in Rwanda the government organizations dealing with information community technologies (ICTs) (e.g. the Rwanda Development Board, the Rwanda Utilities Regulatory Authority, Rwanda National Police) were reported to have departments that deal with cybersecurity and cybercrime. Nonetheless, data protection has not received serious consideration among these agencies. There has also been the lack of laws to safeguard data privacy. These agencies do not have specific institutions that are specially designated to look at data privacy issues (allafrica.com, 2015).

7.2 Privacy, Data Protection and Security Issues Associated with Big Data in Developing Countries

An implicit assumption among many practitioners is that 'privacy and strong data security are luxuries that may matter to us [the rich] but the poor cannot afford' (McKee, 2012). Some analysts pointed out that during the Ebola crisis in West Africa, data from mobile phone companies could have helped to know the pattern of spread of the virus and hence contain the disease. Expressing dissatisfaction regarding the unwillingness of phone companies and the governments to release the data, Kenneth Cukier, data editor of *The Economist*, was quoted as saying that 'phone operators are self-interested, regulations inept and politicians clueless' (Makri, 2015). However, against this argument it is helpful to remember that telephone companies based in the developing world have genuine privacy and business concerns regarding making their customers' data available to third parties.

In countries where inter-ethnic tribal tensions and violence exist or where people are living in the aftermath of a recent civil war, privacy is a genuine concern. Moreover, in countries characterized by conflict, crisis and weak law enforcement, privacy breaches may lead to a physical security risk (Letouzé, 2012).

Some argue that wealthier and more privileged people worry about their privacy and have the ability to afford privacy- and security-enhancing measures such as encryption. It is argued that the digital divide has extended to become a 'privacy divide' (Koebler, 2015). Poor people's lack of capability and resources to defend themselves would make privacy more and not less important for the disadvantaged group.

The Internet of Things (IoT) presents special security risks due primarily to the relative newness and unproven track record of the technology. There has been a lack of clear focus on cybersecurity in the IoT, which means that in the future IoT devices are likely to become larger and attractive targets for cybercriminals, nation states and cyberterrorists. In 2014, a cybersecurity researcher showed that about 200,000 traffic-control sensors in major cities such as Washington DC, New York, San Francisco, Seattle (the USA), Lyon (France) and Melbourne (Australia) were not encrypted and thus were vulnerable to cyberattacks. The researchers demonstrated that it was possible to intercept information coming from these sensors from a distance of 1500 feet away or by a drone (Perlroth, 2015).

IoT devices are even newer phenomena in developing countries. Moreover, less attention is paid to cybersecurity in these countries. Concerns have been raised about new forms of vulnerability associated with the IoT such as physical property damage (Dignan, 2016). Such damages have already been observed in industrialized countries. According to a December 2014 report by Germany's Federal Office for Information Security, hackers caused physical damage to a facility of a steel plant. The attackers had used spear-phishing and social engineering to gain access to the plant's network, and subsequently penetrated the production network (Kovacs, 2014). It was reported that the attack resulted in 'massive' damage (Zetter, 2015). This attack was the second confirmed case (after the Stuxnet attack on an Iranian nuclear facility) in which a purely cyberattack caused the physical destruction of a plant or equipment. While organizations and individuals in developing countries have not yet suffered physical damage from cyberattacks, such attacks are a possibility.

Some BD projects are being planned without giving sufficient consideration to privacy and security. For instance, in August 2014, the Nigerian government launched a pilot programme in which 13 million Nigerians are expected to receive biometric ID cards. The programme was endorsed by the payments and technology company, MasterCard. The card stores scans of irises and all ten fingerprints of the owner, as well as all personal information such as health insurance, tax payments and bank accounts. It also serves as a driver's licence and is a MasterCard. By 2019, all Nigerian citizens above 16 years are expected to carry the cards. Nigeria is arguably the first country in which a major financial institution specifically endorsed the use of a biometric card that is tied to a banking system. The plan is to use the ID system to disburse social benefits, and make deposits and withdrawals. Savings accounts can also be set up through local banks that have partnered with MasterCard for the initiative. MasterCard describes the initiative as a 'financial inclusion project'. The project has a potential to disburse government benefits more efficiently and reduce corruption (O'Grady, 2014).

Critics have raised concerns that the Nigerian government presented no plan to protect citizens' data. A major risk with the biometric ID cards is that they may compromise the privacy and security of Nigerian citizens. The government or a hacker may pose threats. For instance, the card could be an attractive target for cybercriminals looking for personal information.

Misuse and abuse of personal data and information are reported to be key problems facing Chinese consumers who receive credits from BD companies (Kshetri, 2016). Online credit services in China that use BD analytics in extending loans are being accused of abusing personal data to collect debts. One such example is Alibaba's Ant Check Later, which allows users to delay payments and pay in instalments. An online user reported that he was contacted by Ant Check Later for information about his friend who owed money to the payment service. Ant Financial Services reportedly said that the practice of contacting a borrower's friends or relatives to help with collecting debts is common in the financial sector. TMTpost cited a *China Youth Daily* poll which showed that 75.9% of respondents believed there was abuse of BD (wantchinatimes.com, 2015). Users of JD.com reported similar problems. The JD.com financial unit operates JD Baitiao, which is similar to Ant Check Later. In a question posted on online legal advice site 110. com, a JD.com user asked if it was legal for JD.com to give a third-party service his personal information for the purpose of debt collection.

Among the focus areas of this book, it can be argued that compared to environmental data, agricultural- and health care-related data and information are more vulnerable to privacy and security threats. Below we briefly discuss some privacy and security-related considerations that apply in agriculture and health care.

7.2.1 Agriculture

For many years, US farmers shared data on crop yield and soil data with agribusinesses. Their data contributed in a wide variety of ways to help develop technologies that have made US farmers among the world's most productive. Agribusinesses such as DuPont, Monsanto and Deere have developed powerful software that can determine optimal seed spacing or more accurately predict local weather patterns. In the past US farmers did not think about data ownership issues. However, in recent years there has been an increasing concern that big agribusiness companies may now control a massive amount of farming data that may present privacy and business risks to farmers. It was reported that a farmer in the US state of Indiana stores his farm records, which goes back three decades, on a computer without an Internet connection (Singh and Kaskey, 2014).

Farmers based in the developing world have not acquired appropriate tools and mechanisms to protect themselves from the tricks of potential adversaries. The idea of rare enemy syndrome (Dawkins, 1982) provides a helpful perspective for understanding how unfamiliar baits tend to achieve more success. Using the terms that evolutionary biologists use, it can be argued that the enemy's manipulation is so rare that the victim has not developed an effective counter poison (de Jong, 2001). That is, evolutionary development has not yet progressed. To put things in context, whereas farmers in the industrialized countries have had opportunities to learn from their mistakes and experiences, farmers based in the developing world have lacked such opportunities.

7.2.2 Health care

With widespread connectedness and pervasive use of ICTs in health care, consumers based in the developing world have become exposed to numerous and varied privacy and security threats. A hacker in 2012 reverse-engineered transmitters and demonstrated that he can deliver killer shocks to a patient with a pacemaker or implantable cardioverter defibrillator (ICD) who is within 10 m of his laptop (Nielsen, 2013).

The rapid diffusion of new energy smart meters poses new threats to customers' health-care information. According to a European Union (EU) data watchdog, such meters can track whether consumers are at home or not, how they spend their free time and the type of medical devices they use (bbc.com, 2012). When the data are transmitted to electric utilities or stored, potential interception or theft is possible (National Institute of Standards and Technology, 2010). Precise and frequent measurements of utility consumption allow the collection and inference of a huge amount of confidential information, which can be utilized for user profiling on the basis of personal behavioural patterns (Rebollo-Monedero *et al.*, 2014). For these reasons, data transmitted by smart meters are often high value data. It is argued that the electricity consumption data are worth more than the commodity consumed to generate the data (Perera, 2015).

In 2011, US health organizations generated about 150 billion gigabytes of information on patients (Nielsen, 2013). As of 2013, Kaiser Permanente stored about 30 PB of data and added about 2 TB of data every day (Jaret, 2013). While not at the same level as in the US, organizations based in the developing world are collecting and storing huge amounts of data. For instance, as of 2013, Alibaba's three data centres in China had capabilities to process more than 1 PB of data daily (chiconline.com, 2013). A huge amount of data means that security breaches and privacy violations are likely to lead to more severe consequences and losses via reputational damage, legal liability, ethical harm and other issues, which is also referred to as an amplified technical impact (ISACA, 2014).

Manufacturers of health-care products based in the industrialized world also collect data from patients based in the developing world. Consider the ICD made by US-based firm Medtronic. ICDs monitor the heart rhythm, act as a pacemaker and deliver a therapy to correct undesirable and dangerous accelerations in heart rate. Medtronic's ICD products have been implanted in patients in developing countries such as India (Sinha, 2010). An ICD's accelerometer can tell when a patient is asleep, eating or walking around. It also monitors when the patient is speaking or if fluids build up inside the chest cavity. As of mid-2013, Medtronic remotely monitored about 750,000 ICD patients worldwide. The information is transmitted to the manufacturer and not to the doctor, the hospital or the patient. In the case of a problem, the cardiologist receives an alert from the manufacturer. If the condition is serious, the doctor will inform the patient (Nielsen, 2013).

7.3 Variation in Institutionalization of Cybersecurity and Privacy Issues Across Developing Countries and Groups of People

Institutions and the responses of various actors vary widely from the perspective of privacy and security. During the 2014 West African Ebola crisis, the governments of affected countries also differed in their willingness and capacity to make telephone companies release customers' phone records. For instance, an emergency presidential decree was issued in Nigeria that enabled officials to access mobile phone records in order to track down people at risk (USAID, 2014). Other neighbouring countries did not take such a measure.

Whereas strong legal protections for the privacy of personal information exist in the EU and clear laws exist as to how data can be collected, stored and reused, privacy is a 'new luxury' in most cities in Asia and other parts of the world (Townsend, 2013). Likewise, authoritarian regimes of the Persian Gulf view surveillance and data mining as a means to increase their power and control over terrorists, criminal outfits, minority groups and migrant workers (Townsend, 2013).

Relevant laws, regulations, policies and practices of countries differ widely with respect to providing citizens' data to lenders, researchers, non-governmental organizations (NGOs) and other organizations. For instance, whereas anyone is allowed to check anyone else's credit score in China via the website of Credit China, governments in most other countries are cautious and tend to think carefully about sharing citizens' data and information.

Especially in countries characterized by authoritarian political structures, non-government entities, special-interest groups and the civil society are organized loosely. There is little room for these groups to influence national policymaking. Some nascent special-interest groups such as environmental and animal-rights organizations and sports clubs have placed new demands on the state and created competition for resources, attention, status and legitimacy. While such groups provide tremendous societal benefits, their potential for mobilizing people on a regional or even nationwide scale has increased the government's nervousness. Although China's industrial leaders and state science and technology officials have repeatedly appealed to the government to take the measures necessary to increase the participation of the trade, industry and professional associations, unsurprisingly the regime has responded with reluctance and resistance to accept an increased role of the independent civil society.

7.3.1 Variation in consumers' orientation to data security and privacy

The degree of institutionalization of data security and privacy also varies across countries and different groups of consumers. The Omidyar Network conducted an in-depth study of the early adopters of what they refer to as 'Big Data, Small Credit' (BDSC) in Kenya and Colombia. BDSC involves utilization of BD to assess the creditworthiness of potential borrowers. Among Colombian consumers who borrowed from Lenddo, a Philippines-based online microfinance firm, about 70% were willing to share information about social media activity and web-browsing history with the lender in order to improve their chance of getting an initial loan or getting a larger loan. In Kenya, only 5% of respondents were reported to feel uncomfortable about sharing information with a financial institution (Costa *et al.*, 2015).

The study also found that users and non-users of BDSC differ with respect to their willingness to provide private information. For instance, non-users of BDSC in Colombia were significantly less willing to share their social networking data and private information (Costa *et al.*, 2015).

7.4 Institutionalization of Data Privacy and Security Issues in Developing Countries

Here we introduce the concept of institutions' influence on data privacy and security issues in developing countries. Institutions can be defined as the 'macro-level rules of the game' (North, 1990, p. 27), which consist of 'formal constraints (rules, laws, constitutions), informal constraints (norms of behaviour, conventions, and self-imposed codes of conduct), and their enforcement characteristics' (North, 1996, p. 344). Institutions influencing organizations' and individuals' BD-related behaviours exist at different levels: global, national, local, social network, professional, industry, inter-organizational and organizational. We discuss institutions at various levels that are relevant in the context of this book. Table 7.1 compares institutions related to privacy and security issues at various levels in developed and developing countries.

7.4.1 National level

Security and privacy issues associated with BD have attained at least some degree of institutionalization in industrialized countries (Kshetri, 2014). For instance, the gathering of data from sensors on tractors, combines and other farm equipment by large seed companies is receiving the same level of attention as immigration reform and water regulations (foxnews.com, 2014).

Most industrialized countries have more well-developed regulations related to data privacy and security. For instance, in 2004, the Food and Drug Administration (FDA) issued guidelines for RFID (radiofrequency identification) and drug supply chain management (Harpham, 2015). For instance, the EU commission brought forward a draft regulation that would require manufacturers to export data in formats that are easy to use and interoperable. The bill also required the data to be in an open-sourced electronic format (Nielsen, 2013). Vendors and health-care providers are also required to provide patients with access to their data (e.g. particular images, lab results, health records) in a recommended standard (eHGI, 2012). European patients with ICDs have more privacy rights than those in the USA. In EU states the clinic that performed the ICD implant has custody of personally identifiable information (PII), whereas the ICD maker has

Table 7.1. Institutions related to privacy and security issues at various levels: a comparison of developed and developing countries.

Level of institutions	Developed countries	Developing countries
National	Well-developed regulations	Relative lack of regulatory control and enforcement
Industry standards	Relatively well developed (e.g. FDA-approved blood pressure monitor developed by iHealth)	Such standards are nascent and may take years to fully develop
Trade associations	Trade associations such as AFBF are working on data governing policies	Such initiatives are not well coordinated
Professional associations	Some (the European Society of Cardiology) are calling for more transparency in health-care data	This issue has not received attention
Inter-organizational networks	Farmers are developing networks (e.g. teaming up with smaller technology companies) in order to monetize their data	Lack of such networks
Company-specific guidelines	Relatively well-developed mechanisms, tools and systems for handling data (Orange)	Cybersecurity and privacy are not yet a familiar terrain for most companies
Individual	Farmers are concerned about potential misuse of their data	Lack of awareness and understanding of potential privacy and security risks

AFBF, American Farm Bureau Federation; FDA, Food and Drug Administration.

custody of 'technical data' such as the patient's heart rhythms and how much battery life remains. The technical data are 'anonymized' (Nielsen, 2013).

Developing countries are characterized by the relative lack of regulatory control and enforcement in the area of data privacy and security. As noted above, formal institutions do not guarantee privacy. For instance, the Credit China website allows anyone to check anyone else's credit score. Informal institutions are less concerned about privacy, for example, for IoT deployment for the purpose of insurance underwriting or rating. While homeowners in the West can voluntarily provide data related to household management, Chinese consumers may lack awareness of their right to household management-related data and information.

7.4.2 Industry standards

In some areas, there are relatively well-developed industry standards in developed countries. For instance, some consumer products in the USA meet professional health-care standards, which provide compelling economics and minimal business risks. An example is an FDA-approved blood pressure monitor developed by the health-care products maker iHealth. Consumers can buy the product at the electronics retailer Best Buy. Partners HealthCare gives patients a coupon to buy one. There is no data charge, which lowers the costs of Partners HealthCare

(Robert, 2014). Initiatives have not been taken to develop such standards in developing countries.

7.4.3 Trade associations

Farmers are concerned about the potential misuse of information about their farming activities at the firm and at the industry level. For instance, the trade group American Farm Bureau Federation (AFBF) warned its members that seed companies' prescriptive-planting programmes have vested interests in higher crop yields associated with BD's use (Bunge, 2014). The AFBF has put together a 'privacy expectation guide' to educate its members. In addition, it has drafted a policy which has emphasized that data should remain the farmer's property (foxnews.com, 2014).

The AFBF and bureaus in some states such as Illinois and Missouri met with equipment, seed and chemical companies to work on data-governing policies. They asked the companies to provide full disclosure of the intended use of data. They also asked the BD handlers to give farmers multiple chances to opt in or out. Farmers have expressed concerns that the agreements offered by companies are 'confusing' (Singh and Kaskey, 2014).

7.4.4 Professional associations

Some professional associations based in the developed world are calling for more transparency in health-care data. For instance, since 2011 the European Society of Cardiology has been campaigning to bring changes in the European laws governing medical devices. It emphasized that the system of evaluation must be transparent so that physicians, other health-care professionals and patients have full access to relevant information (Fraser, 2015). This issue has not received attention among professional organizations based in the developing world.

7.4.5 Inter-organizational networks

Some US farmers are reportedly contemplating a new initiative to aggregate data on their own so that they can decide the type of information to sell and at an appropriate price. Other farmers are teaming up with smaller technology companies in order to challenge the domination of big agricultural giants in the prescriptive-planting business (Bunge, 2014).

US farmers' dissatisfaction with BD companies has created entrepreneurial opportunities and therefore encouraged entry of start-up BD firms such as Farmobile, Granular and Grower Information Services Cooperative (GISC). The GISC is a farmer-owned cooperative that is reported to be building a platform to collect its members' data. As of August 2015, the cooperative had signed up about 1500 members in 37 states. These organizations have developed systems that enable farmers to capture data streaming from tractors and combines. The data can be stored and marketed to agricultural companies or futures traders. The cooperative arrangement also gives farmers more control over the information generated on their fields (Bunge, 2015).

Farmobile's transmitters, which are about the size of a book, download information from the diagnostic systems of tractors and other machinery and transmit it to a remote server. Farm managers can track their tractors and combines in real time and monitor performance and chemical use. Farmobile charges US$1250 annually for its data transmitter and mobile application. The company plans to open an electronic marketplace in 2016, which allows pesticide companies, tractor makers or commodity traders to search for data on farmers' harvests. Those interested in a farmer's information can quote prices to the farmer to see detailed information. If a farmer sells the information, the proceeds will be split between the farmer and Farmobile (Bunge, 2015).

7.4.6 Company-specific guidelines

Most companies based in the developing world that store consumer data lack mechanisms, tools and systems for handling data compared to their counterparts based in the industrialized world. Cybersecurity and privacy are not yet a familiar terrain for most telephone companies based in the developing world.

In order to provide additional insights into this observation, let us contrast the situation with multinational companies based in the developed world who also operate in the developing world. Take, for example, the French telecom company Orange, which made millions of call data records (CDRs) from Senegal and Ivory Coast available for research use (economist.com, 2014). Note that Orange ranked #196 in Forbes' 2015 list of The World's Biggest Public Companies (http://www.forbes.com/companies/orange/), which had 390,000 employees worldwide. Its market capitalization as of May 2015 was US$43.9 billion with a sales revenue of US$52.32 billion.

Orange took a number of measures and decisions to anonymize and de-identify the data. Firstly, it replaced telephone numbers by identifiers and the data were aggregated. Secondly, the company 'blurred' the data by slightly changing the antenna position and rounding up the timestamp of the call to the nearest minute. Note that data blurring is often essential in location-based services since the actual positions of users may violate their privacy. Blurring the position slightly may preserve key population statistics and enhance customer privacy. While the location of a user cannot be precise, the data are often good enough for relief work. Thirdly, a space–time sampling technique was used as a representative sample, which involves the randomization of time (e.g. day of week and/or segment times during a given day), space (location to which participants are to be drawn from) and individuals (e.g. every *n*th person entering a location). The company tested the resilience of the resulting datasets by assigning them to three external research teams. The external teams were asked to 'attack' the datasets and reveal any potential vulnerabilities. Based on the comments of the external research teams, the company adjusted the sample sizes. Following these procedures, the data became 'perfectly robust' in terms of privacy protection and satisfied the needs of the 160 teams of researchers. The research teams signed a legal contract with Orange in order to mine the datasets (orange.com, 2015). Overall it is a time-consuming and complex process that requires a high level of expertise and experience to correctly carry out.

It is clear that Orange is a company that is capable and willing to undertake the needed work in order to facilitate data sharing. However, not all telephone companies operating in the developing world are in a position to achieve what Orange undertook. For instance, Eritrea Telecommunication Services (see Chapter 2) may lack the technological and organizational resources to engage in the complex and rigorous process followed by Orange. The development of capabilities and competencies among phone companies to appropriately handle telephone data is thus critical in order to encourage them to share CDR data.

US-based food and agricultural companies such as Monsanto, DuPont and other corporations claim that they do not use data for purposes other than providing services requested by farmers. They keep the data secure and they do not sell it (foxnews.com, 2014). Some companies get consent from customers before sharing their data.

The data analytics company First Access (www.firstaccessmarket.com), which works with banks and financial institutions to utilize mobile phone data to predict credit risk for bottom-of-the pyramid consumers, utilizes informed consent. The process involves sending advance notification to consumers regarding the use of their information for a specific transaction. Consumers have the option of accepting or rejecting the use of such information. There have also been attempts to provide supplemental information in physical hand-out format (e.g. a one-page information sheet) (Mazer *et al.*, 2014). In many cases, however, the measures hold little or no meaning and may do little to protect the privacy of the consumer. For instance, some estimates suggest that half of the populations of developing countries cannot speak an official language of their own country (Kenny, 2003). People without experience with data are likely to give consent without relevant knowledge and understanding of the value of their information and severity of consequence in the case of a privacy violation or security breach.

7.4.7 Individual farmers

Some farmers are concerned that big agricultural firms such as Monsanto may influence them to buy specific seeds, sprays and equipment and are likely to profit from the costs of their services and higher seed sales (Seppala, 2014). Another key concern that farmers have expressed is that their data and information could be used by competitors. For example, other farmers' access to the crop-yield information may create direct and unwanted competition to rent farmland, which may cause a new spike in land values and seed prices (Bunge, 2014). The issue regarding who owns farmers' crop data is also of equal concern (Seppala, 2014).

Another fear is that Wall Street traders could use the data to make bets that could hurt the farmers. For instance, if conditions early in the growing season lead to lower futures contract prices, it may reduce the profits farmers could have made from crops by locking-in to sell the futures (Bunge, 2014). Likewise, farmers are concerned that hedge funds or big companies might use real-time data at harvest time from a large number of combines to speculate in commodities markets long before official crop-production estimates are available (foxnews.com, 2014). This fear has some foundation as the developments in BD technologies make it possible to do so. For instance, a group at the MIT Media Lab used location data from mobile phones to estimate the number of people in Macy's parking lots on Black Friday. The model they developed made it possible to estimate the retailer's sales on that day even before Macy's had recorded those sales. Insights like this are expected to provide competitive advantage to Wall Street analysts and managers (McAfee and Brynjolfsson, 2012).

US farmers also have additional concerns. For instance, if agricultural-related companies misuse or accidentally release their information, government auditors may scrutinize their finances or environmental activists may protest about fertilizer and pesticide use (Singh and Kaskey, 2014). However, such concerns have not yet been substantiated in developing countries.

Thanks to high-profile cybersecurity incidents in the USA, farmers in the country are increasingly aware and informed about cybersecurity issues facing them. In 2013, the Environmental Protection Agency, which gathers farm and livestock information to monitor air and water quality, inadvertently released to environmental groups the personal information of 80,000 farmers (Singh and Kaskey, 2014). Such events have provided US farmers with an environment to learn and become more familiar with security and privacy issues involving data.

Such mechanisms are yet to evolve in many developing countries. Farmers in these countries lack awareness and understanding of potential privacy and security risks.

7.5 Discussion and Concluding Comments

Analysts have stressed the importance of providing incentives to individuals to share information such as pricing/offers and improved services. Others have advocated the development of privacy standards and 'opt-out' ability (WEF, 2012). A large proportion of consumers in developing countries are often willing to provide their personal information to BD companies without knowing the value and possible consequence of releasing such information.

Serious economic, physical and psychological harm could arise by the potential abuse and misuse of BD. For instance, in some developing countries, publishing or releasing individuals' data and information open up possibilities of being victimized by dictatorial regimes, rival tribal groups and cybercriminals.

In some developing countries, the state's tendency to trump individual rights and the low priority in enforcing laws and implementation of policies are likely to work as key hindrances to the development of the BD industry. Low ethical standards of businesses may further exacerbate this problem. Whereas industrialized countries have industry standards, company-specific guidelines and performance measures, developing countries lack such metrics, methods and systems.

Many BD suppliers operating in developing countries have claimed that they obtain consumers' consents before collecting data and information from them.

However, due to the newness of BD and a low degree of institutionalization of privacy and security issues, consumers have a low degree of understanding of these issues. A consent has no value unless the individual making his/her decision has been given the necessary and sufficient information about the risks related to privacy violation and security breach.

The relatively low degree of institutionalization of privacy and security issues in the developing world is reflected in the fact that regulations are not well defined and enforced. Data collection activities in most countries currently fall into a regulatory grey area. Moreover, violation of privacy is not yet viewed by many consumers as a harm. Nonetheless, changes are likely to occur in consumers' orientation towards BD. For instance, there has been increased public awareness and activism in developing economies such as China regarding the handling of personal information by BD companies.

During the 2014 West Africa Ebola crisis, it seemed that some researchers, NGOs and other organizations based in the developed world exhibited a sense of entitlement regarding their privilege to CDRs and other data from Ebola-affected countries. However, it might be inappropriate to think that anyone is entitled to have access to any type of data when the data subjects are poor people. It is an unfortunate reality that despite the high degree of usefulness and value of CDRs, many phone companies based in the developing world are simply not in a position to release them due to regulatory and business concerns.

Note, however, that even world powers and rich nations consider exposing critical data as national security threats. For instance, while Google Maps can provide directions for public transport in South Korea, they cannot do so for driving. In order to block information from falling into North Korean hands, South Korean security restrictions put in place after the Korean War prohibit the export of map data. Thus, Google and other foreign companies are not allowed to provide driving maps for South Korea (Pfanner, 2013).

China is concerned about cyber-threats from foreign entities, both state and non-state actors. China views the great amount of metadata produced by smartphones and other devices as a key national security issue. Chinese state media have frequently criticized Apple. They have accused it of providing user data to US intelligence agencies and called for 'severe punishment' against the company. In a July 2014 broadcast, the state-owned CCTV aired an interview with a researcher, who argued that iPhone's 'Frequent Locations' function tracks and reveals 'extremely sensitive data'. The researcher further noted that the data could reveal the entire country's economic situation and 'even state secrets' (reuters.com, 2014). It may be the case that some governments based in the developing world consider national security a bigger threat than the spread of epidemics such as Ebola.

BD deployment in industrialized countries, especially in the agricultural sector, may provide valuable lessons that could be applied to the context of the developing world. Given their longer experience in BD, industrial countries can provide learning opportunities for developing countries. For instance, farmers in the developing world can learn from the privacy and security risks faced by US farmers. While some are irrelevant (environmental activists protesting fertilizer and pesticide use) and some are comparatively less important (possibility of government auditors scrutinizing their finances), others are equally relevant. In some cases, they have some risks that are unique to their locations (e.g. inter-tribal conflicts).

Many organizations believe that making data anonymous before sharing with third parties would make it impossible to identify. The anonymization process involves removing PII such as names, phone numbers, addresses and other personal details such as dates of birth. Many believe that such a record is safe for release to researchers, and even to the public. This is often a convenient but possibly false assumption. Researchers have presented a variety of methods and techniques that can be used to de-identify personal data and re-associate with specific consumers (Brill, 2012). In order to illustrate this point, we consider the following example. An article published in *The Economist* magazine commented on the Australian data scientist Anthony Tockar's mining of a database consisting of taxi-ride details of visitors to the Hustler Club, a gentlemen's entertainment venue in New York. The data did not have any direct identification of the Hustler Club customers involved. However, drop-off points of trips that started at the club were clustered at some private addresses. It was pointed out that by matching the taxi-ride database with voter-registration records, it was possible that the passengers could be people living in those private addresses (economist.com, 2015).

In summary, most developing countries currently have no regulatory safeguard in place to protect farmers and citizens from possible data misuse. Mechanisms, tools and systems for handling data are underdeveloped. Farmers and poor communities lack an awareness of data privacy and security issues. These conditions mean that BD-related issues are being considered in a setting of nascent institutionalization. Farmers in developing countries are even more prone to exploitation by big businesses.

Prior research in economics indicates that political processes tend to have built-in biases that often favour organized groups compared to those that are unorganized (Mitra, 1999). Farmers in developing countries tend to be small and poorly organized. Many developing economies lack associations such as the AFBF or have poorly functioning associations. This situation puts farmers in a disadvantaged position from the standpoint of privacy protection.

References

allafrica.com (2015) East Africa: why Rwanda needs a law on data protection. Available at: http://allafrica.com/stories/201509071166.html (accessed 11 April 2016).

bbc.com (2012) Warning over smart meters privacy risk. Available at: http://www.bbc.com/news/technology-18407340 (accessed 11 April 2016).

Brill, J. (2012) Big data, big issues. Fordham University School of Law. Available at: http://www.ftc.gov/public-statements/2012/03/big-data-big-issues (accessed 11 April 2016).

Bunge, J. (2014) Big Data comes to the farm, sowing mistrust; seed makers barrel into technology business. Wall Street Journal (Online). Available at: http://www.wsj.com/articles/SB10001424052702304450904579369283869192124 (accessed 11 April 2016).

chiconline.com (2013) Alibaba to transform China's 'e-conomy' with $500 billion marketplace. Available at: http://en.chiconline.com.cn/show_news_view/666.aspx (accessed 11 April 2016).

cio.de (2014) India's biometric ID project is back on track. Available at: http://www.cio.de/index.cfm?pid=156&pk=2970283&p=1 (accessed 11 April 2016).

Costa, A., Deb, A. and Kubzansky, M. (2015) Big data, small credit. Omidyar Network. Available at: https://www.omidyar.com/spotlight/what-big-data-small-credit (accessed 11 April 2016).

Dawkins, R. (1982) *The Extended Phenotype*. Oxford University Press, Oxford, UK.

de Jong, W.M. (2001) Manipulative tactics in budgetary games: the art and craft of getting the money you don't deserve. *Knowledge, Technology & Policy* 14(1), 50–66.

Dignan, L. (2016) Internet of Things security years away from being fully baked, says Forrester. Available at: http://www.zdnet.com/article/internet-of-things-security-years-away-from-being-fully-baked-says-forrester/ (accessed 12 April 2016).

economist.com (2014) Mobile-phone records would help combat the Ebola epidemic. But getting to look at them has proved hard. Available at: http://www.economist.com/news/science-and-technology/21627557-mobile-phone-records-would-help-combat-ebola-epidemic-getting-look (accessed 11 April 2016).

economist.com (2015) Can big databases be kept both anonymous and useful? Available at: http://www.economist.com/news/science-and-technology/21660966-can-big-databases-be-kept-both-anonymous-and-useful-well-see-you-anon (accessed 11 April 2016).

eHGI (2012) Discussion paper on semantic and technical interoperability proposed by the eHealth Governance Initiative. Available at: http://ec.europa.eu/health/ehealth/docs/ev_20121107_wd02_en.pdf (accessed 12 April 2016).

foxnews.com (2014) American farmers confront big data revolution Available at: http://www.foxnews.com/us/2014/03/29/american-farmers-confront-big-data-revolution/ (accessed 18 August 2014).

Fraser, G.A. (2015) Clinical evaluation of medical devices: light at the end of the tunnel? *European Heart Journal* 36(2), 64–66.

Gilpin, L. (2014) How big data is going to help feed nine billion people by 2050. Available at: http://www.techrepublic.com/article/how-big-data-is-going-to-help-feed-9-billion-people-by-2050/ (accessed 12 April 2016).

Harpham, B. (2015) How the Internet of Things is changing healthcare and transportation. Available at: http://www.cio.com/article/2981481/healthcare/how-the-internet-of-things-is-changing-healthcare-and-transportation.html (accessed 12 April 2016).

ISACA (2014) Generating value from big data analytics, White Paper. Available at: http://www.isaca.org/Knowledge-Center/Research/ResearchDeliverables/Pages/Generating-Value-From-Big-Data-Analytics.aspx (accessed 12 April 2016).

Jaret, P. (2013) Mining electronic records for revealing health data. Available at: http://www.nytimes.com/2013/01/15/health/mining-electronic-records-for-revealing-health-data.html (accessed 12 April 2016).

Kenny, C. (2003) The Internet and economic growth in less-developed countries: a case of managing expectations? *Oxford Development Studies* 31(1), 99–113.

Koebler, J. (2015) Why mass surveillance is worse for poor people. Available at: http://motherboard.vice.com/read/why-mass-surveillance-is-worse-for-poor-people (accessed 12 April 2016).

Kovacs, E. (2014) Cyberattack on German steel plant caused significant damage: report, December 18. Available at: http://www.securityweek.com/cyberattack-german-steel-plant-causes-significant-damage-report (accessed 12 April 2016).

Kshetri, N. (2014) China's data privacy regulations: a tricky trade-off between ICT's productive utilization and cyber-control. *IEEE Security & Privacy* 12(4), 38–45.

Kshetri, N. (2016) Big Data's role in expanding access to financial services in China. *International Journal of Information Management* 36(3), 297–308.

Letouzé, E. (2012) Big data for development: what may determine success or failure? OECD Technology Foresight. Available at: https://www.oecd.org/sti/ieconomy/Session_5_Letouz%C3%A9.pdf (accessed 12 April 2016).

Makri, A. (2015) Is big data the gold dust of medical aid? Available at: http://www.scidev.net/global/data/scidev-net-at-large/big-data-the-gold-dust-of-medical-aid.html (accessed 12 April 2016).

Mazer, R., Carta, J. and Kaffenberger, M. (2014) Informed consent how do we make it work for mobile credit scoring? CGAP. Available at: http://www.cgap.org/publications/informed-consent-how-do-we-make-it-work-mobile-credit-scoring (accessed 12 April 2016).

McAfee, A. and Brynjolfsson, E. (2012) Big Data: the management revolution. Available at: http://hbr.org/2012/10/big-data-the-management-revolution/ar/1(accessed 18 August 2014).

McKee, K. (2012) What if poor people do care about privacy of their financial data. Available at: http://www.cgap.org/blog/what-if-poor-people-do-care-about-privacy-their-financial-data (accessed 12 April 2016).

Mitra, D. (1999) Endogenous lobby formation and endogenous protection: a long-run model of trade policy determination. *American Economic Review* 89(5), 1116–1134.

Mzekandaba, S. (2014) Cloud computing becoming the norm in SA, says Microsoft. Available at: http://www.itwebafrica.com/home-page/channel/612-south-africa/233259-cloud-computing-becoming-the-norm-in-sa-says-microsoft (accessed 12 April 2016).

National Institute of Standards and Technology (2010) Guidelines for smart grid cyber security: 2(14). Available at: http://csrc.nist.gov/publications/nistir/ir7628/nistir-7628_vol2.pdf (accessed 5 February 2015).

Nielsen, N. (2013) Heart of the matter: who owns your health data? Available at: https://euobserver.com/news/119802 (accessed 12 April 2016).

North, D.C. (1990) *Institutions, Institutional Change and Economic Performance*. Cambridge University Press, Cambridge, UK.

North, D.C. (1996) Epilogue: Economic performance through time. In: Alston, L.J., Eggertsson, T. and North, D.C. (eds), *Empirical Studies in Institutional Change*. Cambridge University Press, Cambridge, UK, pp. 342–355.

O'Grady, S. (2014) Nigeria's Orwellian biometric ID is brought to you by MasterCard. Available at: http://foreignpolicy.com/2014/09/03/nigerias-orwellian-biometric-id-is-brought-to-you-by-mastercard/ (accessed 12 April 2016).

orange.com (2015) The other challenge: providing information while respecting privacy. Available at: http://www.orange.com/en/Press-and-medias/Thematic-features/2013/D4D/Folder/anonymous-data (accessed 12 April 2016).

Perera, D. (2015) Smart grid powers up privacy worries. Available at: http://www.politico.com/story/2015/01/energy-electricity-data-use-113901.html (accessed 5 February 2015).

Perlroth, N. (2015) Smart city technology may be vulnerable to hackers. Available at: http://bits.blogs.nytimes.com/2015/04/21/smart-city-technology-may-be-vulnerable-to-hackers/?_r=0 (accessed 12 April 2016).

Pfanner, E. (2013) Google jousts with wired South Korea over quirky Internet rules. Available at: http://www.nytimes.com/2013/10/14/business/international/google-jousts-with-south-koreaspiecemeal-internet-rules.html?_r=1&. (accessed 28 March 2014).

Rebollo-Monedero, D., Bartoli, A., Hernández-Serrano, J., Forné, J. and Soriano, M. (2014). Reconciling privacy and efficient utility management in smart cities. *Transactions on Emerging Telecommunications Technologies* 25, 94–108.

reuters.com (2014) Apple iPhone a danger to China national security: state media. Available at: http://in.reuters.com/article/2014/07/11/us-apple-china-idINKBN0FG0S520140711 (accessed 12 April 2016).

Ribeiro, V.J. (2014) India's biometric ID project is back on track, http://www.cio.de/index.cfm?pid=156&pk=2970283&p=1 (accessed 12 April 2016).

Robert, L.M. (2014) Internet of Things. *Computer World* 47(7), 12–16.

Seppala, T.J. (2014) Monsanto pushes Big Data-driven planting but farmers are skeptical. Available at: http://global.ofweek.com/news/Monsanto-pushes-Big-Data-driven-planting-but-farmers-are-skeptical-8587 (accessed 18 August 2014).

Singh, S. and Kaskey, J. (2014) Farmers press agribusiness giants for data security. Available at: http://www.bloomberg.com/bw/articles/2014-01-23/farmers-press-agribusiness-giants-for-data-security (accessed 12 April 2016).
Sinha, K. (2010) Now, a shockproof pacemaker. Available at: http://timesofindia.indiatimes.com/india/Now-a-shockproof-pacemaker/articleshow/6039301.cms (accessed 12 April 2016).
Townsend, A.M. (2013) Your city is spying on you: from iPhones to cameras, you are being watched right now. Available at: http://www.salon.com/2013/10/13/your_city_is_spying_on_you_from_iphones_to_cameras_you_are_being_watched_right_now/ (accessed 12 April 2016).
USAID (2014) Use of technology in the Ebola response in West Africa. Available at: https://www.msh.org/sites/msh.org/files/technology_and_ebola_response_in_west_africa_technical_brief_final.pdf (accessed 12 April 2016).
wantchinatimes.com (2015) Online credit services in China accused of abusing personal data. Available at: http://www.wantchinatimes.com/news/content?id=20150927000087&cid=1203 (accessed 12 April 2016).
WEF [World Economic Forum] (2012) Big Data, big impact: new possibilities for international development. Available at: http://www3.weforum.org/docs/WEF_TC_MFS_BigDataBigImpact_Briefing_2012.pdf (accessed 12 April 2016).
Zetter, K. (2015) A cyberattack has caused confirmed physical damage for the second time ever. Available at: http://www.wired.com/2015/01/german-steel-mill-hack-destruction/ (accessed 12 April 2016).

8 Lessons Learned, Implications and the Way Forward

Abstract

The explosion of data is likely to change the way individuals and organizations in developing countries act and interact. This concluding chapter evaluates the appropriateness of BD in the developing world and analyses the meaning and significance of BD. It also considers the ways in which BD-related innovations can trickle up from developing to developed nations. Implications for businesses, policy makers and future research are discussed. It argues that despite the optimistic promises that some consultants and development experts have made regarding the developmental and practical applications of BD, it should not be viewed as a panacea and the answer to all the many and varied problems facing the developing world. There is a need to fully assess availability, appropriateness and effectiveness of BD in addressing development challenges.

8.1 Introduction

Each generation has access to more data and information than the preceding generations. However, the nature and usefulness of the available data and information are distinguishing features of the recent information revolution. Developing economies are experiencing a rapid explosion of data and information due primarily to a diffusion of mobile phones and social media. If history is any guide, this explosion is likely to change the way individuals and organizations act and interact. An analysis of the effects of information overload from the sixteenth to the eighteenth century, indicated that the availability of more information led to the diffusion and development of various learning aids and tools and also affected the way scholars worked (Blair, 2003). It is thus reasonable to expect that BD is likely to have a profound impact on decision-making processes in activities related to agriculture, health care and the environment.

BD has already acted as a transforming force in agriculture, health care and environmental security and other activities. BD is being used to understand and respond to important development issues such as water supply, food security, human health, conservation of natural resources and protection against natural hazards. The above discussion makes it clear that while social media activities have important social aspects and consequences, data from various social media activities also have some economic importance. There have been some recent encouraging developments in the utilization of BD in improving farmers' livelihood and access to services. The cases of Agrilife and other initiatives indicate that BD has promoted better functioning of the market. For many businesses and individuals that have not yet connected to the Internet, however, the biggest impacts of BD are still to come.

There are only limited types of data that can be found for most developing economies (e.g. related to tweets in Indonesia and mobile money transfer data in Kenya). Data unavailability thus remains a major challenge, which has led to a new form of digital divide (Boyd and Crawford 2012). Efforts thus need to be directed towards collecting new data, reassessing existing data and developing methods for analysis.

In particular, climatic data have usefulness in all areas of focus of this book. For instance, the intensity of malaria transmission depends on a number of variables, including topography, altitude, the presence of water bodies, temperature, humidity level (wet, dry and winter seasons) and rainfall (duration and intensity). More rainfall is found to increase the possible breeding grounds for mosquito larvae, resulting in high transmission rates of malaria. Climate data can help assess the effectiveness and necessity of climate-sensitive interventions such as indoor spraying programmes (Thomson *et al.*, 2011). Good climate information is likely to positively influence health-related outcomes. It ensures better timing and location of the distribution of mosquito nets, public awareness campaigns, and medicines that have a short shelf life. Some diseases (e.g. leptospirosis and cholera) follow floods and storms. Accurate prediction of such events could result in better preparedness and response of health-care professionals. Better mapping can also help identify areas that are at risk of epidemics of meningococcal meningitis, which favour a hot, dry and dusty environment (Thomson *et al.*, 2011). Likewise, about 90% of crop losses can be attributed to bad weather (IBM, 2015). Farmers' access to better weather-related data and their capability to act on the data can help minimize the losses and improve farming productivity.

An important point to bear in mind is that the quality of data are more important than the quantity. Countering the argument that data is the new gold rush, the data management technology provider REVER argues that data are 'more like the stones from the river bed that the gold hunter needs to shake in his net to find the real value' (rever.eu, 2015). This phenomenon is likely to significantly change the role of a data scientist. A data scientist is increasingly expected to address issues related to data quality rather than merely acting as a data analyst. In this way, data scientists are likely to play a critical role in protecting an organization from being overwhelmed and confused with excessive amounts of data.

While appropriate analysis of BD may provide valuable insights and information for key policy areas, great care must be taken to ensure that data quality standards are satisfied and that appropriate methodological steps have been taken.

For instance, the use of Twitter application program interface data has been criticized on the grounds that it suffers from questionable quality and serious methodological challenges such as samples of unknown representativeness, a lack of one-to-one correspondence between accounts and users, and a proliferation of tweets created by bots (Crawford, 2009).

8.2 The Appropriateness of Big Data in the Developing World

As noted in earlier chapters, there are proponents as well as opponents of the use of BD in major development activities such as agriculture, health care and the environment. To provide an understanding of both sides of the argument, we provide a comparison of encouraging as well as challenging aspects of BD with the help of many examples and cases discussed in this book.

Rogers (1995) identified various characteristics of a technology affecting its diffusion pattern: relative advantage, compatibility, complexity, observability and trialability. Table 8.1 presents how BD performs in terms of these characteristics.

8.2.1 Relative advantage

Real-time monitoring and accurate forecasting are major relative advantages of BD over available alternatives. For instance, China's Hengqin Island has installed energy-monitoring devices at factories and offices, which help track emissions and energy consumption in real time (Shumway, 2014). Accurate and effective forecasting of the availability of renewable energies can lead to a more sustainable power generation and supply. Nonetheless, due to perceived security, privacy and confidentiality issues, disadvantages may outweigh advantages for some organizations. Organizations worry about hidden costs associated with security breaches or lawsuits tied to data breach. Businesses and consumers are cautious in using cloud computing to store high-value or sensitive data and information.

8.2.2 Compatibility

The convergence of a number of trends, such as innovations in low-cost devices and sensors, has facilitated BD adoption in developing countries. Likewise, the proliferation of low-cost satellites is making it easier and more affordable to get data and information on various economic, social and environmental indicators. Some BD solutions thus meet the low-cost needs of users in developing countries. On the other hand, under-developed infrastructures such as those related to weather forecasting and satellite imaging technologies are incompatible with the use of BD in environmental monitoring and protection in these countries. These challenges limit their capability to utilize BD effectively. A low degree of digitization is one of the biggest barriers.

Table 8.1. Characteristics of a technology influencing its diffusion: the case of BD in developing countries.

Dimension	Explanation	Encouraging aspects	Challenging aspects
Relative advantage	Perceived benefits of a technology over previous technologies and the extent to which it is better than the idea it supersedes	Accurate and effective forecasting More sustainable power generation and supply	Due to privacy and security risks, potential costs are likely to outweigh the benefits in some organizations
Compatibility	The degree to which a technology and the tasks it performs are perceived as being consistent with the existing values, beliefs, past experiences and needs of potential adopters	BD solutions meet the low-cost needs of users	Under-developed infrastructures such as those related to weather forecasting and satellite imaging Culture may not demand high-quality data
Complexity	The level of difficulty of installing and using technology (variety and uncertainty increase complexity)	Some solutions are easy to use (e.g. Agrilife)	Shortage of skills for data-related workforce
Observability	The degree to which the features and benefits of a technology are visible, noticeable and understandable to self/others, the results can be described to non-users	Clearly visible results (e.g. increase in milk productivity using BD in TH Milk facility) In countries such as China, which are characterized by the excessive emission of carbon dioxide and high cost of energy, BD's energy conservation potential will be highly attractive	BD does not necessarily lead to a high degree of effectiveness (a large proportion of sellers on Taobao do not make a profit and many shops are closed down every day)
Trialability	The ability to experiment or try (on a limited basis) before formally adopting	Organizations can try with small datasets or a few types of data	Not possible in mega BD projects

Source: Based on Rogers (1995) and author's research.

8.2.3 Complexity

Some BD companies have developed solutions that are easy to use and understandable to the average user. Some examples include Agrilife and iCow. At the same time, there is a shortage of skills for a data-related workforce in developing countries. People with the lack of appropriate technical skills and qualifications may find BD techniques more complex.

8.2.4 Observability

The results are clearly visible in some projects involving environmental monitoring and protection. As noted earlier, in China's Zhangbei city, the deployment of IBM's supply and demand management system led to a reduction of energy waste from 30% to 20%. However, not all BD projects give observable positive results. For instance, as noted above, a large proportion of sellers on Taobao do not make a profit and many shops on Taobao close down every day.

8.2.5 Trialability

Organizations based in the developing world can use small datasets or a few types of data to try to see the appropriateness and effectiveness of BD projects. However, it may not be possible and feasible to do so in the case of mega BD projects such as TH Milk in Vietnam.

8.3 The Meaning and Significance of Big Data in the Context of Developing Countries

BD may have different meaning and significance for the purpose of development. For instance, BD applications in developing countries may not necessarily involve petabytes of data as used by transnational corporations such as eBay and Walmart. They may also be characterized by a relatively smaller variety of data. Likewise, as to the velocity dimension, a data-processing time of several months may be considered fast enough.

Experts have emphasized the importance of assessing organizations' 'information supply chain to identify and prioritize data management issue' (Laney, 2001, p. 2). This is also relevant to development-related data. Data in different contexts may come from different combinations of sources. The composition and structure of the data may differ across economies. Among developing countries, Indonesia has the most Twitter users (Richter, 2013). More tweets come from Jakarta than from New York, Tokyo, London or São Paulo (Florida, 2012). In Kenya, mobile money transfer is extremely popular and could serve as an important data source (Kaplan, 2013; UN Global Pulse, 2013). Sixty-eight per cent of Kenyan mobile phone users regularly use their phones to make or receive payments (pewglobal.org, 2014).

There is likely to be a wide variation across economic activities and industries in the diffusion of BD. Even within an industry, differences in the diffusion of BD are likely to be significant. For instance, in the agricultural industry, cash crops that are integrated in the modern supply chain are likely to experience more significant impacts of BD.

A comparison of China and Vietnam indicates that local BD companies are important but not essential for an effective deployment of BD in key developmental projects. Unlike China, Vietnam lacks local high-profile BD firms. Nonetheless

Vietnam has effectively deployed BD in key areas such as agriculture and environmental protection.

China's experience indicates that local and foreign BD firms have distinctive and complementary roles that reflect their sizes, origins and missions. According to a Gartner analyst, most Chinese cloud service providers (CSPs) have the capability to provide cloud services to small to medium-sized enterprises or start-up companies. Global players such as Amazon Web Services (AWS), on the other hand, have offerings appropriate for large enterprises or government organizations (Jing, 2014). According to an analyst at Forrester Research in Beijing, key advantages of foreign CSPs concern the richness of product offerings, quality and experience in servicing large-scale clients.

8.4 Big Data and Transparency

Table 8.2 presents BD-led transparency in major areas of focus of this book that were discussed in earlier chapters. With respect to transparency, some important additional points must be emphasized that were not pointed out earlier.

Firstly, whereas transparency is essential to ensure reliability and validity, BD created through the use of social media is often produced by commercial organizations that have closed structures (Driscoll and Walker, 2014). For instance, Gillespie (2011), pointing out the fact that Twitter engages in censorship, has argued that users have displayed a 'misplaced faith' in Twitter Trends and has urged them to stop 'worshiping algorithms'.

Table 8.2. BD-led transparency in major areas of focus of this book.

Area	Possible effect of BD	Explanation
Agriculture	Fighting cruelty to animals	BD helps track actors who commit acts of cruelty against animals in a more systematic way and in a timely manner
	Farmers' expansion of markets	Data can help meet differing standards regarding the amount of pesticides and address concerns about the use of child or slave labour
Environment	Fighting environmental crimes and injustices	Environmentalists are presenting BD-based evidence in order to pressure politicians and corporations responsible for environmental damage, degradation and harm to be transparent and accountable in environmental management (e.g. the 2015 Indonesian fires and deforestation of rainforests in the Peruvian Amazon)
Health care	Breaking the silo mentality and paradigm in various health-care organizations	BD can help health-care actors to be more accountable and responsible and address and resolve major health-care issues
	Increasing the effectiveness of disease prevention programmes	The South African insurance firm AllLife gets data from medical providers to track policyholders' adherence to treatment protocol

Secondly, an important trend that can be seen in the agricultural sector in Africa, Latin America and Asia is the promotion of non-traditional agricultural exports (NTAEs). These include fruits, vegetables and cut flowers that are targeted at the European and North American markets. It is reported that women account for about 80% of the workforce in NTAEs. These are often organized as large-scale 'factory' farms that have worse working conditions than in other factories (e.g. garments) due to the high use of pesticides. Consequently, workers suffer from physical and mental health risks such as birth defects and acute depression (Carr and Chen, 2002). BD-led transparency is expected to address this situation.

8.5 Trickling up of Big Data-Related Innovations from Developing to Developed Nations

Technology countries based in the developed world are gearing up to respond to the huge opportunities created by BD to improve agriculture, health and environmental security in the developing world. Some of the BD tools are currently being trialled in the developed world. They are likely to be exported to developing countries in the future.

At the same time, some breakthrough innovations have been created in developing economies (e.g. Kenya) that have employed new technologies and created new markets with new business models. In a letter to *The Verge*, Bill and Melinda Gates noted that the innovation in mobile money is likely to 'trickle up' from developing to developed nations. Mobile banking innovation is also taking place in the USA after many banks closed branches serving lower-income customers (Popper, 2015). Following the 2008 global financial crisis, US banks had closed 1826 branches as of May 2013; 93% of the closings took place in postal codes where the household income was below the national median (Bass and Campbell, 2013). Indeed, US banks are estimated to lose money on 37% of customer accounts, which means that even those of many middle-income customers are unprofitable (economist.com, 2014).

In 2014, M-PESA was launched in Romania, where about 35% of the population lacks access to formal banking (Shadbolt, 2015). Romanian M-PESA customers can transfer as little as one new Romanian leu (0.22 euro cents) up to 30,000 lei (€6715) per day (vodafone.com, 2014).

8.6 Implications for Businesses

BD can open up many new opportunities for businesses in all economic sectors. For instance, regarding the Internet of Things (IoT), financial firms can identify areas that are linked to financial decisions and the demand for financial services. By tracking and monitoring activities in real-time, immediate financial actions can be taken. Some believe that IoT devices can link health monitors to investment accounts. When IoT devices indicate the sign of a serious health hazard such as a heart attack, investment accounts may be automatically adjusted to relatively high liquidity of investment funds so that the customer can be prepared for future cash needs (Srinivas, 2014).

BD firms based in the industrialized world can internalize and exploit their BD-related knowledge, experience, technology and other resources in the developing world markets. The case of AfiMilk and other Israeli firms in Vietnam indicate that multinational corporations in the BD area can engage in high value-adding activities in developing countries. For instance, it was reported that the TH Milk project is reported to be 11 times larger than the biggest milking facility in Israel with a capacity to produce milk equivalent to 15% of Israel's dairy industry (Udasin, 2015). It is arguably one of the world's largest projects of its kind.

BD firms can also realize economies of scope by deploying health-care-, agriculture- and environment-related BD applications in other economic sectors and activities. Reliefwatch (see Chapter 4) is also looking to expand to government health ministries and has identified the potential for food and disaster aid, as well as agriculture, since the database can track any type of inventory (e.g. wheat, lettuce, bananas) (theguardian.com, 2015).

In some cases, it may be economically justifiable for firms to subsidize or pay for consumers' Internet access. This is important in developing countries because in some of these countries, consumers spend 8–12% of their income on phone plans. Most consumers are on prepaid plans, which means that every call or text costs money. To access African consumers, some multinational corporations offer potential customers incentives such as free cellular airtime for filling out a survey or watching a video. Likewise, in Indonesia, customers purchasing Danone products at Carrefour stores receive a scratch card with a code printed inside. After dialing the code, they instantly receive 5000 rupiahs (about US$ 0.44) worth of airtime credit. They could make another 5000 rupiahs for referring three friends on Facebook. This has led to an increase in the sales of the targeted products by 27% (Caulderwood, 2014).

Regarding established foreign BD and cloud companies' entry in developing economies, it is worth noting that they often offer more sophisticated applications and services than local companies. In order to illustrate this, let us compare Amazon and Alibaba's offerings. According to Alibaba's filing with the US Securities and Exchange Commission for an initial public offering, its cloud was capable of handling 3.6 million transactions per minute in 2014 (Hardy, 2014). On the other hand, Amazon's data storage system reportedly handled 1.5 million requests per second (90 million per minute) in 2013 (Hardy, 2013).

Likewise, as of August 2014, whereas Alibaba had only three BD centres in China and a smaller one in Hong Kong, AWS had 25 big and 52 smaller data centres worldwide (Hardy, 2014). Local companies such as Alibaba, on the other hand, are more effective in providing solutions suitable for local needs. Thus while Alibaba has one of the most advanced BD offerings among developing world-based companies, some BD and cloud companies based in the developed world are in a position to provide even more powerful and sophisticated tools. The examples presented in this book make it clear that in some developing countries such as China and Vietnam, market segments of substantial size exist for BD solutions from firms based in the developed world.

In particular, data from IoT devices can offer operational and competitive advantages to firms. Firms thus need to make investments in products and services that allow businesses to collect data and information from IoT devices and connect this information to other devices and applications. Training needs to focus on integrating IoT with other corporate applications. Businesses need to identify the problematic areas where the existing approaches show some limitations and explore the potential of developing IoT-based solutions that can address those limitations. For instance, if a bank is losing money due to fraudulent behaviours as a result of the inability to verify the identity of a customer, there might be potential of IoT-related solutions to address this issue (e.g. the use of location data as a low-cost mechanism to validate self-reported addresses using a mobile phone's nightly location patterns, as discussed in Chapter 6). Businesses can bring fundamental changes in business models taking advantage of BD, especially the IoT. For instance, as noted earlier, by using sensors, real-time feedback and predictive analysis of behavioural data it is possible to shift the property and casualty insurance business from a 'reimbursement' model to a 'prevention and loss control' model (Schutzer, 2014).

We can also expect a higher level of activism and awareness regarding the handling of personal information by BD companies. For instance, as discussed in Chapter 7, misuse and abuse of personal data and information are reported to be key problems facing Chinese consumers who receive credits from BD companies.

In some cases, businesses need to ask for more than what the data suggests. Some estimates suggest that about half of Africans who have access to mosquito nets do not use them. Many rural people reportedly believe that malaria is also caused by other factors such as mangoes or hard work. The treated nets also fail to consider cultural preferences and geographic issues facing rural Africans. For instance, a major design flaw is that the tight mesh blocks ventilation, which is a serious problem in hot and humid places (Shah, 2010). This highlights the importance of understanding local contexts and conditions.

8.7 Implications for Policy Makers

According to an estimate by McKinsey & Company, the collective economic impact of the Internet of All Things, clouds, mobile technologies and automation of knowledge work will reach US$10 trillion to US$20 trillion annually by 2025 (Bughin *et al.*, 2015). BD capability could be what differentiates nations that are likely to be winners from those that are losers. Developing countries need to understand the promises of BD as well as the consequences of not utilizing it appropriately.

BD obviously offers a number of potential benefits and vast possibilities in developed economies. Nevertheless, developing economies are at a nascent stage and far from a full utilization of the great potential of BD. Benefiting from BD requires a drastically different approach. In order to overcome barriers related to BD adoption, policy makers should ensure various enabling conditions for the creation, availability and use of data. The lack of BD-related skills and competency underscores the importance of moving the focus beyond the numbers of technological devices to the strengthening of national technological capacity to use BD.

The experience of Vietnam indicates that BD projects are more likely to be launched in countries with political will at the highest level of the government. Vietnam is one of the world's biggest exporters of rice, coffee and seafood. However, poor farming techniques often result in high costs to farmers. Moreover, due to degrading quality of water resources and land, several major outbreaks of disease have been reported in animals and sea creatures. These factors have led to a decrease in agricultural production (Shamah, 2012). According to Vietnam's agriculture ministry, the country had 170,000 cows in 2013. The goal is to increase to 500,000 cows by 2020. In addition to low yield, the milk products in Vietnam tend to be of inferior quality primarily due to the fact that farmers use agricultural by-products to feed cows.

Vietnam has exhibited a high degree of reliance on imported materials for its dairy industry. Vietnam was estimated to spend US$812 million on dairy imports in 2012 and about US$1 billion in 2013. The country's annual milk imports are about 1 million tonnes (Hoang, 2013).

Vietnam is thus facing a strong pressure to increase agricultural productivity using information communication technology (ICT). Vietnam has embraced BD enthusiastically in key areas of agricultural and environmental management thanks to the political support at the highest level. Tsafrir Asaf, the commercial attaché of Israel's Economics Ministry in Vietnam, noted: 'Vietnam has a clear understanding at all governmental levels that their objectives will be achieved only through the implementation of advanced technologies in all areas of the agricultural sector. The central government and the provinces are trying to promote this process, and many private companies are also examining ways to improve the product quality of their yields' (Shamah, 2012).

BD has not yet been a priority policy issue for most of the donor agencies nor has this issue been closely tied to national development strategies. While many organizations and data collection processes in industrialized countries constitute a rich ecosystem and serve a wide variety of functions needed to achieve various goals, most developing countries lack such ecosystems. It would be critical for the developing world's governments to get support from key stakeholders (e.g. researchers, international agencies, software developers, data-intensive sectors and venture capitalists) to create and utilize relevant, development-related data and information. Collaboration and cooperation among these stakeholders are essential to foster a data ecosystem for development. Creation of appropriate databases may stand out as particularly appealing and promising to some entrepreneurial firms. Governments, businesses and individuals are willing to pay for data when they perceive the value of such data in helping them make better decisions. In the meantime, policy makers, academics and other stakeholders should make the most of what is available.

Among the half of the world's adults who remain unbanked, more than 35% reported barriers to account use, which may be possible to address by public policy measures (Demirguc-Kunt and Klapper, 2012). The most commonly reported barriers to accessing financial services include high costs, physical distance and lack of proper documentation. Government policies can be important in addressing some of these limitations and problems. For instance, one encouraging aspect is that mobile phones are increasingly being used for birth registration, which means that today's children do not need to face the documentation problem when they grow to adulthood.

It is especially necessary to introduce policies, procedures and interventions to ensure the privacy and confidentiality of sensitive data. To return to the Kenyan example discussed earlier, the open data portal (ODP) was put in place without appropriate legal frameworks in key areas such as protection of data reuse (WEF, 2012). While Kenya's constitution guarantees openness, transparency and participation, which facilitated the establishment of the ODP, many developing countries, especially authoritarian regimes, lack such an environment.

Apart from the obvious direct economic effects, the use of BD is also associated with a number of non-economic benefits. Strengthening transparency by making information public would help monitor and discipline office-holders and fight corruption (O'Neill, 2006). Bentham (2001, p. 277) noted that '. . . the more strictly we are watched, the better we behave'. Initiatives such as Kenya's ODP can thus be seen as a key factor in strengthening the performance of government and public administration in developing countries.

BD companies in some countries, especially those providing some specialized services, have a monopoly or near monopoly position in the market. Due to their dominant market power, these firms may engage in supra competitive pricing by charging customers above what can be sustained in a competitive market. As noted earlier, a large proportion of sellers on Taobao do not make a profit and many shops on Taobao close down every day. Some public policy measures to encourage more BD firms in various key developmental areas need to be adopted.

Many of the problems described in the book are global in scope and will require greater cooperation at the international level. For instance, if telephone companies make call data record (CDR) data available, most such companies operate within national boundaries. This means that they can make CDRs available only if the calls were made within the boundaries of countries where the company operates. However, both internal and international migration are common in times of crisis as well as normal times (Bhartia *et al.*, 2015).

Data consumption and exchange are no less important than data production and analysis. Some argue that the consumption of free data such as time spent on social media and on mobile phones may provide a 'consumer surplus' not captured in official statistics (Letouzé, 2013). The utilization of BD in key development areas hinges critically upon the availability of a workforce with BD competency. It is thus important for national governments and international agencies to direct more efforts towards developing BD workers.

The above discussion suggests some important policy implications that stress the need to emphasize the enrichment of the BD ecosystem and to ensure that appropriate regulations aimed at encouraging organizations' the BD adoption in activities with positive social and economic contributions and outcomes are in place. Due to the public goods nature of data, organizations that invest in data collection cannot necessarily reap all the benefits. While some statistics are gathered several times in different ways, others are rarely or never collected (adb.org,

2013). Appropriate incentives are needed to collect relevant data and overcome the fragmentation among the governments and organizations collecting development-related data.

BD projects focusing on developing countries persistently face a number of challenges and issues. For most BD projects in the agricultural sector of the developing world, it is not possible to find data and information at the desired level of granularity. Normal market forces do not provide strong incentives for the private sector to engage in the construction of some types of databases that are useful to smallholder farmers (e.g. soil test-related databases). Government subsidies may correct this market failure by lowering a company's costs to provide poor people's access to useful data. For instance, a farmer is more likely to benefit if data and information are available at a granular level instead of an aggregate or summary data for the entire village.

The government is a key actor that can drive the BD ecosystem. Civic organizations, mobile app developers and media groups are using the data available at Kenya's ODP to improve the understanding of population patterns and transparency of public services (WEF, 2012). Governments and international agencies need to support the expansion of initiatives such as Kenya's ODP.

From this perspective of interoperability and standardization, governments are in a position to respond to the needs of the market. For instance, the Chinese government is shaping the standardization processes due to its role in control and coordination. In the food industry, China has implemented the 'National Food Quality Safety Traceability Platform', which was a result of the collaboration of the Chinese government between the food-production and ICT industries. The platform utilizes the IoT to improve the quality and safety of food-production supply chains. In order to ensure the traceability of food-safety information, it uses the handle system of the digital object (DO) architecture. A key feature of the DO architecture is that each digital object has a 'unique persistent identifier' (itu4u.wordpress.com, 2014). A malpractice can be traced to the exact source and the responsible company can be identified. The dairy industry was the first to implement the handle system, which is expected to be adopted by other sectors in the food industry (Jian, 2014). The Chinese government has selected the handle system as the core technology for major national projects such as the National Food Quality Safety Traceability Platform and the National Public Service Platform for IoT Identifier Management (Zhou, 2014). This platform will make the handle system available to all industries in order to trace the identity of goods, producers and processes in the supply chain.

8.8 Future Research Implications

Before concluding, we suggest several potentially fruitful avenues for future research. Firstly, in this book, we limited our analysis of BD deployment to agriculture, health care and the environment. Future research may wish to focus on the use of BD in modern economic sectors such as information technology, biotechnology, retail, utilities, medicine research and development, banking, finance, and service organizations. Future research can also compare the roles of BD in the industries examined in this book with those of modern economic sectors in developing countries.

One issue that was raised but not fully addressed in this book is the changing awareness of and concern about privacy protection. As noted in Chapter 7, consumers have been concerned and unhappy about the ways in which BD companies have been handling their data. It is not clear whether and how the data-handling practices of BD companies are likely to change consumers' perceptions of privacy of their personal information. The dissatisfied consumers may also engage in lobbying and other activities, which can lead to regulatory reforms to address consumers' privacy concerns. One approach to study this dynamic would be to focus on formal and informal institutions from the standpoint of privacy and look at the various mechanisms of institutional changes. Institutions are defined in Chapter 7. Notwithstanding their connotation of inertia, resistance to change, persistence, durability and stability, institutions are subject to change. Institutions arguably have a higher propensity to change when they are characterized by contradictions that 'create conflicting and irreconcilable incentives and motivations' (Campbell, 2004, p. 186). It can be argued that these conditions are prevalent in the BD industry and market. Prior researchers have noted that institutional changes can be seen as an outcome of the dynamic interactions of contradictions. Seo and Creed (2002) have proposed four sources of contradiction: (i) legitimacy that undermines functional inefficiency; (ii) adaptation that undermines adaptability; (iii) intra-institutional conformity that creates inter-institutional incompatibilities; and (iv) isomorphism that conflicts with divergent interests. Thus in the future, research scholars may study how these contradictions are linked to institutional changes related to privacy in the BD context.

Consumers worldwide have been reported to differ widely in terms of their emphasis on protecting privacy of their personal information. Asian societies are reported to have a lower degree of concern about privacy than Western societies (Kshetri *et al.*, 2014). Likewise, as noted in Chapter 7, Colombian consumers were reported to be more concerned and aware of risks posed by privacy violation than Kenyan consumers. For consumers whose personal data have been used by BD companies, these observations may no longer hold true. Another intriguing avenue for future research is to compare how consumers with and without exposure to BD companies' data handling differ in terms of the need and preference for privacy.

A fourth area of future research concerns the roles of professional and trade associations, non-governmental organizations (NGOs) and activist groups in shaping the discourses and practices related to the use of BD in key development activities and mobilizing the strategies of activism. As noted earlier, such organizations have played an active role in the fields of agriculture (e.g. the American Farm Bureau Federation), environment (e.g. the Environmental Investigation Agency) and health care (e.g. the European Society of Cardiology). In order to understand the role of professional and trade associations, NGOs and activist groups in shaping nascent industries such as those related to BD in developing economies, it is important to examine such associations *vis-à-vis* other institutional elements – most notably, the state. Note that the state is arguably the most important institutional actor (Groenewegen and van der Steen, 2007). With regard to the state's role in influencing the behaviour of industry in emerging economies, however, it is important to note that the rule of law is 'often weakly developed' or sometimes 'ignored with impunity' in such economies (Bratton, 2007). Secondly, in nascent and formative sectors such as industries related to BD, there is no developed network of regulatory agencies comparable to established industrial sectors (Powell, 1999). In such settings, professional and trade associations may emerge to play unique and important roles in shaping the industry (Kshetri and Dholakia, 2009). Further inquiry is needed to investigate such organizations' roles in shaping the BD field in developing economies.

8.9 Final Thought

Developing economies and firms based in these economies, which have access to high-quality and useful data and the capability to extract meaningful insights from the data and take quick actions, are likely to benefit from the BD revolution. Low-cost or freely available data, tools and applications are essential to catalyse the changes in policies, strategies, investments, technologies and best practices in order to improve agriculture, health care and environmental conditions in developing countries.

The future potential of the IoT is particularly bright in these economies. It is argued that developing economies have fewer legacy issues to grapple with and thus have the potential to leapfrog the industrialized world in some areas of IoT applications (Bughin *et al.*, 2015). For instance, consider the primary sector of the Chinese economy. One estimate suggested that 266 million people or 35% of workers in China are employed in primary sector activities such as agriculture, forestry and fishery. A study indicated that while South Korea has less water and arable land than China, output per farmer in South Korea is 40 times higher than that in China. One key factor behind higher farming productivity in South Korea concerns increased utilization of machinery by farmers (Badkar, 2012). The fact that most Chinese farmers do not utilize machinery makes the IoT-related innovations more attractive for them. Thus, the IoT is likely to offer higher relative advantage to farmers based in the developing world than those in industrialized countries.

The availability of incentives and motivations to engage in capital-intensive strategy such as BD deployment can reduce environmental degradation and combat climate change. These measures can also improve energy efficiency and thus support energy security. In addition, BD deployment can overcome various barriers to access to health care. Appropriate deployment of BD technologies thus needs to be encouraged and supported among the poorest of the poor through education and creation of awareness.

Many firms based in the developing world are also developing BD capabilities not by choice but to meet the demands of their powerful business partners, often from the industrialized world. In many cases, small agribusiness firms may have to adopt IoT not by choice but because it is required or expected of them by trading partners.

Efforts and activities to collect data and information, create databases and associated tools, and identify new and creative uses of existing data can strengthen the BD ecosystem. For instance, anonymized mobile phone data may represent a proxy that is cost efficient and can be used to track population movements. So far the use of such data has been largely limited during crises. However, CDRs are being viewed as a promising proxy for assessing creditworthiness of poor people since the nightly location data can validate self-reported addresses (identity) and travelling patterns. For example, the number of mobile phone masts one passes during the week can indicate the reliability of the individual's financial habits (i.e. ability/willingness to pay debt). Employees with diverse skills, backgrounds and capabilities are needed to implement BD projects. BD projects often require the management of multidisciplinary teams from a number of areas, including operations, IT, analytics, engineering, HR, training, finance, marketing and design. It is also important to consider some key challenges in managing such teams. In most cases, BD projects need to be seen in the backdrop of other infrastructures rather than as a self-contained phenomenon. For instance, BD projects need different levels of physical infrastructures.

Uses of BD that lead to positive social and economic outcomes and those that benefit socially and economically disadvantaged groups need to be promoted. Responsible uses of BD also require the protection of people's dignity and legitimate expectations of privacy and economic interests. For instance, among the key lessons from the overview of risks to farmers over possible misuse of data and information in industrialized countries, is that these concerns are even more pronounced in developing countries due to the lack of data protection regulations. Moreover, most farmers in developing countries lack the degree of self-awareness and organization that can be observed among some farmers based in the industrialized world. For instance, while farming groups in industrialized countries are taking measures to protect against misuse and exploitation of their data, such measures are lacking in developing countries.

BD can help reduce poverty directly as well as through indirect causal chains. Among the indirect effects we can mention the deployment of BD in fighting corruption. Note that corruption and poverty are tightly related and interdependent (McMillan, 2005). In this regard, the examples that we considered in previous chapters indicate that BD is also helping to attack the root causes of poverty by promoting transparency and reducing corruption. In general, BD is forcing everyone, from farmers to politicians, to be more transparent, honest, open and accountable. BD analytics is changing how policy makers, farmers, organizations and activists can make decisions and take actions.

Closely related to the above is the idea that transparency is about sharing information in order to allow the other party to understand and scrutinize the actions of an organization or an individual. Some BD companies providing solutions to consumers based in the developing world have exhibited a tendency to hide information behind a secret algorithm, which means that it is not possible to assess the welfare effects.

Farmers participating in the data collection efforts of BD companies are often not paid in proportion to their efforts. If farmers have a better assessment of the value of their information, they can strengthen their negotiating power *vis-à-vis*

BD companies. One way to improve the welfare of farmers would thus be to create awareness of the value of data they provide to data aggregators. This is also one of the lessons from the US farmers, who are exploring ways to monetize the information.

BD can help better utilize the scarce resources and deal with the various sources of inefficiency that have been frequently cited by critics as among the key obstacles for development in developing countries. For instance, BD can help to reduce the waste of inputs such as fertilizers and increase agricultural productivity and control the epidemics of various diseases. BD can help develop an effective food system that can provide better nutrition and preserve the world's natural resources. BD enables farmers based in the developing world to provide proof of trustworthiness and legitimacy in order to sell their products in the developed world.

Multiple trajectories and diverging trends with diverse impacts exist in the deployment of BD in developing countries. China and Vietnam are among the countries that have already harnessed the power of BD to bring economic transformation and improve the monitoring and protection of the environment. China has intensified efforts and activities to create local BD solutions. The lack of reforms in education and skills formation is likely to act as a major obstacle in utilizing BD to generate broader transformations and organizational changes in Vietnam. For instance, Vietnam does not have a single internationally recognized university. On the other hand, most of the other Southeast Asian countries have at least a few universities of international standing. Vietnam's universities perform poorly in research and publications in international scientific journals (Valley and Wilkinson, 2008). Unsurprisingly most BD projects in Vietnam do not utilize local, indigenous BD and related technologies. The Vietnamese dairy industry, on the other hand, has received a big boost thanks to collaborations of big firms in this industry with Israeli technology companies.

Vietnam's politico-economic system can be described as 'crony capitalism', which is characterized by a close link between business tycoons and top Communist Party officials (Fuller, 2012). This means that while environmentalists and activists are sensitive to the potential damage to the environment caused by mega agricultural projects, the government may ignore the environmental implications of such projects.

Notwithstanding some impressive accomplishments in certain areas, so far the BD situation in the developing world appears to be a 'little too much talk and less action'. BD is still in an early phase of development and deployment in developing countries. Most guidelines for implementation and conclusions related to the economic and social impact of BD are based on limited evidence and experience.

Finally, data by itself has limited or no value. The willingness of relevant government agencies and organizational leaders to take actions based on what the data tell is key in achieving outcomes related to agriculture and food security, environmental sustainability and performance, and health-care delivery. For instance, legislative actions are needed to close the regulatory loopholes and to take action against firms that pollute the environment. Peru's case discussed in Chapter 3 also indicates that contradictory laws must be straightened out so that environmental protection becomes a key element.

References

adb.org (2013) Big Data: vital statistics for development. Available at: http://www.adb.org/features/big-data-vital-statistics-development (accessed 18 August 2014).

Badkar, M. (2012) Why South Korean farmers are 40 times more productive than Chinese farmers. Available at: http://www.businessinsider.com/chinese-farmer-productivity-2012-8 (accessed 17 February 2016).

Bass, F and Campbell, D. (2013) Predator targets hit as banks shut branches amid profits. Available at: http://www.bloomberg.com/news/articles/2013-05-02/post-crash-branch-closings-hit-hardest-in-poor-u-s-areas (accessed 12 April 2016).

Bentham, J. (2001) Farming defended. In Quinn, M. (ed.) *Writings on the Poor Laws*, vol. 1. Oxford University Press, Oxford, UK, pp. 276–290.

Bhartia, N., Lub, X., Bengtsson, L., Wetterc, E. and Tatemc, J.A. (2015) Remotely measuring populations during a crisis by overlaying two data sources. *International Health* 7(2), 90–98

Blair, A. (2003) Reading strategies for coping with information overload. *Journal of the History of Ideas* 64(1), 11–18.

Boyd, D. and Crawford, K. (2012) Critical questions for Big Data: provocations for a cultural, technological, and scholarly phenomenon. *Information, Communication, & Society* 15(5), 662–679.

Bratton, M. (2007) Formal versus informal institutions in Africa. *Journal of Democracy* 18, 96–110.

Bughin, J., Chui, M. and Manyika, J. (2015) An executive's guide to the Internet of Things. Available at: http://www.mckinsey.com/Insights/Business_Technology/An_executives_guide_to_the_Internet_of_Things?cid=digital-eml-alt-mip-mck-oth-1508 (accessed 12 April 2016).

Campbell, J.L. (2004) *Institutional Change and Globalization*. Princeton University Press, Princeton, NJ, USA.

Carr, M. and Chen, A.M. (2002) *Globalization and the informal economy: how global trade and investment impact on the working poor*. Working Paper on the Informal Economy No. 1. International Labour Office, Employment Sector, Geneva, Switzerland.

Caulderwood, K. (2014) Cheap phones, big data and good business. International Business Times (online). Available at: http://www.ibtimes.com/cheap-phones-big-data-good-business-1567731 (accessed 12 April 2016).

Crawford, K. (2009) Following you: disciplines of listening in social media. *Continuum: Journal of Media & Cultural Studies* 23(4), 532–533.

Demirguc-Kunt, A. and Klapper, L. (2012) *Measuring financial inclusion*. The Global Findex Database. The World Bank Development Research Group, Finance and Private Sector Development Team, Policy Research Working Paper, 6025.

Driscoll, K. and Walker, S. (2014) Working within a black box: transparency in the collection and production of big Twitter data. *International Journal of Communication* 8, 1745–1764.

economist. com (2014) A phoneful of dollars: the world's poor need the stability and security that banks have traditionally offered, but increasingly they do not need banks to provide it. Available at: http://www.economist.com/news/briefing/21632441-worlds-poor-need-stability-and-security-banks-have-traditionally-offered (accessed 12 April 2016).

Florida, R. (2012) The world cities that tweet the most. Available at: http://www.theatlanticcities.com/arts-and-lifestyle/2012/08/world-cities-tweet-most/2944/ (accessed 18 August 2014).

Fuller, T. (2012) In Vietnam, message of equality is challenged by widening wealth gap. Available at: http://www.nytimes.com/2012/09/02/world/asia/in-vietnam-message-of-equality-challenged-by-wealth-gap.html (accessed 12 April 2016).

Gillespie T. (2011) Our misplaced faith in Twitter Trends. Available at: http://www.salon.com/2011/10/19/our_misplaced_faith_in_twitter_trends/ (accessed 18 August 2014).

Groenewegen, J. and van der Steen, M. (2007) The evolutionary policy maker. *Journal of Economics* 41(2), 351–358.

Hardy, Q. (2013) Amazon bares its computers. Available at: http://bits.blogs.nytimes.com/2013/11/15/amazon-bares-its-computers/?_php=true&_type=blogs&_r=0 (accessed 12 April 2016).

Hardy, Q. (2014) Alibaba has a computing cloud, and it's growing, too. Available at: http://bits.blogs.nytimes.com/2014/08/04/alibaba-has-a-computing-cloud-and-its-growing-too/ (accessed 12 April 2016).

Hoang, T. (2013) Dairy farming in dire need of high tech. Available at: http://english.thesaigontimes.vn/32197/Dairy-farming-in-dire-need-of-high-tech.html (accessed 12 April 2016).

IBM (2015) Precision agriculture. Using predictive weather analytics to feed future generations. Available at: http://www.research.ibm.com/articles/precision_agriculture.shtml (accessed 12 April 2016).

itu4u.wordpress.com (2014) Lost something on the Internet? Never again with new digital object (DO) architecture. Available at: https://itu4u.wordpress.com/2014/01/06/lost-something-on-the-internet-never-again-with-new-digital-object-do-architecture/ (accessed 12 April 2016).

Jian, Z. (2014) Tracing dairy products with the Internet of Things. Available at: https://itu4u.wordpress.com/2014/12/17/tracing-dairy-products-with-the-internet-of-things/ (accessed 12 April 2016).

Jing, M. (2014) Amazon brings its cloud computing to China. Available at: http://usa.chinadaily.com.cn/business/2014-01/02/content_17210951.htm (accessed 12 April 2016).

Kaplan, E. (2013) Searching for digital signals in Kenya. UN Global Pulse. Available at: http://www.unglobalpulse.org/searchingforsignalskenya (accessed 12 April 2016).

Kshetri, N. and Dholakia, N. (2009) Professional and trade associations in a nascent and formative sector of a developing economy: A case study of the NASSCOM effect on the Indian offshoring industry. *Journal of International Management* 15(2), 225–239.

Kshetri, N., Alcantara, L.L. and Park, Y. (2014) Development of a smart city and its adoption and acceptance: The case of New Songdo. *Communications & Strategies* 96 (4), 113–128.

Laney, D. (2001) 3D data management: controlling data volume, velocity and variety. Available at: http://blogs.gartner.com/doug-laney/files/2012/01/ad949-3D-Data-Management-Controlling-Data-Volume-Velocity-and-Variety.pdf (accessed 18 August 2014).

Letouzé, E. (2013) Could Big Data provide alternative measures of poverty and welfare? Available at: http://www.oecdbetterlifeindex.org/es/blog-es/could-big-data-provide-alternative-measures-of-poverty-and-welfare.htm (accessed 18 August 2014).

McMillan, J. (2005) Promoting transparency in Angola. *Journal of Democracy* 16(3) 155–169.

O'Neill, O. (2006) Transparency and the ethics of communication. In Hood, C. and Heald, D. (eds), *Transparency: The Key to Better Governance*, Proceedings of the British Academy, 135, 75–90. Oxford University Press, Oxford, UK.

pewglobal.org (2014) Emerging nations embrace internet, mobile technology. Available at: http://www.pewglobal.org/2014/02/13/emerging-nations-embrace-internet-mobile-technology/ (accessed 18 August 2014).

Popper, B. (2015) Can mobile banking revolutionize the lives of the poor? Available at: http://www.theverge.com/2015/2/4/7966043/bill-gates-future-of-banking-and-mobile-money (accessed 12 April 2016).

Powell, W.W. (1999) The social construction of an organizational field: the case of biotechnology. *International Journal of Biotechnology* 1, 42–66.

rever.eu (2015) Data quality: when do you have too much data ? Available at: http://blog.rever.eu/blog/data-quality-when-do-you-have-too-much-data (accessed 12 April 2016).

Richter, F. (2013) Twitter's top 5 markets account for 50% of active users. Available at: http://www.statista.com/topics/737/twitter/chart/1642/regional-breakdown-of-twitter-users/ (accessed 18 August 2014).

Rogers, E.M. (1995) *Diffusion of Innovations*, 4th edn. Free Press, New York.

Seo, M.G. and Creed, W.E.D. (2002) Institutional contradictions, praxis, and institutional change: a dialectical perspective. *Academy of Management Review* 27(2), 222–247.

Schutzer, D. (2014) Impact of The Internet of Things on financial services. Available at: http://fsroundtable.org/cto-corner-impact-of-the-internet-of-things-on-financial-services/ (accessed 12 April 2016).

Shadbolt, P. (2015) Africa's mobile money makes its way to Europe with M-PESA. Available at: http://www.cnn.com/2014/11/20/tech/mobile/tomorrow-transformed-m-pesa-mobile-payments/ (accessed 12 April 2016).

Shah, S. (2010) In Africa, anti-malaria mosquito nets go unused by recipients. Los Angeles Times (online). Available at: http://articles.latimes.com/2010/may/02/opinion/la-oe-shah-20100502 (accessed 12 April 2016).

Shamah, D. (2012) Dairy diplomacy yields stronger ties with Vietnam. Available at: http://www.timesofisrael.com/dairy-diplomacy-yields-stronger-ties-with-vietnam/ (accessed 12 April 2016).

Shumway, R. (2014) Randy Shumway: one solution for air pollution: big data. Available at: http://www.deseretnews.com/article/865617771/One-solution-for-air-pollution-Big-data.html?pg=all (accessed 12 April 2016).

Srinivas, V. (2014) The 'Internet of Things' and the financial services industry. Available at: http://www2.deloitte.com/us/en/pages/finance/articles/internet-of-things-financial-services-industry.html (accessed 12 April 2016).

theguardian.com (2015) The cloud-based tool improving healthcare across the developing world. Available at: http://www.theguardian.com/sustainable-business/2015/jan/07/the-cloud-based-tool-improving-healthcare-across-the-developing-world.

Thomson, C.M., Connor, J.S., Zebiak, E.S., Jancloes, M. and Mihretie, A. (2011) Africa needs climate data to fight disease. *Nature* 471, 440–442. Available at: http://www.nature.com/nature/journal/v471/n7339/full/471440a.html (accessed 12 April 2016).

Udasin, S. (2015) Israeli–Vietnamese commercial milking venture nears completion. Available at: http://www.jpost.com/Business/Israeli-Vietnamese-commercial-milking-venture-nears-completion-390874 (accessed 12 April 2016).

UN Global Pulse (2013) Landscaping study: digital signals & access to finance in Kenya. UN Global Pulse. Available at: http://www.unglobalpulse.org/Kenyan-access-finance (accessed 18 August 2014).

Vallely, J.T. and Wilkinson, B. (2008) Vietnamese higher education: crisis and response. Memorandum Higher Education Task Force, Ash Center for Democratic Governance and Innovation. Available at: http://www.hks.harvard.edu/innovations/asia/Documents/highereducationoverview112008.pdf (accessed 12 april 2016).

vodafone.com (2014) Vodafone M-Pesa comes to Europe for the first time. Available at: http://www.vodafone.com/content/index/media/vodafone-group-releases/2014/m-pesa-romania.html# (accessed 12 April 2016).

WEF [World Economic Forum] (2012) Big Data, big impact: new possibilities for international development. World Economic Forum. Available at: http://www3.weforum.org/docs/WEF_TC_MFS_BigDataBigImpact_Briefing_2012.pdf (accessed 12 April 2016).

Zhou, J. (2014) Digital object architecture-based product quality safety information traceability system in infant formula industry: architecture, advantages and impacts. *ITU Event on 'Combating Counterfeit and Substandard ICT Devices', Geneva, Switzerland, 17–18 November 2014*. Available at: http://www.itu.int/en/ITU-T/C-I/Pages/Programme.aspx (accessed 12 April 2016).

Appendix: Integrative Cases of Big Data Deployment in Agriculture, Environmental Security and Health Care

Case 1: Big Data Deployment in the Chinese Health-Care Industry

The Chinese health-care sector is experiencing a number of challenges such as high costs, inefficiency in public hospitals and an increase in the number of patients with chronic diseases (Wang, 2014). Faced with these problems, China is leveraging on BD and cloud computing to transform the health-care system.

From the BD perspective, an issue that deserves mention relates to China's substantial progress in hospital information systems (HIS). According to the Ministry of Health, in 2008 80% of hospitals had implemented HIS (Zhou, 2011). The progress has been slow on the electronic medical records (EMR) front, however. Many hospitals handle patient data on paper. Community clinics and hospitals are plagued by problems such as outdated information technology (IT) equipment, the lack of collaborative operation and the lack of IT workforce. Consequently, Chinese hospitals and clinics are finding it difficult to meet the growing needs of patients, and to do so efficiently.

In light of the above, it is noteworthy that information sharing and EMR are key components of the Healthy China 2020 strategy. The goal is to provide health-care access to every resident by 2020. Regional health-care information networks (RHINs) are expected to play a key role in enhancing information sharing. RHINs also facilitate IT operations among China's community health centres, primary care facilities and hospitals. A RHIN IT platform is expected to provide clinical decision support, cloud-based imaging services and tele-intensive care unit monitoring.

Chinese health-care organizations have focused on the rapid adoption of BD and the cloud in an effort to enhance competitiveness. The Shanghai government deployed China's first 'health cloud' in the Zhabei district, which integrated a 'health-care cloud', 'community health cloud' and 'district-wide health cloud' (cloudcomputinglive.com, 2011). Likewise, in 2011, the city of Dongying had plans to add health-care services to the cloud to centralize patients' records and make them available to health centres if required (Chandrasekaran and Kapoor, 2011). The Shanghai Pudong Health cloud hosts medical records of patients in hospitals and community health centres. The information enables patients to visit outpatient or small regional clinics instead of specialized doctors that are located far away (Chua, 2011). Similarly, any patient visiting a hospital in the city of Jinan receives a card, which is used to register, pay and receive test results via machines in the hospital connected to the cloud (cncworld.tv, 2012).

A1.1 Big Data-based mobile health-care apps

BD-based mobile health care represents the Chinese health-care IT industry's sweet spot. While the majority of China's population has no access to PCs, by the end of 2015 there were 1.306 billion mobile phone subscribers (digitimes.com, 2016).

According to a survey conducted by PricewaterhouseCoopers, 80% of doctors and consumers in China believe that widespread adoption of M-health will be 'inevitable'. M-health will improve doctors' interactions with hospitals and patients, and mobile carriers are capitalizing on this opportunity. China Telecom launched M-health pilot projects in over 200 hospitals. It has also teamed up with Cambridge University in research involving M-health. China Unicom has developed a cloud platform to collect, transmit and retrieve health-care data. The company has also developed systems for M-health rescue positioning and real-time transfer of vital signs such as heart beat, breathing rate, temperature and blood pressure (tmcnet.com, 2012).

A1.2 Resources to create a healthy society

Some health-care players have developed systems and created resources for disease prevention and the creation of a healthy society. Neusoft's health-care management platform, Xikang, is an open platform that connects to health-care services provided by medical centres and community health-care facilities and combines with real-time resources available in the health Internet of Things, health cloud platforms and other sources. The resources available in Xikang include those related to full-lifecycle health-care services and a chronic disease prevention ecosystem to enhance health and quality of life (Neusoft.com, 2015). In 2012, Neusoft also formed a joint venture with Japan's Alps Electric Company to establish Shenyang Xikang Alps Technologies.

A1.3 Government investment as a trigger

The government's health-care investment is an important trigger in the deployment of BD-related solutions in the Chinese health-care industry. In 2009, the government announced plans to spend US$27 billion to create a fully electronic predictive health information network (marketwired.com, 2009). As a component of the reforms, 22 provinces and municipalities in rural regions were selected for a pilot programme to trial a system that can better use and manage EMR. By the end of 2010, about 100 hospitals in those provinces and municipalities had launched EMR pilot tests (WHO, 2011).

In response to the government's call for a wider utilization of IT in the health-care industry, Beijing, Shanghai and other developed cities in the east and south coast have made substantial progress in establishing a unified health-care IT system and have started health-care IT trials. The government's plan to construct new facilities has focused on less developed regions.

State-of-the-art health-care facilities that utilize BD have been started in the country. For instance, in early 2015, Ningbo Municipal Health and Family Planning Commission and Neusoft Xikang Healthcare Technology (Neusoft Xikang) started China's first cloud hospital 'Ningbo Cloud Hospital'. The Ningbo Cloud Hospital utilizes cloud computing, BD and the Internet of Things (prnewswire.com, 2015). Ningbo Cloud Hospital's open platform makes it possible to connect with major hospitals, primary health-care institutions, specialists, community doctors and third-party organizations such as pharmacies and insurance companies. As of March 2015, Ningbo Cloud Hospital connected 100 health-care organizations and 226 doctors and family physicians. There were four 'Cloud Diagnosis Rooms' for hypertension, diabetes, psychological consultation and general practitioners. Ningbo Cloud Hospital has also been linked with local pharmacies and third-party organizations. Prescriptions given by 'cloud doctors' can be transmitted to local pharmacies, where the medicine can be collected (prnewswire.com, 2015).

A problem facing China's health care also concerns the 'information island' (Kshetri, 2013). While many large hospitals completed initial IT initiatives in the mid-2000s, they suffer from fragmentation and incompatibility of information systems between departments, and the inability to communicate and share data. One reason for the slow EMR diffusion concerns the lack of standards.

A1.4 Well-known Big Data companies in the value chain of the health-care sector

China's well-known BD companies are rapidly entering the value chain of the health-care sector, such as online consultations and health data information. The three biggest Internet giants (Baidu, Alibaba and Tencent, the so-called 'BAT') are significant players in the health-care industry. Patients can use platforms, such as Alibaba's Alipay and Tencent's WeChat, to consult doctors, schedule appointments, pay bills and check medical reports (usa.chinadaily.com, 2015).

Alibaba

Alibaba is heavily involved in the medical industry. Alipay has launched a service called Future Hospital, which allows patients to schedule appointments and pay hospital bills online. It is reported that during peak hours, it may take 5 hours or more for a patient to complete the processes in a hospital such as registration, check-up and getting medicine. Using Future Hospital, the process can be reduced to around 1 hour (Zinran, 2014). Guangzhou Women and Children's Medical Centre was the first hospital to adopt the service in June 2014 (Roberts, 2014). As of April 2015, Alipay's Future Hospital was used in 63 hospitals and had 5 million individual patients as users (Cadell, 2015).

The Alibaba Group and Hubei Chest Hospital launched a pilot scheme in March 2015 that allows outpatients to download the hospital's mobile app and then order and pay for prescriptions online. The prescriptions are then delivered to patients' homes. Alibaba's e-prescription system also links up pharmacies within a 3-km radius from the hospital. In early 2015, Alibaba Health Information Technology teamed up with China Pacific Insurance. Alibaba has also announced the possibility of launching Yu'E Bao-like health insurance products in the near future (usa.chinadaily.com, 2015).

In November 2015, Alibaba's cloud computing unit (AliCloud), Intel and BGI, the world's largest genomics research centre based in Beijing, launched a cloud platform focusing on precision medicine, which involves customization of health-care by tailoring medical decisions, practices and products to individual patients. The goal is to create a genomics data centre and analytics platform for the development of a precision medicine industry. AliCloud will provide a cloud computing environment and BD analytics. Alibaba Group affiliates such as Alibaba Health, Ant Financial Services Group, Taobao Marketplace and Tmall.com will handle services such as payment infrastructure, health management and marketing support. Intel will offer computing resources to process and analyse genetic data (enterpriseinnovation.net, 2015). In October 2015, Tsinghua University's Center for Statistical Science established a Medical Big Data Center. The Center's goal is to conduct research in the areas of clinical decision making, health policies, health-care system management and innovation in the health-care industry (Xin, 2015).

Baidu

In July 2015, Baidu signed a partnership with the mobile health-care service provider EZTcn.com, which helps people schedule an appointment with a doctor (usa.chinadaily.com, 2015). Baidu also reported that about 26 million people search for medical information on its website. Baidu uses BD to track disease, which can help hospitals to make vaccines or schedule personnel (news.xinhuanet.com, 2015). For instance, when users search for 'cold', 'fever' or other terms related to flu, the search engine provider watches closely (Chao, 2014). Baidu has also launched Dulife, which is an open-ended platform used to collect primary data from an interface with third-party wearable devices (e.g. weighing scales, blood pressure monitors and wristbands). The data are then processed by the company for health-care practitioners to advise their patients about the potential risks and to improve patient care (Fidelity Worldwide Investment, 2015).

Tencent

Tencent has invested in dxy.cn, which is the largest health-care information sharing website in China, with more than 4 million registered users in 2014. Most of the users are medical professionals. Tencent offers the site's services such as drug information and a network of doctors to WeChat users (Wang, 2014). It also provided funding for Guahao.com ('making doctor appointments' in Chinese), which makes appointments with doctors online. Both of these portals can be accessed via WeChat (usa.chinadaily.com, 2015). Guahao.com has a large database that consists of information on doctors and specialists. It has also formed a partnership with Haodaifu ('good doctor' in Chinese), which is a platform to search for physicians and receive consultations online (WSJ, 2014).

A1.5 Foreign companies promoting BD deployment in the Chinese health-care industry

Major global suppliers of health-care IT solutions, devices and services are focusing their attention on China. Table A.1 provides a brief description of some of the major foreign companies in the Chinese BD market.

Philips

According to the 2014 China Report on Cardiovascular Diseases, there were about 290 million people in China with cardiovascular diseases. As of 2015, Philips had over 2200 engineers in China. The company has been investing more than €110 million for research and development (R&D) annually in the country. Philips Research China is Philips' second-largest R&D institute globally. Philips has teamed up with the Chinese Society of Cardiology to build the China National Cardiovascular Data Repository. Philips is also reported to be working on other databases (Nan, 2015).

IBM

IBM is a major player in the Chinese health-care IT market. In 2009, IBM opened a Healthcare Industry Solution Lab in Beijing for hospitals and rural medical cooperatives. With the help of IBM, the Guang Dong Hospital of Traditional Chinese Medicine (TCM), China's largest TCM hospital that receives about 4 million patient visits a year, has implemented a suite of health-care data-sharing and analytics technologies (IBM.com, 2009). The system, also known as CHAS (Clinical and Health Records Analytics and Sharing), combines the strengths of TCM and Modern Western Medicine (MWM) and blends input from the two types of medicines. It is designed to enable the sharing of EMRs that incorporate TCM and MWM data across the hospital network. It is expected to help the hospital standardize its patient records and perform statistical analyses to assess the effectiveness of TCM treatments (Chao, 2012).

A state-of-the-art 6.2 million ft^2 Cloud Center in Langfang city constructed by IBM and China's Range Technology will also focus on health care. Range

Table A.1. Major global cloud players in the Chinese health-care IT market: some examples.

Foreign multinational	Chinese partner(s)/ collaborator(s)	Examples of achievements
Philips	The Chinese Society of Cardiology	Building the China National Cardiovascular Data Repository and other databases
IBM	The Guang Dong Hospital of Traditional Chinese Medicine (GDHTCM) Range Technology Yi Lian Zhong (YLZ)	Development of the CHAS system with GDHTCM Range has plans to provide Hebei Province with advanced health-care IT capabilities A collaboration between IBM and YLZ involves building a cloud platform to connect 300 million people with a number of networks including medical institutions
Cisco	Peking University	The 'Connecting Sichuan' programnme helped develop Wenchuan People's Hospital as a 'centre of collaboration'
AT&T	China Telecom	AT&T's experience in Medical Imaging and Information Management would be helpful
Microsoft	Medical College of Qingdao University (QDUMH) iSoftStone	Helped develop HIS for QDUMH Agreement with iSoftStone to introduce Microsoft HealthVault
Dell	China Telecom	Offers consulting services to hospitals Partnered with China Telecom to standardize EHR

Technology's data centres will provide EMR and other health-care IT solutions. In particular, Range Technology will also provide Hebei Province with the advanced health-care IT capabilities. Hebei was among the 22 provinces and municipalities selected for the public hospital reforms pilot. Likewise, a collaboration between IBM and China's information services provider Yi Lian Zhong (YLZ) involves building a cloud platform for YLZ to connect to networks consisting of citizens, government agencies, social service providers, medical institutions, private and public organizations, and educational institutions. The platform is expected to facilitate the sharing of public resources and information, support service integration, improve government efficiency and ensure effective administration of citizen services. The services will cover 300 million people (cbronline.com, 2011).

Cisco

Following the 2008 earthquake of Wenchuan in Sichuan Province, Cisco formed a public–private partnership with the Chinese government and launched a corporate social responsibility programme called 'Connecting Sichuan'. A major goal of the programme was to apply information communication technology to improve the quality and capacity of health care in Sichuan and to bridge the urban–rural health-care gap. The so-called 'Wenchuan Model' provides an example to demonstrate the cloud-led collaboration and integration of hospital resources. Wenchuan People's Hospital (WPH), a secondary-level hospital, evolved as a 'centre of collaboration' in the region and has played a key role in integrating primary- and tertiary-level health-care providers. The health-care collaboration technology and cloud platform allowed doctors at WPH to receive guidance from experts at Sichuan People's Hospital and West China Hospital. Doctors at WPH provide support to the 13 township health centres in Wenchuan (cisco.com, 2012).

AT&T

In 2011, AT&T and China Telecom signed a deal that would allow each other to share infrastructures in the USA and China. The Chinese health-care industry is likely to benefit from AT&T's experience in providing access, storage and sharing of cloud-based medical imaging and information management services.

Microsoft

Microsoft is working with Chinese hospitals and health-care IT services providers. In 2009, it formed a partnership with the Affiliated Hospital of the Medical College of Qingdao University (QDUMH). The QDUMH deployed Microsoft Amalga HIS, which is an important component of Microsoft's cloud strategy and integrates EMR, patient and bed management, laboratory and other data management (Kshetri, 2013).

In 2010, Microsoft and China's iSoftStone signed an agreement to introduce Microsoft HealthVault technology to China (Microsoft.com, 2010). HealthVault is a personal health application platform to store and manage health information online in a personal account. The project initially focused on Wuxi city. The Microsoft–iSoftStone relationship envisioned enabling citizens to connect to health systems and services run by government agencies, hospitals, pharmacies and fitness facilities.

Dell

Dell offers consulting services to a number of Chinese hospitals. Dell is also working with several province governments on health-care initiatives involving the cloud (Shah, 2011). The company has partnered with China Telecom to standardize electronic health records (EHR), which involves working with hospitals throughout the country (Chao, 2012).

A1.6 Professional and ethical issues

The lack of professional and ethical standards has been a major concern. Some health-care BD firms in China are reported to be acting in an immoral, unprofessional and unethical manner. In December 2012, the Dean of Nanjing University's pharmacy school allegedly used blood samples from local hospitals without permission and created a private genetic data bank (Abraham and Wheeler, 2012). Some ethical issues have been raised concerning health care and medical uses of BD. Shenzhen's BGI project is also focusing on finding the genetic basis for genius, which has led to concerns of a future of 'designer babies' (Magistad, 2015).

A1.7 Concluding comments

BD has started transforming the Chinese health-care industry. It has improved the quality of health-care services by generating horizontal and vertical collaboration among hospitals and other organizations, providing platforms to store, share and synchronize patient profiles and enhancing efficiency of hospital management. Wide rural–urban discrepancies that exist with respect to health and health-care resources would translate into differential patterns and sophistication of BD deployment in the health-care industry. For instance, BD has enabled doctors and other health-care professionals to collaborate and share information and access reports, scans, EHR/EMR, prescriptions and medical histories (Kshetri, 2013). Likewise, insurance claims, prescriptions and lab reports can be stored on the cloud.

References

Abraham, C. and Wheeler, C. (2012) Why China is a genetic powerhouse with a problem. Available at: http://www.theglobeandmail.com/news/national/time-to-lead/why-china-is-a-genetic-powerhouse-with-a-problem/article6399668/?page=all (accessed 12 April 2016).

Cadell, C. (2015) Alibaba affiliate's 'future hospitals' can access Chinese medical data. Available at: http://technode.com/2015/04/24/alibaba-affiliates-future-hospitals-can-access-chinese-medical-data/ (accessed 12 April 2016).

cbronline.com (2011) IBM to build cloud computing platform for Chinese firm Yi Lian Zhong. CBR online. Available at: http://appdev.cbronline.com/news/ibm-to-build-cloud-computing-platform-for-chinese-firm-yi-lian-zhong-070911 (accessed 12 April 2016).

Chandrasekaran, A. and Kapoor, M. (2011) Frost & Sullivan 2011: market insight. Available at: http://www.frost.com/prod/servlet/cio/232651119 (accessed 12 April 2016).

Chao, D. (2014) Baidu turns to Big Data to forecast flu outbreaks. Available at: http://blogs.wsj.com/chinarealtime/2014/06/10/baidu-turns-to-big-data-to-forecast-flu-outbreaks/ (accessed 12 April 2016).

Chao, L. (2012) IBM works on China's medical records. Available at: http://online.barrons.com/article/SB10001424052748703369704575462653035645256.html (accessed 22 February 2016).

Chua, M. (2011) Huawei hinges cloud dreams on partners. Available at: http://www.networksasia.net/content/huawei-hinges-cloud-dreams-partners (accessed 12 April 2016).

cisco.com (2012) Cisco and Peking University jointly release the impact assessment report of 'Connecting Sichuan' healthcare program. Available at: http://newsroom.cisco.com/press-release-content?type=webcontent&articleId=782178 (accessed 22 February 2016).

cloudcomputinglive.com (2011) Shanghai Government and Huawei inaugurate a health cloud. Available at: http://www.cloudcomputinglive.com/latin-america/images/case_study_shanghai_health_cloud_hd.pdf (accessed 4 May 2016).

cncworld.tv (2012) China's healthcare cloud. Available at: http://www.cncworld.tv/news/v_show/26095_China_s_healthcare_cloud.shtml (accessed 2 May 2016).

Digitimes.com (2016) China December mobile phone user base grows to 1.306 billion. Available at: http://digitimes.com/news/a20160125VL200.html (accessed 12 April 2016).

Enterpriseinnovation.net (2015) AliCloud, Intel, BGI push cloud for precision medicine, gene research. Available at: http://www.enterpriseinnovation.net/article/alicloud-intel-bgi-push-cloud-precision-medicine-gene-research-865302871 (accessed 12 April 2016).

Fidelity Worldwide Investment (2015) China healthcare: innovation and opportunity. Available at:. https://www.fidelity.com.hk/static/pdf/investor/en/market-commentary/Market_20150212.pdf (accessed 10 May 2016).
ibm.com (2009) IBM announces new healthcare industry solutions lab in China. Available at: http://www-03.ibm.com/press/us/en/pressrelease/27394.wss (accessed 2 May 2016).
Kshetri, N. (2013) IT in the Chinese healthcare industry. *IEEE IT Professional* 15(1), 12–15.
Magistad, M.K. (2015) Does a Chinese company's combination of genomics, big data and AI offer hope for a healthier future? Available at: http://www.pri.org/stories/2015-12-17/how-chinese-innovator-hoping-use-genetics-save-and-extend-lives (accessed 12 April 2016).
marketwired.com (2009) MMR Information Systems, Inc. to enter into definitive agreement with Unis-Tonghe Technology in China, November 19, http://www.marketwired.com/press-release/mmr-information-systems-inc-enter-into-definitive-agreement-with-unis-tonghe-technology-1176374.htm (accessed 12 May 2016).
Microsoft.com (2010) iSoftStone signs agreement with microsoft to develop citizen health solutions in China using HealthVault. Available at: http://www.microsoft.com/en-us/news/press/2010/oct10/10-29mshealthvaultpr.aspx (accessed 2 May 2016).
Nan, H. (2015) A 'cornerstone' in health innovations. Available at: http://www.chinadaily.com.cn/world/2015-10/27/content_22292573.htm (accessed 12 April 2016).
Neusoft.com (2015) Xikang healthcare management platform. Available at: http://www.neusoft.com/services/1447/ (accessed 12 April 2016).
news.xinhuanet.com (2015) What's being said on Facebook about China. Available at: http://news.xinhuanet.com/english/2015-08/26/c_134558545.htm (accessed 12 April 2016).
prnewswire.com (2015) China's first cloud hospital 'Ningbo Cloud Hospital' founded. Available at: http://www.prnewswire.com/news-releases/chinas-first-cloud-hospital-ningbo-cloud-hospital-founded-300050189.html (accessed 12 April 2016).
Roberts, D. (2014) China Internet giants Baidu and Alibaba take on overstressed medical system. Available at: http://www.bloomberg.com/bw/articles/2014-06-10/china-Internet-giants-baidu-and-alibaba-take-on-overstressed-medical-system (accessed 12 April 2016).
Shah, A. (2011) Dell traverses China challenges to expand services unit, IDG News Service. PC World. Available at: http://www.pcworld.idg.com.au/article/404265/dell_traverses_china_challenges_expand_services_unit/ (accessed 10 May 2016).
tmcnet.com (2012) China's mobile healthcare industry to witness two-digit growth. Available at: http://cloud-computing.tmcnet.com/news/2012/03/28/6221092.htm (accessed 12 April 2016).
usa.chinadaily.com (2015) Internet giants' healthy future. Available at: http://usa.chinadaily.com.cn/epaper/2015-09/14/content_21851207.htm (accessed 12 April 2016).
Wall Street Journal (2014) Tencent leads financing for Chinese healthcare website Guahao. Available at: http://blogs.wsj.com/digits/2014/10/14/tencent-leads-financing-for-chinese-healthcare-website-guahao/ (accessed 12 April 2016).
Wang, W. (2014) Tencent buys minority stake in Chinese healthcare website. Available at: http://www.forbes.com/sites/ywang/2014/09/02/tencent-buys-minority-stake-in-chinese-healthcare-website/ (accessed 12 April 2016).
WHO [World Health Organization] (2011) China: country health information profiles. Available at: www.wpro.who.int/countries/chn5CHNpro2011_finaldraft.pdf (accessed 2 May 2016).
Xin, Z. (2015) Medical Big Data Center set up in Beijing. Available at: http://www.chinadaily.com.cn/business/2015-10/30/content_22327861.htm (accessed 12 April 2016).
Zhou, B. (2011) Healthcare in China: at a critical transition phase. Available at: http://en.community.dell.com/dell-blogs/health-care/b/washington-report/archive/2011/08/23/healthcare-in-china-at-a-critical-transition-phase.aspx (accessed 12 April 2016).

Zinran, J. (2014) Smartphones help patients cut waiting times. China Daily (online). Available at: http://www.chinadaily.com.cn/china/2014-06/04/content_17560484.htm (accessed 12 April 2016).

Case 2: Big Data Deployment in the Fight Against Ebola

The diverse uses of BD and its powerful effects make it of particular interest in dealing with natural disasters, as well as fighting and controlling deadly infectious diseases such as Ebola. BD solutions can help to increase the degree of citizen engagement and to track the disease's spread and the population movement. This case provides an overview of the diverse actions and roles of a number of BD-solutions providers. For instance, Microsoft had provided cloud-computing platforms (e.g. Azure) and research applications to medical researchers working on the Ebola virus (nbcnews.com, 2014). The cloud-based tool Reliefwatch (Chapter 4) also played a key role in the fight against Ebola. Reliefwatch teamed up with the USAID to launch a programme in Liberia to track Ebola supplies at health clinics (theguardian.com, 2015).

The United Nations Office for the Coordination of Humanitarian Affairs (UNOCHA) received a US$1.02 million grant from the Paul G. Allen Ebola Program in order to integrate data systems and offer data services to its partners in West Africa. The grant is also expected to be used in adding new features for data sharing and analyses in the UNOCHA's open data platform, the Humanitarian Data Exchange (prnewswire.com, 2015).

A2.1 Citizen engagement and analytics system

BD-based tools helped develop and increase citizen engagement during the Ebola crisis. The local telecommunications company, Airtel, IBM Research Africa and Kenyan start-up Echo Mobile teamed up in joint activities to launch a citizen engagement and analytics system in Sierra Leone. IBM developed the cloud and analytics platform required for the service along with Sierra Leone's Open Government Initiative. Airtel set up the toll-free number for citizens to call and send text messages to report Ebola-related issues and concerns. Echo Mobile anonymized the text messge data. Supercomputers, analytics capabilities and the cloud helped to highlight emerging issues across the dataset of messages in order to provide actionable insights about experiences of communities affected by Ebola to develop strategies to control the disease (businesscloudnews.com, 2014).

The location-specific feature of text messages and voice data allowed IBM to graphically present the data and create opinion-based colour-coded heat maps, which correlated public sentiment with location information. For instance, the heat maps showed which regions had large and growing numbers of suspected Ebola cases. These regions required supplies such as soap and electricity urgently and faster response times for body collection and burials. In this way, the platform helped emergency workers coordinate and allocate medical and other resources to areas that were in more urgent need of Ebola-related relief. The system also brought into light the issues related to resource constraints in the diagnosis of Ebola and influenced the government to approach the international community to request more testing facilities and equipment (itnewsafrica.com, 2014).

A2.2 Tracking the population movement during the Ebola crisis

Phone companies use call-data records (CDRs) to manage networks and bill customers. The information included in these records include the caller's identity, the time of the call, the phone tower that handled the call and the number called. Data collected by phone companies can also identify where a phone is even if it is not being used. This is because in order to enable them to receive calls, phones constantly send out signals so that their location is known. To put things in context, CDRs contain information about people's location and their movement patterns, which could be very helpful to epidemiologists. Note that the base station handling a call can be considered as a rough approximation and indication of the caller's location.

Mobile phone data can help track changes in population movement. By comparing the current activity level to historical data, pattern changes can be observed. With an analysis of previously unavailable data, faster responses can be achieved and resources can be deployed in a manner that best serves these populations (Wilson, 2014).

Telecom firms such as Orange worked with data scientists in order to track population movement with the help of phone signal data in countries that were affected by Ebola. Orange made millions of CDRs from Senegal and Ivory Coast available for research use under its Data for Development initiative (economist.com, 2014). For instance, Orange Telecom in Senegal had provided the Swedish non-profit organization Flowminder with anonymized voice and text data of 150,000 mobile phone owners. Based on the information, Flowminder drew detailed maps of typical population movements. The maps helped authorities to identify the best places to set up treatment centres. The government also used the maps to identify the most effective ways to restrict travel in order to contain the disease (Wall, 2014). By monitoring calls to health centres and helplines from mobile phones and looking at the pattern, it is possible to identify problems so that resources can be better deployed.

A2.3 Tracking the spread

A number of tools had been used to track the spread of Ebola.

HealthMap

HealthMap is a data-driven mapping tool that uses algorithms to analyse sources involving a large number of social media sites, local news, government websites, social networks of infectious-disease physicians, websites of international health organizations and governments, personal blogs and others to detect and track the outbreaks of diseases such as Ebola. The algorithm looks at examples of articles labelled by HealthMap analysts and uses those examples to identify key words and phrases associated with actual outbreak. The algorithm is reported to improve continuously based on learning from a feedback loop (Titlow, 2014).

The reliability of news reported in social media may be questionable. HealthMap's algorithm, however, is designed to differentiate the 'noise' from the 'signal', which increases the usefulness and the value of such sources. Irrelevant data are filtered out and the relevant information is classified in order to identify diseases and map their locations (Publichealthwatch.wordpress.com, 2014).

On 23 March 2014, the World Health Organization (WHO) issued its first public statement on the Ebola outbreak. However, on 14 March 2014, HealthMap's algorithms had detected reports about an outbreak of a 'mystery hemorrhagic fever', which had killed eight people in Guinea. On 19 March 2014, the algorithm picked up a local news report of a possible Ebola outbreak, which was believed to be the first such report. It had triggered HealthMap to issue an alert (publichealthwatch.wordpress.com, 2014).

Global Data on Events, Location and Tone (GDELT)

The GDELT 'monitors the world's broadcast, print, and web news' (http://www.gdeltproject.org/). It is another useful tool to track and monitor epidemics such as Ebola. It promises to be the ultimate big database for journalists. It covers news in over 100 languages from nearly every country as of the end of 2015.

A *Foreign Policy* article commented that the first public international warning of Ebola came from a traditional channel: a news item from Xinhua's French-language newswire. A 13 March 2014 article entitled 'Guinée: une étrange fièvre fait 8 morts à Macenta' reported that 'a disease whose nature has not yet been identified has killed eight people in the prefecture of Macenta in south-eastern Guinea'. The article was reporting on a press conference held that day by Dr Sakoba Keita, the director of the Guinea Department of Health's Division of Disease Prevention. The press conference was broadcast nationally on state television. The Xinhua article had also noted that the government of Guinea had formally notified the WHO of the outbreak.

It was reported that GDELT had monitored Dr Keita's press conference and detected an increase in domestic coverage from 14 March 2014, but that did not translate into actionable information, knowledge and initiatives. The main problem concerned the fact that all of the media coverage of what was happening was in French and GDELT lacked capabilities to translate French material at that time.

A2.4 Some challenges

The efforts to use BD to track and control Ebola were constrained by various technological and organizational inefficiencies. Some analysts argued that the availability of more data, especially on the real-time movement of people, would have increased the effectiveness of relief efforts. Researchers have been lobbying with mobile carriers for access to CDR data (Scacklett, 2015). Privacy is a key concern for phone companies to release consumers' data. In addition, these companies may be concerned about the risk of disclosing commercial information to their competitors. Some argued that the governments' actions would have forced phone companies to make call records available for tracking the spread of the disease and take necessary actions. Researchers who access the data need to sign legal agreements with the phone companies specifying the way in which the data may be used. There were complaints regarding the bureaucratic slowness, red tape and the lack of political will to take such actions (economist.com, 2014).

The newness of this phenomenon also worked against the willingness of phone companies to share data. The changes of the magnitude of the Ebola upheaval often created confusion and uncertainty and produced an environment that lacked norms, templates and models about the appropriate strategies and structures (Newman, 2000). In such situations, the institutional context may not provide organizing templates for institutional actors. To put things in context, there was no precedent of using CDRs in an emergency such as Ebola. In order to make crucial decisions such as making consumers' phone data available, people of high political status from the government and executives from the top management level of the phone companies need to be involved. It thus became challenging and confusing to bring the concerned parties together (economist.com, 2014).

Various types of data vary in quality and usefulness. For instance, a major drawback of the data provided by Orange Telecom in Senegal was that it was historical, and thus performed poorly in terms of the speed or velocity dimensions. It would be more helpful if the authorities had been able to map people's movements in real time since the movements tend to change during an epidemic.

Finally, a main reason why developing economies are not getting as much benefit as they deserve concerns the English-language centricity of most apps and global BD projects. For instance, consider Sierra Leone and Guinea, where Ebola was first reported in March 2014. Whereas most monitoring systems emphasize English-language material, the majority of the Internet content in these countries is not published in English (Leetrau, 2014).

A2.5 Concluding comments

During natural disasters and epidemics, BD solutions can help to increase the degree of citizen engagement and can also be used to track the spread of disease and population movements. A key lesson that we take away from this case study is that the efforts to use BD to track and control global epidemics such as Ebola can be constrained by privacy concerns, as well as various technological and organizational inefficiencies.

References

businesscloudnews.com (2014) Mobile, cloud, big data platform helping to contain Ebola outbreak. Available at: http://www.businesscloudnews.com/2014/10/27/mobile-cloud-big-data-platform-helping-to-contain-ebola-outbreak/ (accessed 13 April 2016).

economist.com (2014) Mobile-phone records would help combat the Ebola epidemic. But getting to look at them has proved hard. Available at: http://www.economist.com/news/science-and-technology/21627557-mobile-phone-records-would-help-combat-ebola-epidemic-getting-look (accessed 13 April 2016).

itnewsafrica.com (2014) IBM & Airtel to launch Ebola containment initiatives in Africa. Available at: http://www.itnewsafrica.com/2014/10/ibm-airtel-to-launch-ebola-containment-initiatives-in-africa/ (accessed 13 April 2016).

Leetaru, K. (2014) Why Big Data missed the early warning signs of Ebola. Available at: http://foreignpolicy.com/2014/09/26/why-big-data-missed-the-early-warning-signs-of-ebola/ (accessed 13 April 2016).

nbcnews.com (2014) Microsoft offers cloud-computing tools in fight against Ebola. Available at: http://www.nbcnews.com/storyline/ebola-virus-outbreak/microsoft-offers-cloud-computing-tools-fight-against-ebola-n230201 (accessed 13 April 2016).

Newman, K.L. (2000) Organizational transformation during institutional upheaval. *The Academy of Management Review* 25(3), 602–619.

prnewswire.com (2015) The Paul G. Allen Ebola Program awards $11 million in new grants, continuing its support of innovative solutions to help prevent future outbreaks from becoming epidemics. Available at: http://www.prnewswire.com/news-releases/the-paul-g-allen-ebola-program-awards-11-million-in-new-grants-continuing-its-support-of-innovative-solutions-to-help-prevent-future-outbreaks-from-becoming-epidemics-300155538.html (accessed 13 April 2016).

publichealthwatch.wordpress.com (2014) How a computer algorithm predicted West Africa's Ebola outbreak before it was announced. Available at: https://publichealthwatch.wordpress.com/2014/08/10/how-a-computer-algorithm-predicted-west-africas-ebola-outbreak-before-it-was-announced/ (accessed 13 April 2016).

Scacklett, M. (2015) Fighting Ebola with a holistic vision of big data. Available at: http://www.techrepublic.com/article/fighting-ebola-with-a-holistic-vision-of-big-data/ (accessed 13 April 2016).

theguardian.com (2015) The cloud-based tool improving healthcare across the developing world. Available at: http://www.theguardian.com/sustainable-business/2015/jan/07/the-cloud-based-tool-improving-healthcare-across-the-developing-world (accessed 3 April 2015).

Titlow, P.J. (2014) How this algorithm detected the Ebola outbreak before humans could. Available at: http://www.fastcompany.com/3034346/how-this-algorithm-detected-the-ebola-outbreak-before-humans-could (accessed 13 April 2016).

Wall, M. (2014) Ebola: can big data analytics help contain its spread? Available at: http://www.bbc.com/news/business-29617831 (accessed 13 April 2016).

Wilson, M. (2014) Tracking and tackling Ebola using mobile phone surveillance. Available at: http://betanews.com/2014/10/15/tracking-and-tackling-ebola-using-mobile-phone-surveillance/ (accessed 13 April 2016).

Case 3: Kilimo Salama's Weather-Based Index Insurance for Smallholder Farmers

Microinsurance is not an attractive business for most insurance companies due to the high transaction costs. For instance, consider a farmer who is required to pay an insurance premium of US$1 to insure seeds worth US$10. In the case of bad weather such as drought, an insurance agent may need to visit the farm to verify the farmer's loss. The insurance company also needs to do paperwork to pay US$10 to the farmer. The company's expense is the same irrespective of the amount of the insurance policy, whether it is a US$10 or a US$10,000 policy. It is possible for insurance companies to offer small insurance policies to poor farmers if the costs associated with signing up people, verifying claims and paying for the damages are close to zero.

Insurance companies also suffer from a bad reputation. Many sub-Sahara African-based farmers have not heard of insurance, whereas a small proportion of farmers, who are aware of insurance, have had bad insurance-related experience in the past. Some have been cheated because the insurance company went bankrupt. In some cases, insurance agents took money and then disappeared. In other cases, a broker took the insurance payout money and did not pass it on to the farmer (Rosenberg, 2011).

A3.1 Kilimo Salama's weather-based index insurance

The social enterprise Kilimo Salama (which means 'safe agriculture' in Swahili) has brought together actuarial science, agronomy, climate science, economics and remote sensing to develop a weather-based index insurance in an attempt to serve a vulnerable market that traditional insurance schemes have ignored. Its micro insurance scheme attempts to protect small farmers in Kenya against poor weather conditions.

The insurance programme is offered as a partnership between the Syngenta Foundation for Sustainable Agriculture, the Kenyan insurance company UAP, and Safaricom. Kilimo Salama also gets financial assistance from the International Finance Corporation, which is a sister organization of the World Bank (Rosenberg, 2011).

Kilimo Salama started a pilot project in 2009, insuring 200 maize farmers in the Nanyuki region of Kenya. The project subsequently extended the cover to wheat, sorghum, cotton, beans and coffee crops. As of 2011, it had insured 22,000 farmers and became the largest insurance project in Africa (Rosenberg, 2011). As of 2013, Kilimo Salama had insured over 100,000 small farmers in Kenya and Rwanda (Kalan, 2013). For some farmers the cost of insurance amounts to as little as 1 kg of maize, seed or fertilizer (un.org, 2014).

In order to reduce transaction costs and build trust with clients, Kilimo Salama's index insurance mainly relies on solar-powered weather stations and mobile phones. Kenya's weather stations traditionally employed manual rain gauges. Kilimo Salama modernized 32 of them with solar power and computerized gauges. Weather stations are equipped with wireless SIM cards that transmit data on rainfall levels, sun and temperature every 5 minutes to a cloud-based server.

The insurance is completely automated. Kilimo Salama uses mobile phones for signing up farmers and paying out insurance claims. It does not have to rely on insurance agents. Policies are distributed through dealers who sell seeds, fertilizers and chemicals to farmers. The dealers are provided with camera phones to record the purchase. They use an advanced phone application with camera and phone functions to scan and capture policy information through a code. The information is uploaded to Safaricom's mobile cloud-based server, which administers policies. Farmers instantly receive information about their policy and payouts in text messages (Schneider, 2013). Perhaps the most notable feature of this insurance offering is that at the end of the growing season, payouts go electronically to the farmer's mobile phone account (Rosenberg, 2011).

A farmer who buys insurance is linked to the nearest weather station, which is closer than 20 km. At the end of a season, the data are aggregated and combined with satellite data in order to map out rain patterns. Kilimo Salama works with agronomists to calculate the index and identifies the locations that experienced too much rain, too little rain, or rain at the wrong time. Farmer payouts are calculated based on crops, location and the amount invested in seeds (Kalan, 2013). If the rainfall is insufficient early in the growing season, or too much later in the maize season, farmers in that area get an automatic payout. Farmers are not required to file a claim. In the case of extreme weather that destroys the whole harvest, they get the full amount. No farm visit is necessary (Rosenberg, 2011). Insurance claims are normally settled within 4 days (Gulati, 2015).

Farmers can buy the insurance at the beginning of the season for about 10–20% of the amount they invest in seeds and inputs (Kalan, 2013). However, paying 10% of their costs for insurance is a huge burden for many farmers. Kilimo Salama recruited partners such as Syngenta who cover half the cost of the premium if farmers buy their products. In this way, local firms can facilitate the adoption by creating trust with local communities.

The availability of weather stations and mobile phones dramatically lowered the cost of writing policies. Indeed, sending the text message welcoming the new client has been the biggest component of cost associated with providing insurance for Kilimo Salama (Rosenberg, 2011).

It was reported that a reason why Rose Goslinga, Kilimo Salama's founder, chose Kenya was M-PESA's popularity in the country (Rosenberg, 2011). With the deepening penetration rates of mobile phones and mobile money such as M-PESA in Africa, the markets for Kilimo Salama's insurance products are likely to widen.

A3.2 Appropriateness of index insurance

Researchers and practitioners have advocated the development and use of index insurance contracts to manage the risks faced by farmers and agricultural producers (Miranda and Gonzalez-Vega, 2011). Whereas conventional insurance compensates an insurer based on verifiable losses, under an index insurance scheme such as that of Kilimo Salama, payment to an insured farmer depends on the observed value of a specified index (Miranda and Gonzalez-Vega, 2011). The benefits of index insurance are greater to lending institutions such as agricultural/industrial development banks and microfinance institutions (MFIs) than to borrowers (Skees and Barnett, 2006). Historical data on maize and the other crops insured by Kilimo Salama indicated that payouts based on weather-based index are about the same as payouts for crop damage by bad weather (Rosenberg, 2011).

A3.3 Benefits to farmers

As noted earlier, having insurance to cover damage gives farmers the confidence to invest in agricultural activities that are likely to give higher returns (e.g. cash crops). The benefits, however, go far beyond the increased confidence to invest in high-return crops. Kilimo Salama regularly sends up-to-date climate data to farmers with text messages. Farmers also receive information regarding the ways to increase agricultural productivity and protect crops in the case of bad weather (Omolayo, 2015). Another benefit to farmers is that banks and MFIs are more comfortable in giving loans to farmers thanks to the insurance scheme. In this way, access to essential credit is becoming easier for farmers.

A3.4 Concluding comments

The case of Kilimo Salama indicates that reflecting the background of smallholder farmers, BD solutions targeted to them need to be innovative, low cost and sensitive to their economic conditions. M-PESA's popularity was reported to be a key attracting factor for Kilimo Salama in Kenya. It underscores the central role that a strong BD ecosystem could play in attracting new innovative firms that can provide specialized products.

References

Gulati, A. (2015) Drones and doves. Available at: http://indianexpress.com/article/opinion/columns/drones-and-doves/ (accessed 13 April 2016).

Kalan, J. (2013) Tech fix for Africa's big farming challenge. Available at: http://www.bbc.com/future/story/20130408-tech-taps-africas-farm-potential (accessed 13 May 2016).

Miranda, M.J. and Gonzalez-Vega, C. (2011) Systemic risk, index insurance, and optimal management of agricultural loan portfolios in developing countries. *American Journal of Agricultural Economics* 93(2), 399–406.

Omolayo, O. (2015) These 10 apps will boost agriculture in Africa. Available at: http://venturesafrica.com/these-10-apps-will-boost-agriculture-in-africa (accessed 13 April 2016).

Rosenberg, T. (2011) Doing more than praying for rain. Available at: http://opinionator.blogs.nytimes.com/?s=Doing+more+than+praying+for+rain (accessed 13 April 2016).

Schneider, S. (2013) Five ways cell phones are changing agriculture in Africa. Available at: http://foodtank.com/news/2015/01/five-ways-cell-phones-are-changing-agriculture-in-africa (accessed 13 April 2016).

Skees, J. R. and Barnett, B. J. (2006) Enhancing microfinance using index-based risk-transfer products. *Agricultural Finance Review* 66, 235–250.

un.org (2014) Africa Wired. Available at: http://www.un.org/africarenewal/magazine/august-2014/africa-wired (accessed 13 April 2016).

Case 4: Agricultural Knowledge On-Line (AKOL)

AKOL is an Israel-based agricultural technology BD firm. When AKOL was founded in 1978, the Internet did not exist in the way we know it today. In the pre-Internet era, AKOL's online databases and applications were used by farmers in southern Israel's Kibbutz Bror Hayil in order to improve productivity. The company is regarded as the main force behind the development and achievement in Israel's agricultural success. For instance, thanks to the digitization of farming activities by AKOL and other companies, an average Israeli cow produces 12,000 litres of milk per year compared to the 4000-litre mark for the rest of the world (marketwatch.com, 2011) and 10,000 litres in the USA (Ettinger, 2015). It is reported that AKOL monitors key indicators such as output, health, nutrition, genetics and fertility of every cow in Israel (reuters.com, 2015).

A4.1 AKOL's applications portfolio

Over the years, AKOL diversified its applications portfolio to cover many areas of agriculture such as raising poultry, managing vineyards and producing olive oil (Halevi, 2011). AKOL's tools for information, interaction and communications help to increase productivity and manage resources more efficiently and effectively for average farmers in developing countries.

AKOL applications provide advice on diverse topics such as the most appropriate time to plant and harvest certain crops and the best time to take them to market, the degree of fit of a crop in a geographical area, the best feed mix for cows and other livestock, and the optimal storage procedures for agricultural products for a given climatic zone and condition. Farmers can also get help in tracking the growth of livestock, implementing temperature control procedures in response to changing weather, and generating reports of milk samples for quality control (Halevi, 2011). In 2011, AKOL signed an agreement with IBM to host its applications on IBM Cloud (israeltrade.org.au, 2015).

A4.2 AKOL's emergence as a global agricultural company

As of 2015, AKOL's customers included dairies, vineyards, cattle breeders, chicken growers, and farmers in China, Europe, the USA, Israel and other locations. In May 2015, AKOL signed a joint venture partnership with Microsoft to bring the technology to the developing world (reuters.com, 2015). The partnership involved an undisclosed investment from Microsoft and more than US$10 million from AKOL.

In particular, AKOL's China operations deserve special attention. In fastcompany.com's 2013 list of 'The World's Top 10 Most Innovative Companies in Israel', AKOL was ranked at number five for its role in modernizing Chinese agriculture. In 2012, China's Anhui province began using AKOL's Agro Cloud solution in order to quantify total food production. AKOL's solution, which was developed with IBM, allows local officials to monitor the production of fruit, vegetable, dairy, poultry and meat (Shemer, 2013).

The AKOLogic platform allows real-time monitoring of fruit, vegetable, dairy and poultry production by local officials. This helps to rapidly identify the source of spoiled food and enhances public safety. It also helps farmers based in the developing world to gain access to industrialized world markets. Using the AKOLogic platform, farmers can meet standards and regulations of new markets and comply with them in a cost-effective manner (whatsthebigdata.com, 2014).

In April 2015, the Chinese agricultural authorities signed a deal with AKOL to deploy AKOL's 'agricultural cloud' technology for use in fish farms. Through the AKOL system, fish farm operators can access and analyse the in-depth information gathered via sensors. The system instructs the fish farmers on the appropriate time to clean pools, the amount and time to feed fish, and other information (Shamah, 2015).

A4.3 Incorporating the Internet of Things

AKOL uses sensors that are placed on trees, vines and fields. They can also be attached to cows, milking systems, feed bins or other appropriate locations. Data and information related to temperature, humidity and other factors are recorded in order to assess how much animals are eating and the activity among animals. For plants, data about soil conditions, the level of pests in an area and other indicators are recorded. The data are then analysed and compared with guidelines for ideal production under the circumstances. Specific instructions are then sent back to farmers. For example, dairy farmers may be instructed to increase the amount of liquids given to cows during hot summer days in order to increase cows' milk productivity. Famers may also be provided with instructions regarding specific mixes of feed in order to make them less attractive to pests, bacteria and viruses that may be in the environment. AKOL uses an SAS system using Microsoft's Azure technology (Shamah, 2015).

A4.4 Helping small farmers meet international standards for crops

AKOL is one of the few BD systems for agriculture, dairy or livestock farming that is aimed at small farmers. Its interface is on smartphones, which makes it easy for farmers in the field to access the required information. Farmers record everything in AKOL's database, which can then be used to demonstrate that they comply with the international standards such as good agricultural practices (GAP), which have been adopted by many EU supermarkets. In order to comply with the stringent requirements of GAP, AKOL's system uses computerized information systems that fully and accurately document each crop's entire history involving growing, packaging and delivery stages, and generates relevant reports (Shamah, 2015).

A4.5 Concluding comments

The agricultural sector in the developing world has benefitted from unique solutions, tools and approaches developed by AKOL. The company's BD-based tools help to increase productivity and manage resources more efficiently and effectively. They are especially suited for average farmers in developing countries. AKOL's tools can also help farmers comply with the international standards and thus increase access to markets for their products.

References

Ettinger, Y. (2015) Global kudos to Israel's long term viability. Available at: http://www.theettingerreport.com/Print.aspx?printpath=%2FOverseas-Investments%2FGlobal-kudos-to-Israel-s-long-term-viability (accessed 13 April 2016).
Halevi, D. (2011) Spreading Israel's agriculture miracle. Available at: http://mfa.gov.il/MFA/InnovativeIsrael/Pages/Spreading_Israel_agricultural_miracle-May_2011.aspx (accessed 13 April 2016).
israeltrade.org.au (2015) Israeli companies fight world hunger with innovative technologies. Available at: http://www.israeltrade.org.au/israeli-companies-fight-world-hunger-with-innovative-technologies/ (accessed 13 April 2016).
marketwatch.com (2011) Kibbutznik: what's going down on the Israeli farm? Available at: http://www.marketwatch.com/story/kibbutznik-whats-going-down-on-the-israeli-farm-2011-10-10 (accessed 13 April 2016).
reuters.com (2015) RPT-Milking it: Israel leads the way in dairy tech. Available at: http://www.reuters.com/article/2015/05/19/israel-dairy-idUSL5N0Y44V820150519 (accessed 13 April 2016).
Shamah, D. (2015) Israeli Big Data teaches farmers a cup of joe means better crops. Available at: http://www.timesofisrael.com/israeli-big-data-teaches-farmers-a-cup-of-joe-means-better-crops/ (accessed 13 April 2016).
Shemer, N. (2013) The world's top 10 most innovative companies in Israel. Available at: http://www.fastcompany.com/most-innovative-companies/2013/industry/israel (accessed 13 April 2016).
whatsthebigdata.com (2014) What's the Big Data? Available at: http://whatsthebigdata.com/2014/02/04/satya-nadella-new-microsoft-ceo-on-the-digitization-of-everything-video/ (accessed 13 April 2016).

Case 5: International Center for Tropical Agriculture (CIAT) at the Forefront of Research Related to Agriculture and the Environment

The not-for-profit R&D organization, International Center for Tropical Agriculture or (Centro Internacional de Agricultura Tropical (CIAT) in Spanish), is at the forefront of research in the field of BD. CIAT is backed by the Colombian government and Rockefeller, Ford, and Kellogg Foundations. It was established in 1967 and began research activities in 1969 (https://ciat.cgiar.org/about-us). With headquarters near Cali, Colombia, it also has regional offices in Nairobi (Kenya) and Hanoi (Vietnam). CIAT is among the 15 specialized research centres of the Consultative Group on International Agricultural Research (CGIAR). It is also the headquarters for the CGIAR Research Program on Climate Change, Agriculture and Food Security.

A5.1 Optimizing crop quality and minimizing lost yield

CIAT's R&D activities have already made a major contribution in the Colombian agricultural sector. It monitors various environmental conditions for optimizing crop quality and minimizing lost yield. For instance, in order to provide actionable information to Colombian rice growers, scientists at CIAT analysed a huge amount of data. CIAT's findings indicated that climatic conditions account for 30–40% of crop production variability in some parts of Colombia (Clark, 2014).

Using various data-mining, the researchers provided useful and actionable information to improve agricultural productivity. For instance, a case study of two rice growing areas showed that a key climatic factor leading to a reduction in rice yields is accumulated solar energy during the grain-ripening period. This information can help the farmers to increase the yields by changing the sowing date and adopting rice varieties that are less sensitive to the amount of radiation (Russell, 2014). While many years of field research had reached a similar conclusion, BD produced this result in just one year. Furthermore, BD analysis linked it with climate data in order to provide farmers with actionable recommendations that were timely and site-specific. La Federación Nacional de Arroceros (FEDEARROZ) noted that the results of the BD analysis helped to avoid significant economic losses for about 170 rice growers in Colombia's Córdoba Department (Russell, 2014).

In another study in Colombia, an analysis of historical weather data showed a diverse set of distinct climate patterns occurring in Meta Department. While some of the patterns were associated with favourable growing conditions, others were not. Based on seasonal climate forecasts made by advanced simulation tools, farmers can be provided with reliable recommendations regarding the planting date and rice variety months in advance. Such information is expected to help farmers avoid losses of 1–2 tonnes per ha (Russell, 2014). The future plan is to develop site-specific recommendations for every rice-producing area in Colombia. Incorporation of additional data on soils and other factors is likely to lead to a significantly higher explanatory power and a richer explanation.

CIAT's expertise and experience will soon benefit the agricultural sectors of other Latin American economies. For instance, CIAT researchers also announced a plan to work with the Fund for Irrigated Rice in Latin America or Fondo Latino-americano para Arroz de Riego (FLAR) (http://flar.org/) to scale up the approach with rice growers associations in countries such as Nicaragua and Peru (Russell, 2014). FLAR is a public–private partnership established to improve the competitiveness and sustainability of rice production systems.

A5.2 Favourable political and bureaucratic conditions

Highly favourable political and bureaucratic conditions have been a key to CIAT's ability to make a meaningful contribution to the Colombian agricultural sector. For instance, the scientists at CIAT partnered with Colombia's Ministry of Agriculture and Rural Development (Russell, 2014). The data were shared by FEDE-ARROZ and the Colombian Institute of Hydrology, Meteorology and Environmental Studies, which included information from an annual rice survey, a harvest monitoring dataset and results from experiments on rice sowing date and historical weather data (Russell, 2014).

A5.3 Recent Big Data tools

Perfectify

CIAT has developed a tool, called 'Perfectify', that aims to improve the accuracy of farming recommendations. It involves agronomists, statisticians and data miners crunching data and statistics from a number of sources in order to provide site-specific recommendations that can enable farmers to optimize food production. The key target market for the solution is smallholder farmers in the developing world (Palmer, 2015). The various sources of data used include remote sensing (satellite information), climate and weather information (generated by using various climate models and historical meteorological data) and crop information (from agricultural scientists and farmers).

Terra-i system

CIAT teamed up with the Nature Conservancy, King's College London and Switzerland's University of Applied Sciences and Arts to develop the Terra-i system, which monitors deforestation on a near real-time basis. The Terra-i system was launched in mid-2012. The goal of Terra-i is to help government agencies and other decision makers in Latin America to devise new policies and procedures related to forest and habitat protection. In 2012, the Terra-i team trained technicians from the Bolivian government to use the system (Palmer, 2013).

Terra-i covers the entire Latin America region. The system is based on NASA's satellite information. It can zoom in on Latin America's forests to a resolution of 250 m × 250 m (worldsat.ca, 2016). It can distinguish between losses that are caused by natural disasters from those that are caused by humans. It can also monitor habitat change in savannahs, deserts and other non-forested areas. Anyone can log in and monitor the activities. As of 2013, the images were updated every 16 days (Palmer, 2013).

Monitoring the Terra-i system, scientists have reported some important and intriguing findings on the deforestation of the Gran Chaco (also called the Chaco Plain), which is a sparsely populated, hot and semi-arid region of the Río de la Plata basin, divided between eastern Bolivia, Paraguay, northern Argentina and the Brazilian states of Mato Grosso and Mato Grosso do Sul. It is Latin America's second most-densely forested area. While a lot of international attention is being paid to the Amazon, significantly less attention has been given to the deforestation of the Gran Chaco. Terra-i revealed that during the period 2004–2010, about 1 million ha of forest had been lost in the Gran Chaco primarily due to the expansion of industrial agriculture at the perimeter. The scientists concluded that the damage in the Gran Chaco is much more severe and widespread than observed anywhere in the Amazon (Palmer, 2013).

A5.4 Concluding comments

CIAT has unique specialization in the areas of agriculture and the environment and has developed state-of-the-art tools in its specialization domains. Its expertise and experience are likely to benefit the agricultural and environmental sectors of developing economies. This case indicates that a high level of support from the government is important for a not-for-profit BD organization such as CIAT to innovate and succeed.

References

Clark, H. (2014) How big data is helping farmers save millions. Available at: http://www.gizmag.com/big-data-crops-climate-change/34400/ (accessed 13 April 2016).

Palmer, N. (2013) Eye in the sky: Terra-i keeps track of deforestation, Available at: http://www.ciatnews.cgiar.org/2013/02/14/keeping-an-i-on-deforestation/ (accessed 13 April 2016).

Palmer, N. (2015) Perfectify: Big Data for bigger harvests in the developing world. Available at: https://www.newschallenge.org/challenge/data/entries/perfectify-big-data-for-bigger-harvests-in-the-developing-world (accessed 13 April 2016).

Russell, N. (2014) UN awards big data project for confronting crazy weather in rice production. Available at: http://www.ciatnews.cgiar.org/2014/09/02/un-awards-big-data-project-for-confronting-crazy-weather-in-rice-production/ (accessed 13 April 2016).

worldsat.ca (2016) Satellite Imagery Primer. Available at: http://www.worldsat.ca/pages/10_satimg/intro.html (accessed 10 May 2016).

Index